Custody MD

Fighting for the Woo

Adwoafuaa N, MD

Published by: Writers of the West

Table of Contents

Trigger warning: This novel contains scenes of domestic violence, abuse, and discrimination that might be upsetting for some readers.

The Moment They Took Her

Silence follows devastation. Not the peaceful kind, but the sort that settles deep in your bones when there's nothing left to scream because they've taken the one thing you've been fighting for all along.

I stood there in that archaic courtroom, watching as my daughter—my baby—was led away. My breath caught in my throat, my heart pounding so loudly I was sure everyone could hear it. But I couldn't move, couldn't run to her, couldn't scream like every cell in my body urged me to. The system had rendered its verdict, and my voice meant nothing in that room.

That day, I learned the cruel reality of being a working mother in a system designed to break you down, piece by piece. I'd given everything—my time, my energy, my sanity—to ensure my daughter's future was full of freedom, love, and stability. But as I stood there, helpless, I realized the system didn't care. The courtroom wasn't a place of justice for mothers like me; it was a battleground where being a working mother meant you were already on the losing side. At that moment, I became part of a war I didn't even know I had enlisted in. And this war? It was designed to crush us, one custody hearing at a time.

A Journey Back in Time

Leaving the familiar confines of the city, the drive to Maverick County felt like a journey through a wormhole to another era. As we drove, the landscape transformed from sleek skyscrapers to sprawling fields dotted with dilapidated barns and rusting tractors. The GPS insisted it was only 45 minutes, but with each mile, I felt as though we were slipping deeper into a time capsule set toward the 1900s.

"Are we entering a different century?" I murmured, half-joking to my parents, who sat beside me. The irony wasn't lost on me that we were mere miles from the county that delayed the emancipation of enslaved people—the very reason we now celebrate Juneteenth. Despite President Biden's recognition of the holiday, parts of this region seemed oblivious, stuck in a past that refused to release its grip.

The courthouse emerged on the horizon, an imposing structure built in the late 1870s. Its grand European architectural design was both majestic and foreboding, like a museum relic unaware that time had marched on. As we approached, I couldn't shake the feeling that we were characters in a play set in a bygone era, and the script had already been written without our input.

Inside, the attempt at modernity was almost comical. Security checkpoints with metal detectors stood starkly against the antique décor. Uniformed officers eyed us with the enthusiasm of TSA agents on a slow day. The juxtaposition was almost laughable—if only the stakes weren't so high. Day one began with jury selection, a process that felt as random as a rigged carnival game. Sixty potential jurors filled the room, but the final twelve seemed preordained. Eight men and four women: six white men who looked like they'd stepped out of a country western film, a Hispanic man eager to align himself with the majority, a Native American-looking man who sat stoically, two biracial women whose eyes reflected untold stories, a pregnant white woman gently cradling her belly, and a Hispanic woman who sat with quiet resilience.

"Well, this is quite the ensemble," my lawyer, Marty, whispered to me. Marty Murati was calm and soft-spoken; his intelligence was evident in every measured word. He had a nervous tic—a subtle tapping of his pen—that belied his composed exterior.

"It's like they've cast characters for a play, and we're the unwitting protagonists," I replied, attempting a weak smile.

Across the aisle, the plaintiff's team resembled a strategic war room. Karen Miller, their attorney, orchestrated the scene with all the subtlety of a marching band in a library. Despite her office being in Harold County, she handled the majority of her cases here—a curious fact that hinted at deeper machinations.

Karen was hyperactive and overzealous, her speeches riddled with dramatic pauses as if awaiting applause. Flanking her were two additional team members whose roles were as mysterious as their sudden appearances—extras in a performance designed to intimidate.

Then there was Reginald, my ex-husband. He sat hunched, eyes cast downward, the picture of meekness and sorrow. If I didn't know better, I'd almost feel sorry for him. But beneath that façade was a calculated performance, a ploy to sway sympathies in his favor.

Presiding over this spectacle was Judge Falkenhausen, the self-appointed ringmaster of our little circus. A German-American man with a booming voice that could rival a drill sergeants, he commanded the courtroom with an air of arrogance and condescension. "Order!" he'd bellow at the slightest whisper, his gavel striking like a whip cracking in the air.

The parade of witnesses began, each more surreal than the last. First up was Dr. Azizi Mwangi, appearing via Zoom. A colleague of Reginald's whom I'd never met; his testimony was clinical and detached. Then came Dr. Hannah Pham, another Zoom apparition; her jovial demeanor and sarcastic remarks feeling wildly inappropriate, given the gravity of the situation.

Next was the "nanny cartel": Becky, Andrea, and Elda, three women with conflicting stories but a shared vengeful intent. Two of them had never even worked for Reginald, yet here they were, painting me as some villain in their fabricated tales. They reminded me of the witches from Macbeth, brewing a potion of lies and half-truths.

Our witnesses were few but genuine. Phyllis, our children's nanny, spoke hesitantly but truthfully. My best friend, Denise, testified with the conviction of someone who'd known me for over forty years. My parents, Comfort and Paul, sat stoically, their worry etched into every line on their faces. They spoke of love and stability, of family and support. Perhaps the most baffling absence was Katherine Kaye. Despite being lined up as the new nanny and having her name surface repeatedly throughout the case, she never testified. That, more than anything, was the most shocking revelation. Rumors swirled about her—a mysterious woman with a baby of uncertain paternity. It felt like a subplot from a soap opera had invaded the courtroom.

As the day wore on, the weight of the proceedings pressed down on me like a lead blanket. The turning point came when Judge Falkenhausen declared, "I know it's the law, but I don't care about the law." The words hung in the air, heavy and inescapable. It was at that moment I realized this wasn't just a personal battle; it was a confrontation with a system designed to break me.

Marty leaned over, slipping me a note: "We are going to have to appeal." I met his gaze, the unspoken apology in his eyes both comforting and disheartening. We were up against more than just a biased jury or an unscrupulous ex; we were fighting a system that saw my independence as a threat.

The War Against Working Mothers

I never imagined that my decision to be a working mother would one day be weaponized against me. Society loves to tell women we can have it all—a thriving career, a happy family, personal fulfillment. But when push comes to shove, the very qualities that make us strong and independent are used to paint us as neglectful or unfit. The courtroom wasn't just a battleground for custody; it was a stage where outdated stereotypes played out with devastating consequences. My commitment to my career was twisted into a narrative of selfishness.

My financial independence was portrayed as a threat to the traditional family structure. It became clear that the system favored a version of motherhood that required self-sacrifice to the point of self-erasure. As I sat there, listening to the distorted portrayals of my life, I realized this wasn't just about me. It was about every working mother who's been told she's not enough or inversely that she's too much. Too ambitious. Too independent. Too focused on herself.

The legal tactics used against me were designed to wear me down emotionally and financially. Endless court hearings, surprise witnesses, and mounting legal fees—all part of a strategy to break my spirit. It felt like a modern-day lynching, not with ropes and mobs, but with legal jargon and biased judgments. But I refused to be silent. I refused to let their circus define me or dictate the future of my children. This memoir is my way of reclaiming my voice, of shedding light on the systemic biases that countless women face every day.

A Call to Arms

To you, my confidant, I share this journey not just to unburden my soul but to shine a light on a shadowed corner of our society. The war against working mothers is real, and it's waged in courtrooms like the one I stood in, under the gavel of judges like Falkenhausen, against the backdrop of outdated systems that refuse to acknowledge our worth.

I want you to know that you're not alone if you've felt the sting of injustice, the weight of a system stacked against you. This fight is bigger than custody battles; it's about challenging the narratives that diminish us, about demanding a world that recognizes the strength in our independence, not one that fears it.

In the pages that follow, I'll share not just my story but the stories of others like me. We'll delve into the systemic biases that permeate our legal system, explore the emotional toll of such battles, and uncover practical strategies to navigate this treacherous terrain.

This isn't just a tale of struggle; it's a testament to resilience. It's about finding the strength to stand firm when the ground beneath you is shaking. It's about forging a path forward, not just for ourselves but for the generations of women who will come after us.

So, I invite you to join me on this journey. Let's peel back the layers of this antiquated system and expose the cracks that need to be filled. Together, we can find strength in our collective voices and work toward a future where being a working mother is celebrated, not condemned.

We are stronger together, and this is a fight worth fighting.

Chapter 1:
The Beginning of Us

We've all heard the phrase *love at first sight*, that cinematic moment where two souls lock eyes and the world fades away. But what happens when you don't even notice someone the first time you meet? Is that the universe's gentle way of tapping you on the shoulder, whispering, "Darling, maybe skip this one"? Or perhaps it's more like a neon warning sign flashing "Danger Ahead," and I'm the pedestrian strolling right past it.

Perhaps it's human nature to ignore the subtle signs, especially when we're caught up in our own whirlwind. I was so focused on starting medical school, juggling single motherhood, and proving to the world that I could do it all that I didn't have time to notice the quiet storm brewing on the horizon. Or maybe I chose not to see it. After all, who wants to admit that the path they're on might be leading them straight into chaos?

So there I was, confidently striding into the next chapter of my life, completely unaware that I was about to co-author a story filled with twists I didn't see coming. If not noticing someone at the first meeting is the universe's way of hinting at trouble, then consider me officially oblivious. But honestly, when has a little thing like a bad omen ever stopped anyone from diving headfirst into disaster?

In the end, perhaps the joke was on me. The universe tried to send a memo, and I let it get lost in the spam folder of my life. But if there's one thing I've learned, it's that sometimes you have to walk through the fire to appreciate the warmth. Or, in my case, stumble into it wearing gasoline-soaked shoes.

A New Beginning

The summer of 2004 wasn't just hot; it was punishing. The kind of heat that clings to your skin and makes every breath feel like work. You start questioning why you thought moving to a city with humidity so thick it could choke your ambition was a good idea. But for all the swampy air and relentless sun, I felt something I hadn't in a long time: excitement. I had just survived a brutal summer pre-matriculation program—the academic version of boot camp—that earned me a place at the University of Illinois at Chicago School of Medicine. This wasn't just a step forward for my career. It was a leap over every barrier life had thrown in my path.

As a first-generation Ghanaian-American woman, getting here felt monumental. My deep ebony skin and almond-shaped eyes told the story of a rich Ashanti lineage—one filled with warriors and queens: Women like Yaa Asantewaa, the fierce leader who led the Ashanti in resistance against British colonial forces (Beesley, 2022). Her refusal to surrender, even in the face of overwhelming odds, had always been my inspiration. I needed that same unshakable spirit because the year leading up to this moment had been nothing short of a battle.

The previous year—2003 to 2004—was a chapter of my life I sometimes still struggle to talk about. I was a homeless single mother, raising my daughter out of my car. It didn't matter that I'd graduated from Northwestern University, one of the top schools in the country. That diploma couldn't shield me from the harsh reality of living on food stamps and piecing together odd jobs just to survive. Substitute teaching. Temporary clerical work. Whatever I could find to keep us afloat. To make matters worse, my relationship with my mom was at its breaking point. We clashed over how to raise my daughter, and eventually, she told me to leave. I was heartbroken, humiliated, and, above all, angry. How could I have achieved so much on paper yet felt so aimless in real life?

Thankfully, God Almighty had other plans for me. He placed me in the path of a community program on the South Side of Chicago—a program at 79th and Jeffries, in a neighborhood many dismissed as *dangerous*. This wasn't just a shelter. It was a haven run by a bold, God-fearing African-American lawyer and activist who believed in rebuilding families. She saw something in me that I couldn't see in myself at the time. "You're going to med school," she said firmly, pushing me to study for the MCAT. She didn't give me a choice, and maybe that's what I needed. Through her support and by God's grace, I made it. The University of Illinois at Chicago accepted me—not without conditions, but I was in. And that was enough.

Now, here I was, in the summer of 2004, with orientation just days away. I prayed to God for strength and resilience and for grace to thrive in a world that often felt stacked against me. The orientation was a blur of nervous introductions, stacks of forms, and—of course—icebreakers. I'm convinced these were created by someone who thrived on watching people squirm. We were shuffled into a freezing lecture hall, the kind where you start wondering if hypothermia is part of the curriculum, and divided into small groups. The task? Discuss our summer reading assignment: *The Spirit Catches You and You Fall Down* by Anne Fadiman.

The book was all about cultural competence in medicine—a heavy but vital read. And a book I fully intended to finish. Really! But between late-night feedings, diaper changes, and convincing my toddler that broccoli wasn't poison, it never happened. That book sat on my nightstand, gathering dust and silently judging me every time I glanced at it.

When our group discussion began, I panicked. There was no way I could contribute anything meaningful without giving myself away. So, I did what any overwhelmed, underprepared mom would do: I faked it. I kept my head down, avoided eye contact, and prayed I wouldn't be called on. Blending in wasn't easy for me. People notice me when I walk into a room—it's just how it is. Maybe it's the way I carry myself, with my shoulders back and head high, something my mother drilled into me growing up. Pride in our Ashanti heritage, she'd always say. But at that moment, I wanted nothing more than to disappear into the institutional carpet.

Miraculously, my strategy worked. I escaped the discussion without revealing my secret. Or so I thought. Across the room, Reginald, a quiet observer, had noticed everything. He sat in the same circle, unassuming and watchful, blending into the background in a way I could only dream of. At the time, I didn't even see him. I was too busy surviving the day. But later, he'd remind me of this moment with a sly grin, like it was his little inside joke.

First Real Interaction: Anatomy Lab Encounter

A few weeks in, the anatomy lab became our first real crucible of medical training. Thirty metal tables, each bearing a silent, donated teacher. The overwhelming smell of formaldehyde, the hush of rookie med students not wanting to botch a dissection—an atmosphere both reverent and unsettling. Our assigned cadaver lay second from the door, a blessing if I needed a quick exit in case of queasiness.

It was here I first truly noticed Reginald. While I reviewed a nerve diagram, he leaned over our cadaver, scalpel in hand, dissecting with more force than finesse. He nearly mangled the brachial plexus. Alarmed, I stepped in, guiding his scalpel away and showing him a gentler approach. His shoulders tightened, eyes darting with embarrassment. He apologized softly, stuttering a little.

I recognized the sincerity behind his awkwardness. Over the next sessions, he adjusted his technique, handling the body with increased respect. He was a short, shy, and seemingly humble Chinese American student in a sea of flashy classmates. Worn-out clothes and scuffed shoes told me he wasn't from a wealthy background, and his stuttering suggested a self-conscious streak. In a place where confidence and competition thrived, he seemed overshadowed. Yet I found his presence oddly reassuring—someone content to learn quietly, reminding me not everyone in med school was an ambitious showboat.

But I had bigger worries: balancing single motherhood, devouring textbooks, praying I didn't dissolve from stress. My parents—though we'd clashed in 2003—remained supportive at heart, proud I'd forced my way into med school. They understood the stakes, reminding me daily I was forging a new legacy for my daughter, proving that no slump, not even homelessness, could silence my aspirations. That resolve carried me through the monotony and intensity of cadaveric dissections, with Reginald mostly a subdued partner who listened intently and practiced calmer technique.

Building a Fragile Rapport

As the semester wore on, we occasionally studied together out of sheer necessity. Library sessions extended late into the evening, him quietly reading, me scribbling notes, both lost in the crush of upcoming exams. We discovered we were both big foodies, sampling new cuisines at Chicago's countless eateries whenever we escaped the library. Over saganaki or ramen, we chatted about alternate dream lives—he joked he'd have become a chef if not for medicine; I teased that I might have pursued print modeling, given my height. Such musings felt surreal, a break from the tension of dissected bodies and multiple-choice questions.

Then came our first official date. Reginald surprised me by asking if I'd like to grab dinner off campus. I'd never dated outside my race before, so it stirred both curiosity and excitement. We ended up in Greektown, a Chicago gem where "saganaki" and "Opa!" shouts abound, a perfect playground for two stressed med students craving good food. Over plates of moussaka and spanakopita, our conversation remained somewhat minimal—he was shy, after all—but not awkward. I did most of the talking, and he listened with earnest eyes, occasionally offering a quick, stuttering reply. It was refreshing, gentler than the loud, showy men I was used to.

After dinner, we caught *Ocean's Twelve* at a nearby theater. The film's themes of elaborate heists and trickery would later feel like foreshadowing, but that night, I just chuckled at George Clooney's suave bravado while Reginald sat quietly, occasionally nibbling popcorn. We left the theater in relative silence, yet it felt intimate rather than uncomfortable. Something had blossomed during that evening, a sense that we could be more than just lab partners or library study buddies. I drove home thinking how novel it was to date someone so reserved, so seemingly grateful for any moment of connection.

The following day, our newly formed closeness led to a vulnerable moment. He mustered the courage to say, "Why would someone like you ever want me? I'm… ugly." My heart ached at the sadness in his voice. He pointed to his pinky fingers—a condition called clinodactyly, where both distal joints curved inward. "They don't straighten," he said quietly. "Looks weird, right?" Gently, I took his hand, kissed the bent pinky, and assured him it was a unique quirk that might even help in surgery someday. I teased, "Your specialized pinky might give you a better grip on tools!" Relief flickered in his eyes, and we laughed softly. But underneath, I sensed how deeply self-conscious he was, convinced that a single deformity made him undesirable. The moment built a deeper thread of trust; my acceptance of his perceived flaws reassured him he wasn't an outcast.

Some classmates, of course, felt compelled to comment, fixating on superficial differences. I heard rumors about how they teased his stutter or labeled him a *muppet.* It enraged me. I saw Reginald as a man who helped me feel safer walking to my car at night, who quietly embraced the complexities of med school, and who appreciated a calm dinner instead of a flashy scene. If that was *ugly*, I was happy to be the odd one out. I preferred sincerity over arrogance any day. Yet, just when I thought our bond might strengthen, he vanished out of nowhere near the end of our first year. Or maybe he vanished specifically from me.

One day, he simply stopped responding. That was how our delicate rapport stalled: a promising date in Greektown, an intimate conversation about his insecurities, a blossoming closeness, and then a ghosting orchestrated by parental decree. Looking back, that first date shimmered with the possibility of kindness, curiosity, and mutual respect. However, illusions can die early, and my illusions about Reginald being unaffected by family pressure died that summer. I assumed it was the last I'd see of him. Med school, however, had other plans, eventually drawing us back into a more complicated entanglement of closeness, conflict, and unsolved tension.

Running for Co-presidency

In the meantime, life didn't stop moving forward. I channeled my energy into other challenges, hoping to carve out a sense of purpose while the ache of unresolved emotions with Reginald lingered in the background. Medical school was already a monumental load, but I decided to take on more. Running for co-presidency in a predominantly African-American med student organization felt like the right step—a chance to focus on something bigger than my personal frustrations and to support aspiring minority students.

The previous year, I'd served as treasurer, throwing myself into fundraising for scholarships and celebrating our success in raising an impressive amount of money. It was a rare bright spot in a high-stress environment. Yet, as I stepped into this new leadership role, I discovered a different side of things: infighting and tension within the group. I envied how the Hispanic organization seemed more unified. Maybe I'd been naive, expecting a united front among Black students. My experiences in high school, a mostly white Catholic environment, had been the opposite: The small group of Black classmates banded together for moral support.

At Northwestern, the unity was even stronger—an oasis of bright, like-minded individuals who shared resources. But here, ironically, I found myself mired in internal disputes. It was disheartening—like discovering the dream team you'd yearned for turned out to be fractious. Still, I refused to resign or concede. I fought to maintain a sense of community, trying to replicate the best parts of my undergrad experience. That fight for unity, ironically, mirrored the emotional conflict with Reginald. In both realms, I tried forging bonds, only to find frustration. But I refused to walk away from either challenge.

Outside of school and my co-presidency campaign, I kept myself busy that summer. I was involved in a research program and spent hours analyzing data, staying immersed in academic life. When I wasn't in the lab, I leaned on my friendships. Medical school had introduced me to an eclectic group of people, but my closest bond was with

Aaron Ito, my best friend. Aaron, a chill and highly intelligent Princeton grad, had a knack for grounding me when things felt chaotic. With his mixed Japanese and Caucasian background, his perspective on the challenges of navigating identity always resonated with me. Aaron wasn't just insightful; he was adventurous, too. That summer, we traveled together, ticking off places I'd dreamed of visiting—Italy, Spain, the United Kingdom, Uruguay, Argentina. He even convinced me to visit California for the first time. I still remember hanging out on the UCLA campus, laughing over coffee as he alternated between cracking jokes and sharing some profound observations in one of the many languages he spoke. Sometimes, it was hard to tell when he was joking or dead serious, but that was just Aaron. His ability to blend wit and wisdom made every conversation with him feel like a masterclass in perspective.

Even though I probably annoyed him by talking about Reginald too much, Aaron never judged me for dating him. Instead, he listened patiently, offering advice when I needed it and giving me space when I didn't. He'd warned me about the challenges of dating someone with family pressures like Reginald's, sharing his own struggles with being biracial. His only goal was to prepare me, not discourage me.

Looking back, that summer was a mix of everything—leadership challenges, academic responsibilities, heartbreak, and the kind of friendships that help you keep moving forward. If nothing else, it reminded me that life's complexities don't pause for you to figure them out. You just have to keep showing up.

Reconnection and Intimacy

When classes resumed, awkwardness replaced the silence. We moved in the same academic circles again, but any interactions between Reginald and me were stilted and tense. Clinicals required us to pick a buddy, and I chose Aaron—someone I could focus on sans the emotional baggage. Reginald and I hadn't even spoken since his ghosting, and seeing him for the first time in months was more uncomfortable than I'd anticipated.

One of my girlfriends, who'd traveled with me that summer, summed up the situation bluntly: "He's just not that into you," echoing the title of a popular book at the time. Her comment hit a nerve, leaving me embarrassed enough to confront him. "Why did you just stop talking to me like that?" I demanded one day.

His answer was equal parts infuriating and baffling: His parents had told him to focus on his studies and avoid the distractions of having a girlfriend. Hearing that from a 23-year-old man left me appalled. How could someone so intelligent and capable still surrender so much autonomy? It dawned on me that Reginald wasn't ready for an adult relationship. He felt like a man-child, still tethered to his parents' commands, and it was clear he needed time to grow up.

For the remainder of that second year, we interacted minimally as he focused on his studies—or perhaps just avoided me altogether. I buried myself in the mounting stress of medical school, especially with the USMLE Step 1 exam looming ahead. But when it came time to buckle down and prepare, Reginald and I fell back into our old rhythm. Shared anxiety over the boards eclipsed our earlier conflicts, and we formed a fragile study alliance once more. We spent long, grueling hours in the library together, dissecting practice questions the way we'd once dissected nerves in the lab. Sometimes, we studied for over 10 hours a day, breaking only for naps or quick meals. Somewhere in that haze of stress, exhaustion, and tentative reconnection, we crossed a boundary physically.

I was cautious, mindful that Reginald was a virgin, and determined not to push him into something he wasn't ready for. But when it finally happened, it felt surprisingly… normal. He was unexpectedly strong, lifting my then-120-pound body with ease, and the lingering stereotypes about Asian men's anatomy dissolved into irrelevance. The intimacy was satisfying, even comforting in its simplicity. For a moment, it felt like we'd carved out a space where the outside pressures didn't matter.

That reprieve didn't last. After the exam, our scores came in lower than we'd hoped, jeopardizing our chances at competitive specialties. He'd dreamed of becoming an orthopedic surgeon while I had my heart set on otolaryngology. Both fields demanded top-tier metrics, and neither of us had hit the mark. There were other ways to achieve our goals—performing spectacularly during rotations could open doors—but it meant a grueling fight to prove ourselves.

Our rotations scattered us across the country, pulling us out of the forced proximity that had reignited our connection. Reginald landed an orthopedic rotation at Case Western Reserve in Ohio, where he met a fellow med student who was also pursuing otolaryngology. They hit it off, and he told her about me, though he neglected to mention we'd been romantically involved. To my surprise, she later showed up during my rotation at UIC, gushing about how funny and wonderful Reginald was.

I wasn't jealous, just annoyed. It felt like Reginald had orchestrated this situation as if to prove his desirability or spark some kind of reaction from me. My girlfriends, also on rotation, were shocked by her obliviousness to my history with him. Whether it was calculated or simply clueless, his actions left me irritated. Even then, I didn't see it as a lack of empathy; I felt pity instead. I blamed myself for his struggles, wondering if our relationship had distracted him from excelling on the boards.

Neither of us matched into our desired fields, leaving us scrambling for open positions. I secured a preliminary general surgery spot at Northwestern McGaw Medical Center while Reginald managed to scramble into Rush University's general surgery program. He was devastated, his disappointment palpable. I tried to stay optimistic, viewing it as just another hurdle to overcome.

I encouraged Reginald to make the most of his internship and to show everyone what he was capable of. To his credit, he rose to the challenge, becoming one of the most impressive general surgery interns at Rush. But as I watched him thrive, I couldn't shake the feeling that we were drifting toward an inevitable end.

Approaching the Finish Line

As I prepared to step into residency, I knew my med school journey had ended far from perfectly. I hadn't matched my dream specialty or emerged with the picture-perfect partnership. But I had come out stronger, with a deeper understanding of myself and a reservoir of resilience I hadn't known I possessed.

By the time I crossed the finish line of medical school, I realized that life's narrative rarely unfolds as neatly as we'd like. The perfect ending might never come, but we can choose how we respond to the chaos along the way. For me, that meant embracing the humor in life's twists and finding pride in the messy, unpolished journey.

If nothing else, the years from 2004 to 2008 had taught me to face storms head-on and laugh at the absurdity of it all. Love at first sight might be a myth, but so is the idea that a single setback—or even a dozen—can define your life. I walked away from medical school not unscathed but unbowed, ready to take on whatever challenges residency would throw my way.

Because if there's one truth I hold onto, it's this: No matter how many illusions shatter, you can always rebuild something stronger in their place. And sometimes, the most important thing you carry forward isn't perfection; it's the quiet, persistent courage to keep going.

Chapter 2:

The Unraveling

Residency—or, in my case, a *preliminary internship*—was brutal: an endless parade of scutwork, sleep deprivation, and attendings who seemed to delight in testing the limits of human endurance. During general surgery orientation, one mantra stood out: *Do not neglect your family.* It was practically stamped on our souls. The attending surgeons relayed cautionary tales of broken marriages and ghosted loved ones, all sacrificed at the altar of the OR. Their advice was surprisingly practical: keep your relationships intact, even if it means letting an OR nurse take an emergency call while you're scrubbed in. I tucked the lesson away, determined not to let the grind swallow me whole.

Reginald, on the other hand, existed at the blurry edges of my life. We were in the same city, nominally in the same specialty, but our chaotic schedules and complicated history kept us at arm's length. The past four years felt like a messy script—early camaraderie, ghosting, the rekindling during Step 1 prep, that brief, tension-laden intimacy. Now, we were somewhere between casual acquaintances and estranged lab partners who occasionally exchanged pleasantries.

Then, like a rare celestial event, our schedules aligned for an entire weekend off. It felt like fate—or maybe just dumb luck—but I wasn't one to overthink serendipity.

We ended up at his place near the hospital, a townhouse tucked behind gates in one of the wealthiest enclaves in the city. At the time, I hadn't fully registered the contradiction—how a supposed *resident on a budget* lived in a home surrounded by armed guards just a stone's throw from the mayor's estate. The immaculate space lacked any personal touch, eerily pristine in a way that didn't quite match the man I thought I knew.

The evening unfolded slowly, our conversation meandering from the unglamorous drudgery of general surgery to the frustrations of being bottom-tier interns. We were both exhausted, frayed at the edges, clinging to the thin thread of normalcy that connected us.

At some point, the conversation gave way to something wordless, as if the sheer weight of being alive at that moment demanded comfort. We ended up in bed, two overworked residents grasping at fleeting solace. The sex wasn't passionate or particularly memorable.

It was more like checking a box labeled *human connection.* Still, there was a certain tenderness in the act, a shared exhaustion that dulled the sharpness of the world outside.

Afterward, I fell asleep next to him with a flicker of cautious optimism. Maybe, just maybe, we could turn this into something real, something less fragile than the tangled mess we'd left behind in med school. It wasn't much to go on, but when you're running on fumes, hope can be surprisingly buoyant.

The Cheating Revelation

That hope died a swift and merciless death before dawn. Half-asleep, I heard his voice drifting from the next room—soft, hushed tones as if he didn't want to wake me. My groggy mind pieced together fragments: unmistakable intimacy, plans being made, and a tone far too warm for a casual chat between friends. My stomach churned as the realization sank in: He wasn't just talking; he was planning to meet someone else.

I froze, my heart pounding, as the sting of betrayal washed over me. Hours earlier, we'd shared a bed, and now he was plotting his next move. The irony would have been laughable if it didn't hurt so much. I stayed still, unwilling to confront him while still half-asleep, hoping that morning would bring clarity and reveal my next move.

At breakfast, I masked my simmering suspicion with a calm exterior. "Do you have plans later?" I asked casually as if my chest weren't tight with dread. He barely met my eyes, muttering something vague about meeting two friends—friends we both knew. When I asked if I could join, he brushed me off with a weak excuse: "It's more of a guy thing, you know, bro time." I let it go, offering no challenge. Trust is a fragile currency, and without proof, I wasn't ready to declare emotional bankruptcy. I went home, uneasy but determined to let time reveal the truth. A few days later, our schedules aligned again, giving us another evening together. As he stepped out briefly to grab something from his car, I noticed his jacket draped over a chair and absentmindedly slipped my hand into the pocket.

My pulse quickened. Proof obtained. Case closed.

When he returned, I confronted him, holding the receipt like a scalpel under bright operating room lights. "Care to explain this?" I asked, my voice calm but laced with steel. His reaction was textbook: first denial, then defensiveness, and finally escalation. His voice grew tight, his body agitated, and then he snapped. He grabbed my shoulders, shaking me violently, his hand striking me hard enough to leave me stunned.

Fear surged through me—sharp and undeniable. If physical intimidation was his response to being caught, then I had all the answers I needed. I stepped back, steadying myself as tears burned in my eyes. "We're done," I said firmly, grabbing my things and heading for the door. The city's neon lights blurred through my tears as I walked away, but my resolve was clear.

If he thought violence could silence me, he'd clearly underestimated my strength and backbone.

Aftermath of Betrayal and the Tap-Dance of Regret

I expected that to be the last chapter with Reginald. Surely, no resurrection could follow. But instead of fading into the background like a bad memory, he lingered—relentless, like a misguided salesperson pitching a defective product. He insisted I'd misunderstood, that the other woman was harmless, and that I was conjuring mountains from molehills. My eyes nearly sprained from rolling. Did he honestly think I'd forget the sting of that smack?

Desperate to rebuild trust, he staged a series of meet-ups where I could meet this elusive *harmless* woman and see for myself that there was *nothing amiss.* Equal parts curious and foolish, I agreed to the first meeting, half-mocking the circus I was certain awaited me. As expected, she didn't show. The second time? Another no-show. By the third attempt, it had crossed from awkward into humiliating. Trust doesn't regenerate by watching someone fail at illusions three times over.

After the third flop, Reginald finally broke and confessed the whole truth about this mysterious woman. During an interview for a general surgery residency in New Orleans, he'd met her. They'd gone out after the interviews, and he admitted to getting so sloppily drunk that he'd vomited all over himself. She had helped him remove his clothes and placed him in a tub to bathe himself. He swore nothing sexual happened, emphasizing that she had a boyfriend, but he wanted to give me *full disclosure.*

I listened, cold and unmoved. "Boyfriend or not, she doesn't seem interested in just being friends," I told him. "And clearly, she doesn't care much for me if she couldn't bother to meet me." I left the decision of what to do with that information in his hands. I wasn't giving ultimatums; I didn't need to. I was already done, regardless of what he chose.

Later, while scrolling through Facebook, I stumbled across a post from her. It wasn't subtle: a thinly veiled jab about *insecure girlfriends* forbidding their boyfriends from having female friends. The audacity felt like a slap in the face. She clearly wanted me to see it. So I responded, not publicly, but in a private message. If she had something to say about me, she could say it directly, not broadcast it to her audience.

To my surprise, Reginald cut ties with her shortly after. He didn't tell me about the conversation or its fallout, leaving me to piece together the details through her final Facebook rant. It seemed she wanted the last word as if trying to land one last blow. I gave Reginald a slow clap—not literally, but mentally—for taking the step. He earned a few brownie points in the process, though it wasn't nearly enough to erase the damage he'd done.

Hospital Intervention: Winning Me Over Again

Just when I thought the madness couldn't get any worse, my older daughter, Liza, added another twist to the story. I found myself at Rush University Hospital—Reginald's stomping ground—because my daughter had been admitted. At that moment, balancing motherhood and residency felt like trying to walk a tightrope over a pit of flames. My heart pounded with worry, and her fragile health suddenly made every past betrayal fade into the background. Between grueling rotations, endless call shifts, and countless rushed visits to her bedside, I was running on pure exhaustion and raw concern.

Then, out of nowhere, Reginald showed up at her bedside. Using his residency connections, he ensured she received the urgent care she needed and even sped up consults. The hospital staff, recognizing him as a colleague, gave her extra attention. It wasn't a grand gesture or a performance;

it was quiet, focused help, and in that moment, I couldn't ignore its impact.

Even the normally maddening discharge process—usually a bureaucratic nightmare—went smoothly. Paperwork was finalized without friction, consultations wrapped up, and my daughter went home with a clear care plan. Standing in that sterile hospital corridor, I managed a tentative "thank you" as Reginald passed by, and something inside me shifted. For all his faults, here was a man who stepped up when it truly mattered.

Yet, the memory of him shaking me still haunted me. I couldn't reconcile the Reginald who tenderly cared for my daughter with the one who had lashed out in anger. Even as I witnessed him quietly supporting her recovery, a flood of questions stirred within me: Was this the real Reginald—a man weighed down by insecurities and desperate to meet impossible expectations—or just another calculated performance, another attempt to win me over?

The Final Tap-Dance

Reginald wasn't done trying to redeem himself. His next move in this absurd tap-dance of regret was to introduce me to his parents. Usually, meeting the family is a milestone in a healthy relationship, not a desperate last-ditch attempt to patch up a broken one. But I agreed—half out of curiosity and half to see just how far he'd go.

Meeting them was surreal. Their home had this meticulously ordered vibe that screamed wealth, discipline, and an underlying rigidity. Every surface gleamed with perfection—I half expected their cleaning routine to rival that of an operating room. I walked in with neutral expectations, fully aware of the cultural tensions he'd mentioned before: His parents, Asian immigrants, held strict views about who he should date. As a first-generation Ghanaian-American, I was no stranger to navigating cultural landmines, and I wasn't about to let subtle racism—or worse—ruffle my feathers.

His mother greeted me at the door with a formal smile that never quite reached her eyes. She was the epitome of a "tiger mom": poised, controlling, and relentlessly efficient. I could tell she ran the household like a well-oiled machine, managing not just the chores but the entire family narrative. There was no genuine warmth in her greeting—just the bare minimum of courtesy. Our conversation stayed surface-level and safe. Compliments? None. Insults? Subtle at best. Yet her icy reserve spoke volumes.

In contrast, Reginald's father was quieter—his presence neutral and equally distant. He seemed content to follow his wife's lead, speaking only when absolutely necessary and never directing his words toward me. It wasn't overtly hostile; it was just plain indifferent. Sitting there, sipping tea and nibbling on perfectly arranged snacks, I absorbed their family dynamic. They had three children, with Reginald among them, but it was clear his mother ran the show. From childcare to household management, she was the nucleus—the living embodiment of traditional values enforced with an iron grip.

It wasn't surprising, then, that Reginald had been fast-tracked into medical school straight out of high school.

That achievement explained both his social awkwardness and the immense pressure he carried. He'd never really existed outside the confines of parental control, moving directly from childhood into the rigid world of medicine without the messy, unpredictable process of growing up on his own terms.

Understanding his upbringing didn't make his behavior any more acceptable, though. Trauma might explain bad behavior, but it never justifies betrayal or that slap.

The visit felt less like a warm family introduction and more like a cultural standoff. Whether his mother's chilly demeanor stemmed from disapproval of me being Black, a single mother, or simply because I didn't fit her strict idea of a *proper partner*, I couldn't say. Perhaps this was just her natural state—unrelenting and unapproachable. Either way, it didn't work in Reginald's favor.

When I left their pristine home, one thing was clear: If Reginald had hoped that this introduction would repair the wreckage he'd caused, he'd miscalculated spectacularly. Meeting your partner's parents after cheating is like trying to patch a gaping wound with a flimsy band-aid—too little, too late, and completely out of context.

The Campaign of Nostalgia

Despite the lukewarm reception from his parents, Reginald wasn't ready to give up. His next strategy was to weaponize nostalgia. He recalled our late-night study sessions in med school, the laughter over coffee and highlighters, and the evenings we'd spent exploring Chicago's eclectic cuisines.

At times, his efforts almost worked. Somewhere in the back of my mind, I could still picture the quieter, kinder Reginald from those library nights, the one who'd stumbled through his shyness with a disarming awkwardness. But every time a warm memory surfaced, it was quickly overpowered by the memory of that sushi receipt and the brutal recollection of that forceful slap.

No amount of sentimental reminiscing could erase the sting of betrayal or silence the nagging thought that things might only get worse.

Still, I couldn't completely dismiss the flicker of hope that maybe, just maybe, he could change. What if he could revert to that calmer, kinder version of himself?

That thought nagged at me—a persistent whisper I tried to ignore, but one that I couldn't quite silence.

A Proposal and the Weight of Second Chances

As 2009 approached, Reginald intensified his efforts to mend what he had broken. His next move was a grand one—a proposal. It was a gesture that could either solidify our bond or expose how fragile it truly was.

Before the big moment, he arranged a dinner with my two childhood best friends, Denise and Savannah. It was a calculated move, meant to display his commitment not just to me but to the life he envisioned for us. Over dinner, he painted an idyllic picture of our future: five children, a stable home, and a lifetime of love and support. He spoke earnestly about how he'd care for and cherish our family, weaving his fatherly aspirations into the story.

Denise and Savannah, knowing everything I had been through, were ecstatic. Their genuine happiness and hope for my future temporarily eclipsed my own doubts. Through their eyes, I saw a different Reginald—one who seemed earnest, family-oriented, and ready to build a stable life. Their enthusiasm was contagious, and for a moment, I allowed myself to imagine the possibility that the dream he described could become reality.

Not long after, Reginald orchestrated a private dinner at Del Frisco's, an elegant steakhouse perfect for romance. We were tucked into a cozy corner booth, surrounded by dim candlelight and the hum of hushed conversations. The ambiance should have been magical, but the weight of our rocky past—the betrayal, the slap, and the mistrust—made it feel strangely out of place.

As the evening unfolded, I felt a mix of apprehension and detachment. The lavishness of the setting contrasted sharply with the turbulence of our history. Then, halfway through dinner, he launched into a heartfelt speech. He called me his best friend, his life partner, and the person he couldn't imagine living without. He admitted his mistakes, though not in detail, and promised to rebuild what he had broken.

Then, he pulled out a ring.

My fork nearly clattered onto my plate. The diamond caught the candlelight, sparkling as if to underline the seriousness of the moment. I stared at it, torn between cynicism and a faint tug of hope. Was this another performance? A grand gesture to distract from the cracks in our relationship? Or did he truly mean it this time?

Memories flashed like warning signs: the sushi receipt, the woman in New Orleans, the physical and emotional scars. But alongside them came moments of tenderness: his care for my daughter during her hospital stay, the months he helped with my rent, and the quiet patience he had shown at times.

Strangely, I said yes.

The proposal wasn't where Reginald stopped. Shortly after, he approached my father to seek his blessing. My father, a devout Catholic who had once considered priesthood, carried a deep moral compass. At the time, he was training to become a deacon, embodying faith and integrity in every aspect of his life. His approval meant everything to me as a lifelong daddy's girl.

Reginald met him with humility and grace, pledging to protect me, provide for me, and love me wholeheartedly. My father listened intently as Reginald vowed to be a stable partner, and ultimately, he gave his blessing.

Later, in private, my father expressed his optimism with a hopeful smile. "Chinese men are usually loyal and don't cheat," he said, clearly reassured by Reginald's demeanor. I didn't have the heart to tell him the truth about the past. Instead, I nodded and let it slide, not wanting to tarnish his faith in what could be a promising future.

Reginald's upbringing was a stark contrast to mine, and his privilege was evident in every aspect of his life. His family owned a townhome in a gated community so exclusive that it housed Chicago's mayor, and it was guarded by heavy security.

During our relationship, his financial stability occasionally bridged the gap between us. While I struggled to make ends meet in a tiny 500-square-foot studio apartment on the Magnificent Mile, Reginald helped me cover rent during tough months. Parking alone at my building cost $30 a night, and though the train was convenient, I needed to shuttle between downtown and the suburbs where my parents cared for my daughter. His support was practical and appreciated, but it also underscored how different our lives had been. Accepting his proposal wasn't a fairytale moment. It was a calculated decision, made with eyes wide open. I knew the risks of giving someone a second chance after such deep betrayals. Another violent outburst or an affair would confirm the futility of it all.

But life had taught me that second chances, while risky, could sometimes lead to growth. I thought back to the mantra drilled into me during residency orientation: *Don't neglect your family.* As a surgeon, I knew my career would be demanding, but I refused to let my personal life crumble under the weight of ambition. Reginald, for all his flaws, seemed just as determined to keep us afloat.

That night, as we left Del Frisco's, the ring sparkling under the streetlights, I felt an odd duality. Fear of repeating past mistakes warred with a fragile hope that we could create something new. My mother had always taught me that unwavering faith could move mountains, and my father's blessing reinforced that belief.

So, I took the risk.

Reginald often spoke of building a family, fantasizing about five children and a future where we would never want for anything. It was an ambitious vision, almost laughable given our history, but his earnestness softened my skepticism.

This engagement marked the start of a new chapter—one filled with both promise and uncertainty. I carried with me the lessons of the past: to remain vigilant, to trust actions over words, and to rely on God Almighty to guide my steps. Resilience had brought me this far, and if there was even a slim chance that love could find a foothold in the ashes of our tumultuous history, I was willing to take that step.

Chapter 3:

Becoming a Mother Amidst Violence

By early 2009, I floated in a warm haze of excitement. Reginald had proposed the year before, and though our story was riddled with complications—ghosting, cultural tensions, and flashes of subtle control—I convinced myself that love had triumphed. After all, if we'd survived the rapids of medical school while juggling personal chaos, surely we could tackle the next stage: residency. My optimism felt almost giddy as I pictured a life of shared ambitions, cozy family dinners, and mutual support as we navigated the whirlwind of becoming real doctors.

Both of us had adjusted our career dreams, veering away from our original specialties and settling on general surgery. Reginald landed some impressive interviews, and I often accompanied him to "meet the residents" dinners as his glowing fiancée.

I was thrilled—yes, I'll lean into that cliché—because it felt surreal to be introduced as his partner. I stepped out in my best outfits, chattered confidently, and eased into the small talk that made those gatherings less awkward. Reginald hovered nearby, radiating a newfound self-assurance, watching me charm seasoned surgeons and interns alike.

Maybe he needed my sociability to shine, but in those moments, I only felt pride.

I thought: This is the life we'll build, he and I, complementing each other's strengths, forging a bright, united future.

Still, cracks shimmered beneath the polished surface. At one dinner, a resident casually asked, "What if you two match in different states?" Before I could answer, Reginald jumped in. "She'll follow me anywhere," he said confidently. A flicker of discomfort registered, sharp and distinct, though I brushed it aside. I told myself his confidence was romantic, not an omen. After all, hadn't I already said yes? Wasn't I committed to forging this path together?

We chose not to couples match, leaving our fate to the algorithm. I believed I was flexible enough to handle any outcome—ready to adapt. As always, fate had its own plans. It delivered a strange alignment: I secured another preliminary general surgery spot—not ideal, but manageable—and Reginald matched at one of his top choices, Baylor in Houston. His joy was infectious, and for a moment, it reignited my optimism. It wasn't perfect, but it was close enough.

Then, an unexpected opportunity surfaced: a transitional year affiliated with a neurosurgery program at a University of Texas hospital near Baylor College of Medicine. The idea of returning to neurosurgery reopened old wounds. My younger brother had died of a brain tumor, making the specialty both deeply personal and unbearably painful. But the thought of living close to Reginald outweighed my hesitation. Proximity felt like the key to letting love flourish.

So, I chose Houston. I chose him. I told myself it was a fair sacrifice; after all, we were building a future together, weren't we?

Moving in Together and Early Tensions

Moving to Texas wasn't just a geographic shift; it was a whole new chapter for Reginald and me. It marked the first time we lived together, and I had illusions of romantic cohabitation. I pictured us exploring Houston's incredible food scene, cooking together, and returning to a cozy apartment where love would flourish. The reality hit me like a bucket of cold water.

Reginald had moved first, and when I arrived a few months later, the cracks in my fantasy became glaringly obvious. He was messy—shockingly so. Clothes were scattered across the floor, crusty dishes were piled in the sink, and medical journals were stacked haphazardly under the coffee table. It dawned on me that his previously immaculate townhome in Chicago must have been maintained by a housekeeper. I'd foolishly assumed he'd kept it spotless himself.

I tried to accommodate his chaotic schedule as a surgical resident. I cooked meals for him, and he genuinely appreciated it. When the relentless Houston heat made cooking unbearable, even with the air conditioning blasting, we'd indulge in Tex-Mex or barbecue, exploring the city's diverse culinary scene. But between his rotations and our frequent eating out, we both gained weight—a physical manifestation of the indulgent but stressful life we were leading.

Reginald's hygiene became another challenge. He'd go days without bathing, blaming his grueling schedule. It wasn't just an issue of personal discomfort; I worried about how his colleagues in the operating room might perceive him. I eventually brought it up, framing it as a matter of professionalism, and he promised to do better. But his follow-through was inconsistent, leaving me frustrated.

One day, as I worked on the computer, I stumbled upon something that shook me: his internet history. He hadn't even bothered to delete it. Every link pointed to videos of blonde-haired, blue-eyed women. Porn itself didn't bother me, but the pattern was undeniable. It left me questioning everything. If that was his ideal, then what did he see in me—a first-generation Ghanaian-American woman with dark skin and curly hair?

I confronted him, confused and hurt. He brushed it off, claiming it was meaningless. "Porn is just porn," he said. "I'm not looking for a specific type of woman; it's just something to pass the time." He even described himself as asexual, insisting it had nothing to do with attraction. I sought advice from some male friends, who echoed his sentiment: "Don't overthink it. It's all fantasy." Despite their reassurances, I couldn't shake the quiet unease that lingered.

As if that weren't enough, I stumbled upon a letter from his father that cut even deeper. In it, his father begged him to end our relationship, bluntly stating that there would be time for "messing around with women" later. It was a stark reminder of the disapproval I'd sensed from Reginald's parents all along. His father's words reduced our relationship to a fleeting distraction and echoed the same parental pressures that once prompted Reginald to ghost me in med school.

Although I confronted Reginald about everything else, I never told him I'd seen the letter—not then, not now. The words stayed with me, though, lingering in my mind like a cautionary tale. I watched him closely, curious about whether he'd rise above his father's judgment. To his credit, he pushed forward.

Meanwhile, I was navigating my own challenges. I was working in the Department of Neurosurgery, completing a transitional year. It wasn't as grueling as a residency, but the cases still weighed heavily on my empathic heart. Neurosurgeons, to my surprise, had calm and collected demeanors, even under immense pressure. I admired their grace, but certain cases haunted me: the college student who fell unconscious from alcohol poisoning and had to be taken off life support, the weekend warriors who rode motorcycles without helmets and collided with cars or trucks. Each tragedy felt like a heavy stone in my chest.

But Reginald's father wasn't the only one disappointed by our choices. My old professor, Dr. Hawkins from Northwestern University, had high hopes for me. She had envisioned a different path—one where I stayed in general surgery, where my name would be attached to groundbreaking cases, and where I wouldn't compromise my potential for anything or anyone. When I chose to move to Houston instead of taking the general surgery position and later pivoted from Neurosurgery to Family Medicine, her disapproval was swift and cutting. Unlike Reginald's father, she didn't put her disappointment in a letter. She simply stopped reaching out. For years, I heard nothing from her. The silence spoke volumes. It wasn't just Reginald's family resisting our future; I had people in my own corner who couldn't understand why I was choosing a different path.

Living with Reginald only amplified my emotional exhaustion. Liza, my daughter, had moved to Texas with us by then, making my decision about my career path even clearer. I'd seen female neurosurgeons juggle motherhood and their careers, but I knew myself well enough to realize I couldn't do both without one suffering. I chose family over ambition and decided to apply for Family Medicine programs instead—a more lifestyle-friendly specialty that aligned with my priorities.

By 2010, I was accepted into the Family Medicine Program at Methodist Hospital, ready to carve out a path that balanced my professional aspirations with being a present mother.

The wedding we'd been planning was delayed again, this time due to excuses from his family. His father didn't want a destination wedding, citing an unwillingness to travel, while the rest of his family showed little enthusiasm for the union. Their disinterest felt pointed as if they were dragging their feet in subtle protest. I couldn't help but remember the letter and his father's warning, wondering if this resistance would ever truly fade.

Despite these mounting challenges, Reginald and I still had fleeting moments of warmth. We shared late-night conversations about residency and laughed over hospital mishaps. Some nights, we'd come home from a Tex-Mex binge, collapse on the couch, and exchange tired but genuine smiles. Those moments kept me holding on, convincing myself that maybe, just maybe, we could still build the life we'd envisioned.

The Journey to Parenthood

After settling into Houston and adjusting to our new routines, Reginald and I began talking seriously about starting a family. The plan was clear: We'd wait until after the wedding. But that didn't mean we weren't preparing for it. We started doing our *homework*—not just the obvious part, but everything else that might set us up for success. We knew the healthier we were, the better our chances. Unfortunately, Houston hadn't been kind to our waistlines.

We'd both gained weight since moving south. Back in Chicago, walking was second nature. Public transportation was easy, and the city itself kept us active. Houston, with its sprawling layout and car-dependent lifestyle, was a different beast entirely. Long commutes and sticky heat didn't inspire evening strolls. The gym felt like a distant memory, and we both felt the effects of our increasingly sedentary lives. When my gynecologist confirmed the struggle we were facing, it wasn't a surprise, but it still hit hard.

A fertility workup revealed I had PCOS, and Reginald's sperm count was low. The verdict was blunt: IVF was likely our only chance to have a child. That news carried a weight I wasn't ready for. I hadn't struggled to conceive before—quite the opposite. In college, I'd had an unplanned pregnancy and an abortion after Liza was born. Now, years later, it felt cruel to be on the opposite side of that experience.

Determined not to let the diagnosis defeat us, we set weight loss as our shared mission. Reginald and I joined a gym, carving out time from our chaotic schedules to prioritize our health. Slowly, the pounds started to come off. I also found a new passion: aerial aerobics at Innerme Studios. It was a combination of dance, core strength, and upper-body workouts that left me feeling alive. I wasn't flexible or graceful, but somehow, it came naturally. It became my sanctuary, a place where I could escape the stress of fertility struggles and residency.

Reginald supported me, even encouraging my new hobby with a thoughtful gesture: One Christmas, he surprised me with a pole for the garage. It was one of those rare moments when I felt truly seen by him.

In addition to fitness, I explored other ways to improve our chances. I'd read that walnuts could boost male fertility, so I added them to Reginald's diet, jokingly calling them "super sperm snacks." It felt silly, but we were willing to try anything.

Despite our efforts, a year passed without results. I meticulously tracked ovulation cycles, cervical mucus changes, and body temperature, but nothing worked. We started to live with the reality that IVF might be our only option and postponed treatment until we were financially ready. We tried not to let the disappointment overshadow our daily lives, focusing instead on what we could control.

Then, it happened.

One morning, I stared at a pregnancy test in disbelief, the two faint lines confirming the impossible. After everything—the diagnosis, the lifestyle changes, the walnuts—we'd conceived naturally. It felt miraculous.

But the timing was… complicated.

A Trip Full of Surprises

By March 2011, I was juggling residency and pregnancy when Reginald and I made one of our regular trips back to Illinois to visit family. It felt like a chance to pause, reconnect, and breathe in the familiarity of home. What I didn't expect was for this trip to turn into something much bigger—a wedding.

Looking back, I can see the hints were there. The courthouse they chose was in a quiet, unfamiliar county on the outskirts of Illinois, far from where I grew up. I hadn't completed any paperwork for a marriage license—at least, not that I could remember. At the time, I chalked it up to pregnancy brain, being too tired and distracted by work to think much of it. Only later did it click just how meticulously planned this *surprise* had been. The ceremony itself was simple, intimate, and quick. After the ceremony, we went to Reginald's family home, where the day's surprises continued with a series of traditional rituals.

The first custom began as soon as we stepped out of the car. We were handed oranges and instructed to rub them on ourselves. The bright, citrus scent filled the air as we followed the gesture meant to symbolize wealth and prosperity for our marriage.

Next, his uncle appeared holding a red umbrella, carefully positioning it over us as we walked toward the house. I later learned that the red umbrella is an important symbol in Chinese weddings, offering protection and blessings for the bride as she enters her new home.

Once inside, we performed a tea ceremony, one of the most significant traditions in Chinese culture. Reginald's sister and I prepared tea, pouring it into delicate cups and presenting it to the elders as a gesture of respect and gratitude. This ritual formally welcomed me into their family, solidifying our union in their eyes.

Though I was exhausted—pregnancy and residency don't exactly mix well—I went through each step, trying to honor the traditions that meant so much to Reginald's family.

That night, we stayed in Reginald's childhood bedroom. The rocket ship wallpaper and shelves of stuffed pandas made it feel like I'd stepped into a time capsule of his boyhood.

As I lay there, surrounded by whimsical reminders of his childhood, I reflected on everything that had happened.

I was married.

A Violent Night

By June 2011, life felt like a relentless juggling act. I was seven months pregnant, still deep in residency, caring for Liza—now living with us—and trying to adjust to being a wife. Each day felt like a blur; my energy stretched to its limits. But one suffocatingly hot night, the fragile sense of balance I had been clinging to shattered in a way I never could have anticipated.

I woke to a sharp jolt, Reginald's fists pounding against my pregnant belly. Terror ripped through me, jolting me upright. For a moment, I couldn't comprehend what was happening. Then he froze, his wide eyes darting between me and my swollen abdomen. He stammered out an explanation: He'd been dreaming about trauma cases at the hospital, lashing out at invisible attackers.

The room felt like it was spinning. My mind reeled, trying to reconcile his panicked apologies with what I had just experienced. Was it possible that he truly didn't know what he was doing? Could this really have been an unconscious reaction, a flail brought on by exhaustion and stress? Or was this something darker?

He swore it was an accident, that he never intended to harm me or the baby. I wanted to believe him—needed to believe him. After all, this baby wasn't just any child; he was our miracle.

The memory of everything we went through to conceive flashed through my mind: the fertility issues, the diagnosis of PCOS, the low sperm count, the hours spent tracking ovulation, charting cervical mucus, and trying to lose weight. Reginald had even administered my weekly progesterone injections to help me carry the baby to term. Why would he intentionally sabotage what we'd fought so hard to achieve?

But another thought crept in, one I tried to push away. I knew the statistics: Domestic violence rates surge during pregnancy. I'd read the data during my medical training, had even seen the warning signs in patients. Could this be part of that pattern? Or was I projecting, twisting a nightmare into something it wasn't?

The next day, fear and doubt gnawed at me, and I decided to check on the baby. I visited a friend who had access to an ultrasound machine. I lied to her, saying I had lost my balance and fallen forward onto my belly. She examined me carefully, her expression softening with relief as she told me there were no signs of internal bleeding. The baby's heartbeat was strong, and everything looked stable.

Relief washed over me, but it was fleeting. The guilt of hiding the truth clung to me. I couldn't stop replaying the moment in my head—his fists, his explanation, his apologies.

Could this really have been an isolated, unintentional horror? I told myself it had to be. I stayed silent, trying to bury my fears for the sake of my baby.

The Baby's Arrival

In August 2011, the world shifted as we welcomed our baby boy. The chaotic rhythm of labor pains, the hum of hospital lights, and the flurry of white coats all faded when I heard his first cry. Holding him ignited a love so fierce it momentarily drowned out every lingering fear and doubt.

Reginald surprised me by stepping into fatherhood with unexpected enthusiasm. He changed diapers, rocked our son through sleepless nights, and handled the countless little tasks that come with a newborn. His mother, observing this, remarked with faint astonishment that her husband had never helped with their children. Seeing Reginald break that pattern gave her a sense of pride, one she didn't hide.

When Reginald's family visited, the baby wasted no time making his mark—literally. He pooped on Reginald's sister, and everyone laughed as someone declared it a sign of good luck. His sister later joked that the moment must have worked; she went on to have three healthy children of her own.

Liza slipped seamlessly into her role as a big sister. She adored her baby brother, doting on him with a sweetness that melted my heart.

Our home became a whirlwind of baby bottles, toddler toys, and medical textbooks.

Adjusting to the New Normal

The months following our son's birth brought visits from Reginald's parents, who offered plenty of advice—some of it helpful, much of it unsolicited. I played the role of the polite daughter-in-law, nodding along while quietly following my own instincts.

My mother worked to keep the peace, aware of the delicate balance I was trying to maintain. Between motherhood, residency, and marriage, my life felt like a high-wire act, with no room for missteps.

Reginald's father remained distant, his disapproval palpable even in silence. His mother, though initially cold, softened when she saw Reginald actively stepping into fatherhood. She openly praised his involvement, calling it a sign of progress and a break from the detachment she'd endured in her own marriage.

Amid their quiet judgments and subtle shifts, life pressed on in its chaotic rhythm. I juggled Family Medicine rotations, postpartum demands, and caring for Liza while Reginald navigated the grueling hours of general surgery training. Our days blurred together, a mix of sleepless nights, diaper changes, and hospital obligations. At times, we found fleeting moments of connection—a shared laugh over dinner or quiet exchanges during the baby's naps.

But more often than not, we functioned like two ships passing in the night, tethered to the same storm but charting separate courses.

Reaching 2013: Milestones, Motherhood, and Mixed Emotions

By 2013, life felt like a whirlwind of milestones, challenges, and the beautiful chaos of a growing family. I was six months pregnant with our second child, counting down the final stretch of my Family Medicine residency. The juxtaposition of closing one chapter while preparing for a new life filled me with a mix of pride and uncertainty.

Graduation day came with a swirl of emotions. Some family members stayed away, their disappointment over my career shift from neurosurgery still palpable. To them, it was a step down; to me, it was survival. But my brother's unwavering support stood out. He traveled from Illinois to cheer me on, a quiet affirmation that my journey mattered, even if it didn't look the way others imagined.

Crossing the stage, diploma in hand and baby bump prominent beneath my gown, I felt a profound mix of relief and pride. I had chosen a specialty that aligned with who I was—a field that let me connect deeply with patients, offering care that felt personal and grounded. This wasn't the path I'd initially envisioned, but it was the one that allowed me to keep going, to balance my career with the demands of motherhood and life's unexpected twists. Reginald stood off to the side, holding our toddler.

He didn't say much, but his presence felt steady, almost as if he understood the significance of the moment. The sight of him doting on our son brought a flicker of reassurance, a reminder that, for all the complexities in our relationship, we were building a life together.

Finding Joy in the Chaos

Life during those years was chaotic but not without moments of lightness. I found solace in humor—laughing at the absurdities of parenting, work, and the sheer unpredictability of it all. It wasn't always easy to find joy amid the challenges, but when it surfaced, it was powerful enough to sustain me.

Reginald's better qualities became my focus. He was an attentive father, eager to support me through the highs and lows of parenting. Watching him embrace the role of a dad brought glimpses of the man I hoped he could fully become. Some days, it was enough to quiet my doubts. Other days, the uncertainty lingered, a quiet hum in the background.

Still, I clung to the victories. I had carved out a career that suited my values, nurtured a growing family, and found moments of connection amid the chaos. For all its imperfections, our family was held together by threads of love, persistence, and a shared determination to move forward.

Chapter 4:

Control and Isolation

By 2013, I was certain I had finally crossed a major threshold. Graduating from my Family Medicine residency meant stepping out of the grueling grind of endless rotations and barely-there paychecks. For the first time in years, I could see a path forward with a sense of control over my career and family. No more scrambling for what felt like survival; this was stability. Or so I thought.

July came, and with it, a spark of clarity. "I want us to have a real wedding," I told Reginald one evening, almost testing the waters. To my surprise, he didn't shrug it off or offer excuses about time or expense. Instead, he nodded, saying, "Let's do it in December." His agreement came so easily that I blinked, half wondering if he was serious. But I let the moment carry me. After all, it felt like a chance to rewrite the script—not the courthouse wedding I'd endured under his parents' watchful eyes, but something joyful and intentional.

A Lull… Sort Of

What followed was a brief lull in the chaos, or at least it felt that way. Reginald's research hours during this time were less punishing than the rotations he'd slogged through before. He started attending a few of Liza's school events, enough to earn her curious questions about whether she might be part Chinese. The innocence of her confusion made me laugh, even as I gently reminded her of her Ghanaian roots.

Meanwhile, our family continued to grow, with baby number three due in September. This time, Reginald seemed more engaged in the process. He helped set up cribs and cooked when my body refused to cooperate with the demands of pregnancy. Occasionally, we'd find moments of connection in the small routines—him rocking our toddler to sleep while I tried to keep up with my clinic schedule or us joking about how the vow renewal might just give us the clean slate we both secretly wanted.

It was around this time that I received a letter from my aunt congratulating me on finishing residency but warning me not to ignore any red flags. "Don't let your guard down if you sense darkness," she wrote. I tucked her words away, trying to reassure myself that everything felt steady enough for now. Yes, Reginald's mother still hovered in the background, and his father's silence remained a steady presence, but there were glimmers of progress. Reginald's hands-on approach with the kids and his willingness to help around the house—these were signs that perhaps things were finally shifting.

In September, our daughter arrived, completing our trio of children. Liza embraced her role as a big sister with the same enthusiasm she'd shown when her brother was born, eagerly helping with bottles and bedtime stories. Holding our newborn, I couldn't help but feel a fragile hope take root. Maybe we were turning a corner. Maybe the shadow of that horrifying night in June 2011 could finally recede. Reginald seemed a bit more present. He even started showing up at family dinners with my parents, a gesture that didn't go unnoticed. My father remarked on it once, saying, "I think he's really trying now." I clung to that observation like a lifeline, willing it to be true.

As the weeks passed, my mind turned increasingly to the vow renewal. December felt just close enough to make it achievable but distant enough to plan something meaningful. I envisioned a Christmas-themed wedding with frosty backdrops, flickering lights, and a fusion of our cultural traditions. Ghanaian elements would blend seamlessly with Reginald's Chinese heritage, all under the umbrella of our shared Catholic faith. It was ambitious, but I'd pulled off more difficult feats during residency. What was one wedding?

The Big Wedding Plan

Of course, nothing about planning a wedding—especially one involving Reginald's mother—was simple. She immediately made her presence felt, swooping in with declarations about what was *appropriate* and *respectful.* When I suggested flying lanterns as part of the decor, she dismissed the idea with a wave of her hand. "That's not Chinese," she said, her tone carrying more authority than the topic warranted. The menu became another battlefield. I'd suggested including chicken alongside the other entrees, thinking it was an easy addition. She visibly recoiled. "You won't embarrass me," she snapped, as though poultry were some great social offense.

Reginald's sister joined the fray, supporting their mother's vision at every turn. If I wanted silver tablecloths to match my winter wonderland theme, she pushed for red. If I suggested Christmas-inspired touches, she insisted they were "too much" and needed toning down for the sake of elegance. One day, the wedding planner approached me with an apologetic expression. "They want to spend a thousand dollars on a Chinese dragon cameo," she said hesitantly, as though bracing for my reaction.

I shrugged, too exhausted to argue. If they wanted to spend their money on a fleeting spectacle, I wouldn't stop them. I was determined to focus on the parts of the wedding that mattered to me—bringing my family together, honoring our cultures, and celebrating how far we'd come.

Reginald, to his credit, surprised me with how cooperative he was. When I floated the idea of a father-daughter dance and a choreographed number for the two of us, he agreed without hesitation. We even started taking weekly dance lessons, something I hadn't expected him to commit to.

As we practiced spins and dips, I found myself softening toward him, letting my guard down just enough to believe in the possibility of a fresh start. For a man who rarely expressed his emotions openly, his willingness to participate in this part of the process felt like a quiet apology for the times he'd let me down. Meanwhile, I navigated the logistical minefield of planning a wedding in just six months.

Between clinic shifts, midnight feedings, and managing the older kids, I juggled endless phone calls, emails, and in-person meetings with the wedding planner. Reginald's mother found ways to insert herself into every decision, insisting on overseeing the flower arrangements and vetoing anything she deemed *cheap*. I let most of it slide, telling myself that if compromising on decorations kept the peace, it was worth it.

As December approached, the whirlwind of planning intensified. But there were moments that made the chaos feel worthwhile—Reginald practicing his dance moves with surprising dedication, my older kids excitedly trying on their outfits, and my father beaming with pride at the thought of finally walking me down the aisle. These glimpses of joy reminded me why I wanted this vow renewal in the first place. It wasn't about erasing the past but about reclaiming our story and making it something worth holding onto.

By the time December arrived, I was equal parts exhausted and exhilarated. The wedding planner, sensing my nerves, gave me a reassuring smile during our final meeting. "We'll get through this," she said. I nodded, holding onto her words like a mantra.

For all the challenges and compromises, I believed that this day could mark the beginning of something new. If nothing else, it would be a celebration of survival—of love that had weathered storms and a family that was still standing despite everything.

The Wedding Day

Despite my last-minute mania, I somehow pulled off a decently grand event in mid-December—an elaborate production with over two hundred brave souls defying Chicago's notorious winter. There I stood, drowning in a giant Cinderella gown (a.k.a. a self-contained sauna), half-lamenting the weight of satin and sequins, half-giddy that this was not a forced courthouse circus for once. The church itself sparkled in silver and white, reflecting every glimmer of the holiday lights outside. My heart pounded, but a rush of triumph coexisted with the cold air burning my lungs.

I'd endured so much leading up to this: meddling in-laws, father-in-law's stares, mother-in-law's demands, and a bit of a bridesmaid meltdown. One of my friends—someone

I'd "trauma-bonded" with during our brutal general surgery intern year—had originally pledged to stand by me, only to drop out at the eleventh hour. She claimed pregnancy complications, but part of me wondered if that was code for "I'm just not that invested." Meanwhile, Reginald's sister was pregnant herself and still participated fully. The timing felt fishy, but I had no bandwidth to investigate. I needed a replacement, fast.

I ended up recruiting my best friend Aaron's wife—also pregnant, ironically—who swooped in with heroic composure. I had actually been a bridesmaid at her wedding in Hawaii, so our bond already felt destined. She fit into the maternity bridesmaid dress so perfectly that I nearly believed fate had intervened on my behalf. It was heartbreaking to see how easily my original friend had bailed, but sometimes, you realize that a "trauma bond" doesn't equate to genuine loyalty. Live and learn, right?

My father—the same father who never got to officiate that clandestine courthouse fiasco—now walked me down the aisle, silver and white draping every pew. In a special twist, I used my three-month-old baby girl as my *bouquet*, cradling her in place of flowers, and drawing a wave of aww from the congregation. Once I reached the altar, I handed her off to my mother. My father swapped from paternal escort to deacon officiant—complete with vestments, Scripture readings, and a brief homily about unity. Reginald stood at the altar, giving me a nod that said, *We've got this.* I breathed in, feeling the moment's weight: At last, a wedding day on my own terms.

We exchanged vows with surprising ease. Reginald had taken Catholic classes and completed the required retreat, though his parents' home was littered with Buddha statues—who knew how that all reconciled? Still, sincerity triumphed over contradiction in that moment. A hush of peace settled as my father pronounced us husband and wife (again), and I silently recalled the forced vow fiasco of 2011. I felt triumphant, or at least I allowed myself to pretend it was a pure fairytale.

Then came the reception, a swirl of cultural mash-ups. I was still gasping for air in my tight gown, but at least we had a meticulously choreographed first dance. Reginald and I managed not to butcher it—only two near-collisions, which I count as a victory. Guests hollered in delight—some combos of "Opa!" mixing with Ghanaian cheers—while confetti drifted like plastic snowflakes. My father, having finished his deacon duties, stood aside proudly. My mother-in-law' insisted on a thousand-dollar Chinese dragon cameo that pranced for five minutes, bizarre but entertaining; I later learned that the Chinese dragon dance was meant to drive away evil spirits and bring good luck and blessings to the couple. Meanwhile, Ghanaian drummers pounded mesmerizing beats. The synergy was wild: a swirl of Catholic blessings, Chinese dragons, and African rhythms jammed into one wedding. I half-laughed at the spectacle, at least relieved we weren't huddled in a remote county for a surprise vow ceremony.

The mother-in-law still found ways to overshadow me; she reminded me not to disclose how much money she and Reginald's sister contributed, as if secrecy was essential to preserving face. We'd asked guests to donate to a children's brain tumor fund in memory of my brother, so the mother then demanded a ledger of who gave how much, scoffing at smaller amounts. I tried ignoring her negativity, focusing on the cause itself. Guests milled around, enthralled by balloon artists, face painters, and the comedic blend of cultures.

Of course, no wedding in my world could end without an extra dollop of chaos. Just as I let myself breathe,

Reginald's brother rose for the best-man speech. In what felt like a twisted sequel, he decided to deliver a *roast*—except it devolved into insulting Reginald, calling him "fat and dumb." Half the crowd laughed awkwardly; the other half wore expressions of shock. My cheeks burned with anger. *Why humiliate him in front of 200 guests?* I recalled how this brother never invited Reginald to his own wedding, supposedly because of racist in-laws. Maybe this roast was long-simmering sibling hostility. Either way, it clashed harshly with the fairytale vibe I'd fought so hard to create.

Reginald's face reddened, but he forced a polite grin. I wanted to sprint onto the stage, yank the mic from his brother's hand, maybe fling it into the nearest Chinese dragon costume. Instead, I stood there, a stiff smile plastered on my lips, scanning the crowd. My father caught my eye and offered a sympathetic shrug from across the room. Another fiasco to survive, I thought, ironically finding comedic solace that after forced vows, meltdown dinners, and mother-sister combos, a best-man roast seemed almost mild by comparison. Still, it seared away the last illusions of a perfect day.

Yet I refused to let that overshadow everything else. My new bridesmaid glowed at my side, laughing off the roast as if it were mere background noise. My best friend Savannah gave a radiant toast, praising how far I'd come since the hush-hush fiasco in 2011 to this snowy wonderland. She'd also been present at the birth of my baby girl just a few months prior—her unwavering support a reminder I wasn't alone in navigating these swirling storms.

By the time the night wound down, swirling confetti and half-melted ice sculptures formed the final backdrop. The synergy of Chinese dragons, Ghanaian drummers, Catholic officiation, and the best man's roast was an apt metaphor for my entire relationship: comedic, jarring, a tad absurd, yet laced with fleeting magic. Sure, my mother-in-law overshadowed me, my father-in-law lurked, and Reginald's brother decided to publicly roast him. But I clung to the pockets of real joy—my father officiating with pride, my baby as my *bouquet*, the drummers blending into the frigid Chicago air—and reminded myself, illusions or not, I'd earned this Cinderella moment. Even if real life would come crashing in soon, I savored the fleeting sense of triumph as the bride in the frosty wonderland I'd long dreamed of.

Building a Home for Three Children

By 2014, life as a married mother of three looked deceptively polished on the outside. Inside, it felt more like I was trying to hold a house of cards together during a windstorm. Liza had embraced her role as the big sister, my toddler son brought an energy that could power a small city, and my baby girl was an adorable cooing machine. Meanwhile, I was juggling a demanding Family Medicine career and a marriage that increasingly felt like a solo act with a sporadic guest star.

Reginald's research schedule gave him more downtime, which meant he showed up a little more often—sometimes to read bedtime stories or build Legos—but he still managed to leave the heavy lifting to me. Morning chaos? My job. School drop-offs? Me again! Doctor's appointments, late-night feedings, and the endless toy explosion in the living room? All mine. Reginald's contributions were like rare cameos in a long-running sitcom. Sure, they got a laugh here and there, but they didn't change the plot.

The real kicker? His mother still hovered like an overly invested stage director, pulling strings from the wings while I managed the spotlight. And, of course, Reginald let her. No boundaries, no pushback. Just me, playing the default buffer, quietly dodging her critiques and redirecting her *helpful suggestions* while trying to keep the household running.

Odd Incidents and Quiet Sabotage

It wasn't just the constant meddling; it was the unsettling moments that made me question everything. Like the time Reginald decided to dismantle our baby girl Veronica's playpen while she was still inside it. I froze mid-step, staring in horror as he casually took it apart, oblivious to the fact that a whole human child was trapped in his *project.* And then, as if the situation couldn't get worse, he fumbled, and Veronica tumbled out. The baby was fine—more than fine, it turns out—but my nerves were shot. When I confronted him, he shrugged and said he was "reassembling it differently." Differently? She wasn't Ikea furniture!

Of course, we rushed her to the doctor, terrified we'd broken our baby girl. But the doctor, a calm and unfazed pro, took one look and said, "Don't worry—babies are bouncy." My mom, never one to miss an opportunity for gallows humor, latched onto that phrase immediately. To this day, she jokes about how Veronica bounced right into brilliance, starting to say her first words at just one month old and walking by eight months. "See? That's what happens when you drop them early—superpowers!" she says, laughing. I have to admit, I get my morbid humor from her, and it's served me well. Back then, though, I relied on that humor as a lifeline to keep from spiraling.

Then, there was his father, whose online behavior became a new source of discomfort. At first, I dismissed it as a harmless misunderstanding of Facebook etiquette—an older man fumbling with the platform. His constant *likes* on my photos were a little odd, but I brushed it off. Then he began poking me.

Not once, not twice, but repeatedly. I ignored it, chalking it up to an awkward attempt at connection. But the last straw came when he started liking bikini photos. That wasn't just awkward; it was gross. I mean, who does that to their son's wife's photos?

Relatives started to notice. Friends messaged me, asking if I was okay. Even my older brother, who rarely commented on such things, quietly asked how it made me feel and what Reginald planned to do about it. The truth? Reginald did nothing. When I brought it up, expecting at least mild outrage on my behalf, he snapped. "Well, maybe don't post those photos," he said, his tone colder than I'd anticipated. It was the verbal equivalent of being handed a paper towel after someone spilled wine all over your dress. Not once did he offer to talk to his father or even acknowledge how deeply unsettling it was for me. Instead, he turned stone-cold, spewing venom like I was the problem.

That moment marked a major shift in my perception of him. I lost a lot of respect for Reginald that day. His father's actions didn't just make me uncomfortable; they triggered deep memories of my own history of abuse, memories I'd worked hard to bury. The realization hit me like a freight train: If I couldn't rely on Reginald to protect me in this situation, how could I trust him to safeguard our daughters?

I tried confiding in his sister's mother-in-law, hoping for some validation. She stayed vague, but her actions spoke louder than her words. Shortly afterward, she stopped bringing her young daughter to family gatherings. My gut told me it had something to do with Reginald's father, though she never confirmed it outright. The avoidance was enough of a confirmation for me.

Back on social media, I started noticing something even more troubling: Reginald's father's page was full of photos of young girls, many of them in pageant outfits that made my skin crawl. They looked like tiny JonBenét Ramseys. I couldn't unsee it. The more I observed, the more uncomfortable I became. Blocking him felt like my only option, so I did. It wasn't just about protecting myself; it was about drawing a boundary where none had existed before.

My older brother, who knows my history of abuse, was livid. He wanted to confront Reginald's father himself, but I talked him down. "You've already survived so much," he said, his voice thick with frustration. "Why should you have to deal with this, too?" His words stayed with me, a reminder that I deserved better than the quiet erosion of safety and respect happening in my own home. The final straw came during a holiday visit to Reginald's parents' house. His father called both of us into a room, insisting on lecturing Reginald about his weight and overall health. The conversation was awkward, uncomfortable, and laced with tension. Reginald grew visibly irritated and stormed out, leaving me alone with his father. My skin crawled as I sat there, the seconds stretching into what felt like hours. Thankfully, Reginald's mother walked in, pretending to tidy up but clearly sensing the discomfort in the room. Her presence gave me an excuse to slip out. For once, I was grateful for her meddling.

From that point on, I started building walls—not just figuratively but emotionally. I avoided being alone with Reginald's father at all costs. I began setting boundaries in ways I never thought I'd need to in a marriage—steering clear of certain conversations, keeping my distance during family gatherings, and relying on small acts of defiance to reclaim some sense of control. But the damage was done. The days when Reginald would walk me to my car, telling me about his Chinese wrestling history, felt like a distant memory. He wasn't the man I thought I'd married. He wasn't my protector. And I couldn't unsee that.

Where Did 2014 Leave Me?

By the end of 2014, everything felt heavier—though I suppose three kids, a marriage that was more "guesswork" than a partnership, and a creeping sense of isolation will do that to a person. My relationship with Reginald was fraying, unraveling one ignored red flag at a time. His father's social media antics, Reginald's refusal to address them, and the unspoken tension in our home had chipped away at whatever trust I had left. I felt less like a wife and more like a single mother of three, stuck navigating a maze of subtle sabotage, unresolved trauma, and the occasional Lego minefield. The cracks in our marriage were no longer surface-level; they were cavernous. Something had to give. I just didn't know what—or if I'd have the energy to push for it.

Control and isolation were sneaky like that. From the outside, we probably looked like a busy but functional family, the kind of household where the biggest problem is running out of milk on a Monday morning. But beneath that façade, there were constant presences, quietly shaping my decisions and dictating my days. I told myself I was managing it, but the truth? It felt like trying to steer a sinking ship with a ladle.

Still, I found small ways to push back. When Reginald's mother demanded we host a grand Chinese New Year celebration that would rival a festival, I politely declined and blamed the kids' schedules. (Kids are excellent scapegoats for dodging awkward obligations.).

When she criticized my parenting or my household choices, I mastered the art of the "smile, nod, and do whatever I want anyway" response. These micro-boundaries weren't earth-shattering, but they were my way of reclaiming a little control. But even with my small victories, the isolation was impossible to ignore.

Reginald's family dynamics left no room for me to assert myself. His father's lurking presence, his mother's relentless meddling, and his sister's unsolicited opinions created an environment where I felt more like an intruder than a wife. Even when Reginald tried to support me—helping with the kids or showing up to Liza's school events—it felt more like a cameo appearance than a real commitment.

I clung to the moments that made it all feel worthwhile: Liza's infectious enthusiasm as a big sister, my toddler's belly laughs, and my baby girl's wobbly first steps.

These flashes of joy reminded me why I stayed and why I kept fighting to create something that resembled stability. But those sweet, fleeting moments didn't erase the truth: I felt less like a partner and more like a caretaker, less like a part of a family and more like a very tired stagehand behind someone else's performance.

By the time 2015 arrived, I was staring down the cold, hard truth. The illusion of a perfect marriage had shattered, leaving a glittering mess that no amount of holiday magic—or mother-in-law micromanaging—could fix. But I hadn't given up on the idea of carving out something better. I was determined to reclaim my voice, even if it meant speaking over the noise of meddling relatives, toddler tantrums, and a husband who seemed more comfortable in the shadows than stepping up.

If there's one thing I had learned over the years, it was this: Survival isn't just about gritting your teeth and hanging on; it's about rewriting your story, even when the chapters ahead feel daunting. And for the first time in years, I felt ready to start writing a new one.

That's how I found myself standing at the edge of what would become *The Turning Point.*

Chapter 5:

The Turning Point

By the start of 2015, I had finally made it; I was a practicing Family Medicine physician. That title had once felt like an impossible dream, something far off in the distance as I trudged through residency, pregnancies, and a rollercoaster of family dynamics. In theory, I was now free to design a life that fit my passions, patient care, and, hopefully, an actual partnership with Reginald.

After all, stability was the light at the end of that long, grueling tunnel.

Or so I thought. Because, as I'd come to realize, stability and normalcy are like unicorns: lovely ideas, but they rarely show up when you expect them.

I was pregnant again—our third child, making me a mother of four. April was on her way, and I was still adjusting to life as a new physician. To say I felt overwhelmed would be like calling Houston "a bit warm" in the summer. But I clung to one comforting thought: my mother.

She had been my saving grace during every postpartum period, swooping in from Illinois to cook, clean, and calm the chaos. Surely, with a stable job and more predictable hours, I could manage this, right?

The Final Woo Baby: A Crash Course in Disappointment

Then labor hit.

Contractions slammed into me, and I told Reginald we needed to get to the hospital immediately. He nodded, calm as ever, and then—for reasons that still boggle my mind—decided that Veronica and Reginald Jr. needed a bath. Right then.

Picture me doubled over, clinging to the counter, gasping through contractions as Reginald herded the kids into the bathroom. Was this his version of nesting?

Did he really believe that clean siblings were a prerequisite for a successful birth? I'll never know. All I could do was grit my teeth and wait as the contractions intensified, silently daring him to move any slower. My glare practically screamed: *If we don't leave soon, you'll be delivering this baby yourself.*

By the time we finally got in the car, my labor was so advanced that we barely made it to the hospital. April arrived in a blur—so fast that my own OB didn't even make it. An on-call doctor stepped in, calmly handling the delivery as I struggled to keep up with my body's urgent demands.

Reginald, meanwhile, decided this was the perfect moment to offer his *help*.

"Can you give her a husband stitch?" he asked the doctor mid-repair.

If you've never heard of the *husband stitch*, it's an archaic, misogynistic suggestion where the vaginal opening is tightened for the man's benefit during postpartum repair. In that moment, I wanted to summon every bit of strength to fling something at him. Instead, I focused on surviving the birth. Thankfully, the doctor ignored him and continued with standard care, sparing me further humiliation.

After April's arrival, my mother swooped in—as she always did—to help me navigate those early postpartum days. Her calming presence was a balm, and for a few precious moments, I could finally breathe. But that evening, Reginald left the hospital, promising to return the next day. And then… nothing.

No flowers. No balloons. Not even a text.

The hospital was physically connected to his workplace by underground tunnels; he could've visited without even stepping outside. But he didn't.

I sat in that hospital bed, cradling our newborn, a storm of heartbreak and rage swirling in my chest. This was the same man who eagerly volunteered to cover shifts for his colleagues with newborns, the guy who always made sure they had time to bond with their families. So why couldn't he spare an hour for his own wife and child? And it wasn't just his absence; it was the context. The "husband stitch" comment still churned in my mind, a lingering slap of misogyny echoing his mother's mantra:

"A woman's job is to keep the home and produce children." It wasn't the first time I'd heard those words from her, but now they felt like the subtle script Reginald was determined to follow.

At work, he loved playing the hero—volunteering for extra shifts, solving problems, and basking in the gratitude of his colleagues. At home, however, where responsibilities weren't as glamorous, he was either absent or fumbling through the basics. The contradiction gnawed at me, feeding a quiet resentment I hadn't yet learned how to address.

By the time I got home, I buried the pain under a layer of comedic exasperation. *Typical Reginald,* I told myself. *Saving the day for everyone but me.* It was easier to laugh than to confront the truth: that this was just another hurdle in his training, another promise that things would eventually settle once residency was behind us. He'd show up. He'd become the attentive partner and father I desperately wanted him to be.

Yet, as the days wore on, the pattern remained unchanged. People joked that we were trying to recreate "Eight is enough." I forced a smile, too tired to explain how surprising this latest addition really was. Reginald had reentered his research years—a time that should have meant fewer intense hours. Instead, he used it as an excuse to play superhero at work, covering shifts for colleagues who needed family time. The irony wasn't lost on me: He was the go-to guy for everyone else's emergencies but rarely for mine. Most mornings, he left the house at 5 a.m. and returned well after the kids were in bed, beaming with pride as he recounted how much he was helping others.

Meanwhile, I juggled a full clinic schedule, the fatigue of postpartum recovery, and the chaos of three kids in our 4,000-square-foot "monument to bad decisions." My mother—blessed with endless patience—offered moral support and hands-on help, yet even her efforts couldn't lighten the weight of it all.

Reginald had his grand plans, of course. He'd occasionally remind me that once he finished all his training, he'd pay off my student loans, buy us a bigger house, and maybe even splurge on something nice for my parents—a *rich life* for everyone. But as he outlined this glittering future, I couldn't help but think: *You left me alone after baby number three; what makes you think I can trust you to step up now?*

The truth was, 2015 felt eerily similar to every other time I had hoped for change—that stability was finally within reach. But deep down, I knew better. If there's one thing I'd learned from Reginald, it's that his words were often grander than his actions. And as much as I wanted to cling to the illusion of a supportive partnership, the cracks in our foundation were growing impossible to ignore.

From Bills to Graduation: A Slow-Burning Storm

By 2016, life was a blur of responsibilities and unmet expectations. I was now juggling three kids and a full-time clinic schedule. In theory, Reginald's research schedule should have given him more flexibility, but somehow, he managed to stay busier than ever—just not with us.

One day, overwhelmed by the mounting expenses of our household, I handed him a simple task: Pay the water bill. "Just this one," I told him. "I'll handle the rest." He nodded, and I dared to hope this tiny delegation might lighten my load. But weeks later, I got a frantic text from the nanny: The water's been shut off. She couldn't even wash the baby's bottles. My cheeks burned with embarrassment. Here we were in our huge house with no running water because Reginald forgot to pay a bill.

He tried to make amends. In his typical style, he launched into the "tap-dance of regret," telling me he'd pick up extra shifts at the local jail to funnel more money into my account. On paper, it looked generous. But as I watched him pour his energy into helping others while I struggled to keep our home afloat, the gesture felt hollow. It wasn't that he didn't want to help; it was that he seemed incapable of stepping into the day-to-day trenches of family life.

Meanwhile, his father continued his odd behavior online, liking my photos and occasionally sending *pokes* that felt more predatory than friendly. I blocked him repeatedly, but he'd pop up again with a new account, sending requests like an unwelcome ghost haunting my social media. The last straw came when he left heart emojis on my bikini pictures. His mother, subtle but insistent, added her own layer of tension. She'd call with pointed comments like, "If you had more children, you wouldn't need to keep working."

Her vision of my life mirrored her own—three kids, endless devotion to home, no room for a career. But I wasn't her, and the thought of trading my independence for domestic servitude made me physically recoil.

By 2016, the cracks in our foundation were widening. I'd wake up at 4 a.m., feed three kids (with a fourth kicking in my belly), drop one off at daycare, leave the others with my mother or the nanny, and head to the clinic. Reginald left the house at 5 a.m. most mornings, returning well after bedtime. He'd smile, talking about how proud he was to lighten his colleagues' loads—to cover their shifts. Meanwhile, I wondered: *Who's lightening my load?*

Reginald's big plans for our future didn't help. He'd remind me of the glittering life ahead: He'd pay off my student loans, buy us a bigger house, and ensure my parents were comfortable in their old age. It all sounded wonderful, but his actions rarely aligned with his words. After baby number three, he left me alone in the hospital. Why would baby number four be any different?

By 2017, the routine of chaos had settled in. Reginald occasionally helped with errands, though his efforts were scattershot at best. He'd pick up groceries but forget half the list. He'd promise to take the kids to school functions but disappear to cover a co-worker's shift instead. My mother and the babysitters filled the gaps he left, but the emotional strain was palpable.

Reginald's surgical residency graduation loomed in May 2017, and with it came a mix of hope and dread. He often said, "Once I'm done, we'll finally be stable."

But I wasn't sure what "stable" even meant anymore. Would he step up as a father? Or would his ambitions pull him further away from our family? Graduation Day felt surreal. Reginald stood on stage, beaming as he accepted an award. He scanned the crowd until his eyes landed on me, mouthing, "Hang in there three more years." My stomach dropped. Three more years? Nearly a decade of training already behind us, and now another fellowship on the horizon?

Later, his sister confronted him. "You might lose your family if you keep chasing career goals like this," she said bluntly. For once, I found her meddling oddly comforting. She'd said what I couldn't, what I was too exhausted to articulate.

That day, I let him have his moment in the spotlight. But as he reveled in his accomplishments, I couldn't shake the feeling that another storm was brewing. His promises of a better future felt like echoes of past illusions. The cracks in our marriage weren't just visible; they were threatening to swallow us whole. I braced myself, knowing the calm of graduation day was only temporary. Something was coming, and I'd need every ounce of resilience to face it.

Hurricane Harvey and the Emotional Storm That Followed

August 2017 was the month Hurricane Harvey turned Houston into a waterlogged disaster zone, and my life followed suit. The city drowned, the power flickered, and I juggled four kids, hospital patients, and the ever-looming threat of my sanity running out. Our home survived the flooding, but my mental bandwidth? Not so much.

Reginald, ever the visionary, refused to evacuate. "I need to be here in case I have to go to work," he declared with the kind of conviction you'd expect from someone about to discover the roads were impassable. Spoiler alert: They were. As the city's infrastructure buckled, we were stuck in a house rapidly running low on supplies. It was a situation that demanded teamwork, resilience, and… oh, never mind.

Instead, I walked into the kitchen one evening to find Reginald drinking the last of the milk. From the carton. Despite being lactose intolerant. With three small children under our roof and no grocery stores open for miles. My mother, visiting from Illinois, stood in silent horror, her disapproving glare a masterpiece of restraint. I couldn't even muster the energy to argue.

The milk carton drained, he wiped his mouth like a cowboy in an old Western and wandered off, leaving me to wonder how someone so educated could also be so clueless.

We eventually hired a full-time nanny during the post-Harvey chaos. I didn't care if it raised an eyebrow or two. My options were nanny or total nervous breakdown. Reginald, strangely, didn't complain about the extra help. Maybe he assumed it was temporary, just until I caved to his not-so-secret agenda of me quitting my job entirely to *focus on the kids.*

A Perfect Time for More Ambitions

It didn't take long for him to strike. One evening, amid the wreckage of post-Harvey life, Reginald decided to pitch his dream again. "You should quit medicine," he began, his tone gentle, like a lion about to pounce. "We have four kids now; maybe we'll have five or six. My mom stayed home, and look how well my dad did. It's the key to success. We can pay off your loans and buy your parents a mansion."

I stared at him, half-expecting a punchline that never came. He was serious. My stomach lurched.

"I— I— can't do that," I stammered, my breath catching. "I love my job, my independence. Traveling. Seeing patients. I'm not your mother."

He blinked, startled. Maybe he thought I'd swoon at the promise of financial stability. Instead, my frustration boiled over into a full-blown meltdown.

"I'm done replicating illusions!" I snapped. "I won't be some subservient housewife while you chase ambitions or forget the basics—like paying the water bill. I'm not living your mother's life."

Reginald tried to soothe me, launching into his best impression of a motivational speaker. "You'll never regret being a stay-at-home mom," he said, painting a picture of an idyllic home life that might've worked on someone else.

Not me.

"No," I cut him off, my voice firm. "I've worked too hard for this. I'm not you. I'm not your mother. I'm me."

For years, I'd bitten my tongue, laughed off the frustrations, and told myself that Reginald's actions came from stress or ignorance, not indifference. But now, standing in our kitchen amid the ruins of Hurricane Harvey, I saw everything clearly.

Reginald stood frozen, looking like a man who'd accidentally wandered onto a battlefield. Maybe he'd thought I'd just nod, lured by promises of wealth and ease. Instead, I let years of resentment tumble out.

The kids, oblivious to the storm brewing in the kitchen, played in the other room. My mother quietly busied herself, giving me the space to say what needed to be said. Outside, Houston's streets were a mess of debris and floodwater.

Inside, it felt like the emotional equivalent.

Harvey may have spared our house, but it exposed the cracks in our foundation. And for the first time, I wasn't interested in patching them up. I wasn't going to drown in Reginald's illusions or his family's expectations anymore.

The storm outside subsided, but the one inside? It was just beginning.

Aftermath and Quiet Resolve

In the days that followed, we barely spoke. I continued with my routine: waking early, juggling clinic duties, and caring for four children. He left at dawn, possibly trying to re-cement his "model physician" persona or perhaps just avoiding me. The nanny stayed to help, especially after I recounted how I nearly broke under postpartum loneliness in 2015. This meltdown changed something fundamental: Illusions no longer sustained me.

If my father-in-law messaged again, I'd block him. If my mother-in-law repeated, "Have more children, quit your job," I'd politely tune her out. Reginald, sensing the shift, tried to revert to *damage control*—whispering he might skip the cardiothoracic fellowship he once coveted and might settle for a laparoscopic fellowship with better hours. He also tried funneling more money my way, paying random bills on time for once.

But I'd grown adept at spotting these "tap-dance of regret" maneuvers. I'd seen them after every big misstep—cheating fiascos, overshadowed weddings, postpartum vanishings, unpaid water bills, father's ghostly presence.

The difference now was that illusions no longer comforted me. I recognized that if illusions had once been my emotional band-aids, they'd now peeled off, leaving raw wounds in need of real healing.

Embracing a New Dawn

And so I ended 2017 with a meltdown fresh in my mind and Reginald tiptoeing around me, uncertain how to reassert illusions. My father stood in the wings, supportive but far away. My aunt's wise caution about boundaries echoed each time my mother-in-law tried to meddle. I'd learned that illusions can carry you only so far; real solutions demanded I stand firm.

That's how Chapter 5 concluded: me no longer willing to submerge my identity. The meltdown signaled a pivot—my refusal to adopt the "perfect mother at home" scenario, my declaration that I'd keep practicing medicine, traveling, and forging a life that aligned with my values. Whether Reginald stepped up or not, I had changed. I was done swallowing illusions and praying for small breadcrumbs to sustain me.

Walking into 2018, I felt both trepidation and newfound strength. I'd glimpsed how illusions I'd once coddled—like him paying off everything once he was done—were heartbreakingly hollow. I'd glimpsed that I'd have to stand up for my needs or risk drowning again in postpartum loneliness. If illusions were the scaffolding, I'd now discovered the real steel of my own resolve beneath them. Perhaps that steel would carry me forward, guiding me through the next big storms that inevitably lay ahead. Because in my story, illusions might fade, but comedic vantage and motherly grit would remain, forging a path for the four children who needed me to be real, not a ghost in someone else's dream.

Chapter 6:

Filing for Divorce

By February 2018, I had long since run out of patience with Reginald's controlling whims, emotional antics, and occasional outbursts. Yet, I clung to some remnants of civility, more out of habit than hope. On paper, we were cohabiting—like housemates sharing a mortgage but barely speaking—juggling kids, schedules, and a fragile semblance of normal. But that month, he decided to give one last performance, demonstrating how little he cared about *normal* or *civility*.

I'd planned a rare night out with a girlfriend, Alexis, someone I desperately needed to confide in so I could feel like a human separate from my marriage and motherhood. Alexis and I were pole sisters; we'd bonded through aerial aerobics classes, forging a friendship that embraced empowerment and defied stale norms. She was going through a separation, too, so we often commiserated.

The day before we were due to meet for dinner, Reginald must have smelled the scent of independence in the air. A few hours before I was supposed to leave, he flared up in a screaming match. Actually, that's too gentle a phrase; he screamed, yelled, punched walls, and pinned me against one in front of our daughter Veronica, who watched from the corner, wide-eyed and silent. It was that special brand of rage that makes one half of your brain scream "Run!" while the other half is too shocked to move. All I could think was: Where did we go so wrong that he's trying to keep me from a simple girls' night?

Bizarrely, after unleashing his fury—punching and pinning me like some twisted demonstration of power—he quieted the instant I signaled I would still go out. In his mind, the damage was done: my nerves were shredded, Veronica was traumatized, and the night would be ruined. I left anyway—stubborn me—but I couldn't focus on laughter or cocktails. Alexis noticed how distant I was and pressed me for the truth. When I finally told her about the pinning, the wall-punching, and the raw terror in Veronica's eyes, she grabbed her fork at the restaurant, jammed it onto the table, and declared, "It's time to stick a fork in it!" A dark but fitting metaphor for concluding a rotten situation. I forced a half-laugh, though tears blurred my vision. I'd fooled myself for years, believing if I tiptoed, maybe the worst wouldn't happen again. Now, the worst felt painfully close.

No One Will Want You (March 2018)

It was no surprise that his violent meltdown in February shoved me closer to seeking legal help. But I needed a final push to jump that cliff. A few weeks later, in March, Reginald glowered at me and said he'd kill me if I ever cheated on him. The calmness in his voice sounded less like hyperbole and more like a promise.

It didn't matter that cheating wasn't on my horizon—living under that threat was intolerable. I filed for divorce almost immediately. I'd done it mentally a hundred times, but physically signing papers felt like leaping into an abyss: terrifying, yet exhilaratingly freeing. Naturally, Reginald responded with his own meltdown, sneering, "No one will want you with three kids," then offering, "But if you stay, once I get money, I'll buy you a big house and pay off your loans." The arrogance jammed my brain. Sure, financially, I wasn't Scrooge McDuck, but I was a working doctor. Meanwhile, he showed me how little he respected me beyond child-rearing and housekeeping duties.

He then performed his favorite party trick: crying on cue. As I served him divorce papers, he sobbed with his hands over his eyes, except I saw him peering through his fingers for my reaction. The instant he realized I wasn't swayed, the tears vanished, replaced by a stiff mask. I guess I was supposed to crumble in remorse.

Instead, I pictured dissecting a pathology sample: *Homo Sapiens Woo, a sub-type manipulator* known for ephemeral crying and feigned helplessness.

Secret Exits and Public Slanders (Late March–April 2018)

Around late March, while I was at work, Reginald moved out in secret, damaging walls—some final yanks at nails, I presume—and took the family gun, some jewelry, and even a few of my dresses and photo albums. He introduced a new girlfriend to my children—blonde, blue-eyed, reminiscent of the old porn history I'd discovered—without my knowledge. The brazenness nauseated me. But I was too busy drafting custody petitions and trying to keep a routine for the kids.

One of the nannies, Becky, kept calling that day, telling me Reginald was moving out. She knew I had no clue. I'd gone to work that morning thinking everything was normal, only to discover he was packing up behind my back. Becky and the other nannies found themselves in the crossfire of our crumbling marriage; Reginald once despised the idea of nannies, calling them "stupid," insisting he didn't want strangers raising his kids. Yet he abandoned me and the children, so I needed them more than ever. The irony was thick.

From that point, he smeared me publicly. He tried persuading my family that I was bipolar, psychotic, and going through a midlife crisis. He turned my parents against me initially; my father, not understanding the behind-the-scenes abuse, wondered why we were divorcing at all. My mother tried comforting him, saying I'd come to my senses eventually. Meanwhile, Reginald's family turned their backs on me. They apparently funded his new apartment and threatened him that if he returned to me, they'd cut him from their will. Good riddance, but it stung to see them close ranks against me.

I had to rely on a few stalwart allies—my mother eventually recognized nonsense, my father, too, once he saw how broken I was, but my brother and sister-in-law—evidently swayed—sided with Reginald. That burned worst of all. I'd always believed blood was thicker than water, but illusions die hard. Reginald also unleashed new suits against me even after the divorce was final, roping my parents and siblings in as witnesses as if to prove some twisted point about me being *unstable.*

We tried marriage counseling once, on April 24, with a Christian counselor named Arthur Johnson. I told him I no longer wanted Reginald's touch—that I refused to exist in a *sexless marriage*, which felt like a grim prison. Reginald shrugged, "That's fine. We can stay married without sex." The counselor's jaw dropped. He asked Reginald to step out, then quietly confessed he usually encouraged couples to reconcile, but this marriage alarmed him. We never returned. Some fiascos transcend therapy's reach.

A Mother's Day to Remember (May 2018)

That Mother's Day dawned deceptively calm. Despite having moved out, Reginald appeared to cook a taco dinner for the kids, acting like a model father. Then he left, presumably returning to his new girlfriend or apartment. Exhausted from single-parenting three kids, I dozed off.

Around midnight, the smell of rotten eggs jolted me awake—gas.

Panicked, I ran to the stove and found it left on. I dialed the fire department, who told me to yank open windows, avoid electronics, and remove the kids immediately. The entire house reeked. We spent the night in my car; nothing like sleeping in a sedan with three frightened children, adrenaline-pounding, wondering if your soon-to-be ex had the capacity to *accidentally* kill you.

Police arrived but claimed they couldn't prove intent, though my lawyer, Melissa, recognized the intimidation pattern immediately. She helped me secure a restraining order right after the gas stove fiasco.

The next day, May 14, Reginald crept back to the house, presumably thinking I was at work. I happened to be off, so I caught him peering through the windows. After that, I refused one-on-one encounters. I arranged friends, family, or nannies for any child exchanges. I'd learned that if I wanted physical safety, I needed witnesses.

Smart Home Terror and Summer Threats

In June, Reginald found fresh ways to terrorize me, sending cryptic texts and popping up randomly. Then, on June 15, he manipulated our *smart home* system. He remotely flicked lights off at night, turned the heat up to suffocating levels, and armed or disarmed the alarm. I was paying the bills, so I called the provider, changed every code and password, and removed his access. He still wormed in occasionally until I replaced the equipment—a maddening reminder that I was financing a house where I felt chronically unsafe.

By July, Reginald uprooted the kids, dropping them off with his parents in Illinois and refusing me phone contact. He didn't even plan to be with them himself, just abandoned them to the grandparents, who withheld them from me all summer. Meanwhile, he returned to Texas to finalize his residency or research obligations. I sank into an isolated, lonely home, left childless and anxious. The big house felt like a haunted mansion. My boss at the clinic noticed I never used my PTO, and worried I'd burn out. That's when I planned an ill-fated girls' trip to Miami for my birthday.

I invited my childhood best friends—Savannah, Layla, and Denise—to join me for a much-needed escape: sunny beaches, great food, and a chance to leave all the heartbreak behind for a few days. It felt like the getaway we all desperately needed after everything life had thrown at us. But just days before we were set to leave, I got the call that shattered everything: Savannah had suffered a brain aneurysm and lapsed into a coma. The shock left me paralyzed. She'd already endured so much in her life; how could this possibly be how her story unfolded?

I canceled the trip immediately. The thought of sipping cocktails on South Beach while Savannah lay unconscious was unbearable. My depression deepened as the weight of it all settled in: my stolen children, the silence of my empty home, and now the possibility of losing my dearest friend.

It felt like grief was layering itself over me, thicker and heavier with each day. After weeks of sinking further into despair, my therapist gently suggested something unexpected: Maybe I should try re-entering the dating scene. At first, I balked at the idea—especially when she recommended I try Tinder, which I immediately dismissed as just a hookup site.

In my uncertainty, I turned to my aunt. A formidable Ashanti and Fante Ghanaian woman, she had raised her three children on her own after divorcing their father. All her children were college-educated—one even went to Stanford—and she was an incredibly successful professional. I'd always dreamed of mirroring her strength and independence, yet she warned me not to compare my life to hers. Instead, she admitted that one of her biggest regrets was not embracing dating after her divorce and urged me to give it a try.

Her words, combined with my therapist's encouragement, began to resonate. I gave it some thought. If I hadn't lost the kids, and if Savannah hadn't fallen ill, I probably wouldn't have considered it.

But with my home echoing with silence and my heart desperate for some light, I figured, why not? My therapist promised it wasn't about finding the one right away; it was about giving myself permission to exist outside the grief.

So, reluctantly, I decided to try.

Dating in the Midst of Chaos

At first, I was clueless about where to start. I downloaded a dating app and set up a profile with zero filters, which resulted in an overwhelming swirl of matches—men, women, couples, and everything in between. It was chaos. I ignored most of it; my heart was barely in it until I matched with Greg.

Greg was ten years younger than me, a chemistry lab manager at a plant, and also West African—Nigerian, while I'm Ghanaian. He looked Black American at first glance, but once he spoke, his Igbo roots shone through. We bonded over our shared love of STEM and education, as well as our surprisingly similar experiences with manipulative exes. Greg had escaped a toxic relationship without children while I was neck-deep in a custody nightmare.

Our connection felt natural, though I was cautious. By December 2018, our friendship had blossomed into something deeper, though I often felt guilt creeping in. What if Reginald found out? What if he retaliated? I explained to Greg that Reginald had a vindictive streak, warning him that threats about taking the kids or worse weren't beyond him. Greg, however, shrugged it off. "He can't be that bad," he said with an easy laugh.

But Reginald *was* that bad. When he eventually met Greg, he dismissed him outright, assuming he was some maintenance man at my house. When I clarified that Greg was my partner, Reginald sneered, "You're dating a Black guy?" as if it were the most shocking thing in the world.

Coming from him—someone whose children with me were Black—it was a bizarre, racist insult that underscored just how warped his worldview had always been.

Family Drama and My Mother's Divided Loyalties

My mother, initially on Reginald's side, found it hard to embrace Greg. She clung to the hope I'd reconcile with Reginald. She'd even feed Reginald his favorite Ghanaian dishes—peanut butter soup, jollof rice—behind my back, telling him how my grandmother left her unfaithful husband, had a baby with another man, then eventually reunited with the first. She offered him that story as a glimmer of hope I might do the same.

Meanwhile, she actively shooed Greg away, sometimes starting arguments or refusing him entry. She told him she'd "get rid of him for Reginald." I was livid, telling my mother she had to step aside. I had zero intention of returning to the man who gassed my house with me and our kids inside, who withheld them in Illinois all summer, who once pinned me to a wall in front of Veronica. She relented eventually, though she never wholly warmed to Greg. Divided loyalties die slowly.

My father also felt torn. He'd officiated my second wedding, believed in Catholic permanence, and found divorce perplexing, especially not seeing the full extent of Reginald's mental and emotional abuse.

At the same time, Reginald was claiming "Catholics don't divorce," ignoring how selectively he'd always used his faith. My dad saw the hypocrisy, but it took time for him to accept that the marriage was unsalvageable. Over those months, he watched Reginald refuse to pay bills, secretly funnel money into a 401(k) while I struggled, and ignore fatherly duties altogether. Recognizing such callousness convinced him there was no sense in clinging to illusions. Eventually, my father admitted the divorce was necessary, although not without heartbreak.

Finalizing the Divorce and the Continued War

Finally, September 25, 2018 arrived: the divorce's final hearing. Reginald didn't bother showing. He'd fought to pay only $500 monthly for three kids. The judge shrugged, hammered the gavel, and it was done. Legally, we were free of each other—or so I hoped. I remember when my girlfriend Denise asked if I was hurt that Reginald hadn't even bothered to fight for our marriage. I told her he was probably too busy working, so, no, I wasn't surprised or hurt.

But if illusions taught me anything, it's that a signed decree is rarely the end. Sure enough, the real war raged on: drive-by sightings, father-in-law's new attempts to infiltrate my social media, and random meltdown phone calls. He tried to bribe my oldest daughter, Liza, with lavish gifts—a computer, a prom dress—only to withdraw them if she wouldn't divulge my personal life. Classy. I saw him circle back to old manipulative tactics, ironically confirming that divorcing him was the right choice. The children, especially my older ones, saw his manipulations for what they were. That emboldened me to maintain minimal contact. I recognized he could still lash out, but at least now the law was on my side.

My new partner, Greg, once believing Reginald harmless, started to see glimpses of his malice. Reginald threatened to blow up the house if Greg was there, resulting in more calls to CPS by a mandated reporter. This was my new normal: official divorce on paper but an ongoing siege for custody or intimidation.

Finding Strength in the Aftermath

By May 2019, I'd adapted to the post-divorce battleground. The kids lived primarily with me. I updated locks, replaced door cameras, and kept my father-in-law perpetually blocked. My mother and father, once naive about Reginald, now grasped the depth of his manipulations. He roped them into lawsuits, but seeing him in action shattered their illusions. Meanwhile, my brother and sister-in-law, who'd once sided with Reginald, gradually realized how unhinged his behavior was.

At times, I glimpsed comedic irony: "No one will ever want you with three kids," he'd sneered, yet I was building a stable connection with Greg, a man ironically from the same West African heritage that Reginald found unworthy. I recognized the stark difference: Greg's kindness, calm presence, and unwavering respect for me as a professional and a mother contrasted with Reginald's repeated sabotage. Reginald probably sensed that difference, too, fueling his anger further.

Still, the illusions we once clung to—like maybe Reginald could be reasoned with or that father-in-law might relent—were all dead. And I recognized illusions needed to die for me to stand firm. I found that *scalding, messy exorcism* best described the divorce process. It ripped away the final illusions I'd used to cushion forced weddings, postpartum betrayals, overshadowed vow renewals, and paternal creeper emojis. In place of illusions, I discovered a raw sense of freedom. That freedom came with daily battles, sure, but it also brought a gritty peace each morning I woke up not legally bound to him.

My comedic humor (thankfully!) remained: I told close friends how, ironically, Reginald's meltdown in February 2018 had birthed the final path to divorce or how my father-in-law's endless Facebook attempts only reaffirmed that blocking him was the right choice. This comedic lens was how I refused to let him define me as a victim. He could threaten bombs, manipulate the nannies, or vanish with the kids for a summer, but I was forging a life on my own terms. Slowly but surely, that life included Greg, new friendships, and a reestablished bond with my parents, no longer hoodwinked by Reginald. If illusions and heartbreak once overshadowed me, by mid-2019, I recognized illusions were better left behind.

The illusions that a piece of paper or a vow would change him, that father-in-law might back off, that mother-in-law might ease up, all illusions. The reality was a continuing fight for autonomy and child safety. Yet I found strength in the rawness of that reality: I'd survived forced weddings, postpartum desertion, violent episodes, father-in-law's *pokes*, and controlling nannies who turned on me.

Ironically, it ended just as a new tempest was beginning. On paper, the divorce was final by September 25, 2018, but the real saga—custody battles, sabotage attempts, and father-in-law's random reappearances—persisted. By May 2019, I'd learned to park in the garage, keep a watchful eye for suspicious cars, block father-in-law at the slightest sign, and respond to Reginald's new threats with calm legal measures. Freed from illusions, I found power in small daily triumphs: changing a code, returning to the clinic to see patients, and ignoring his meltdown rants. Even though the heartbreak and illusions that pinned me for years occasionally stung like phantom pains, I discovered a resilient core that refused to yield.

And in that resilience lay a quiet sense of victory. Sure, I might carry scars—like the memory of him pinning me to a wall in front of Veronica or the day he left the gas on—but I also carry comedic grace. If illusions lulled me once, now I'd awakened, forging a path that demanded constant vigilance but offered genuine self-respect. Because illusions, once shattered, can never again imprison you the same way. And that was the ultimate gift of *Filing for Divorce*.

Chapter 7:

False Accusations and Escalation

If you had told me in early 2019 that I would, within months, ditch my cavernous 4,000-square-foot Farland home—and be living with my boyfriend, Greg—I might have waved away the idea as more illusions. But illusions or not, June 2019 found me doing just that. My three children and I drove away from that house, never to sleep there again. The mortgage alone was choking me: $3,000 a month in mortgage payments, taxes, and upkeep. With Reginald, my ex-husband, absent both physically and financially, I felt pinned under an impossibly large overhead. A practical approach was needed.

So, when I told Reginald I'd be moving in with my then-boyfriend in June 2019, you'd think I had announced an imminent apocalypse. True to form, Reginald claimed I was "disrupting the children's environment." Never mind that he was rarely around to cover any part of that environment's cost. I wanted him to meet Greg formally—they were both adult men, after all—but in classic Reginald style, he blew off my suggestions. He specialized in "Disappearing Acts," a trick honed since his medical school days. And so, on the day of our big move, I half-expected him to pop up and pick a fight or feign father-of-the-year concern. Instead, it was silence. I remember standing in the now-empty living room, echoing and half-lit by boxes, feeling an odd mix of relief and dread.

Relieved because leaving that place might reduce my financial strangulation, yet dreading the new wave of conflict that Reginald would certainly conjure once he caught wind of me sharing a roof with another man. It's almost laughable how illusions can keep you hopeful: Illusions told me maybe Reginald wouldn't sabotage; illusions told me maybe he'd step up to co-parent. But illusions and I had a rocky history, and deep down, I knew the next drama was only a phone call away.

For the time being, though, I left that house behind with the kids, trusting that selling it—whenever that happened—would sever yet another string to my ex. But at that moment, I had no clue it would take a full year to offload the property—and no clue about the fiascos that would unfold before the final sale in June 2020. Meanwhile, our new living arrangement with Greg felt like a breath of fresh air, even if we had limited privacy and were stepping on each other's toes while learning a new routine. I clung to the notion that love and common sense might converge for once.

Reginald's Initial Reaction—and Non-reaction

Given Reginald's unpredictability, I sent him a polite message: "I'd like you to formally meet Greg at some point since he'll be around the kids regularly." No response. Two days later, I tried again, explaining we had to vacate the old house due to finances.

Again, silence. It was eerily anticlimactic. I braced for condemnation or a meltdown, but he vanished into the background. Perhaps he'd reappear with a flourish, or maybe he'd sink further into absent-father mode. Time would tell, I thought. Meanwhile, the Farland property stood empty, waiting for a buyer who never seemed to come. I found myself paying a mortgage on a place I never intended to step inside again. Even illusions couldn't disguise how impractical that was. I told myself: *You'll see, a buyer will appear soon.* But illusions are illusions, and that monstrous house sat on the market indefinitely, mocking me with every monthly payment.

A (Surprising) Year of Calm: Summer 2019 to Early 2020

Surprising is the best word I can think of to describe the lull that descended from about January 2019 to February 2020. In hindsight, it's almost bizarre how quiet Reginald went. Sure, he tossed an occasional menacing text or phone call, mostly about nonsense: "How's the new boyfriend?" or "You'll regret ignoring me." But compared to meltdown dinners, random gas leaks, or forced vow renewals, these potshots felt mild.

June 2019: An Alaskan Escape

Amid all that stress of uprooting from the Farland house, I somehow orchestrated a trip to Alaska—my kids, Greg, and I flew north to meet my best friend, Aaron, along with his wife and their children. Aaron had been my rock for ages, defined by his snarky humor, unwavering loyalty, and zero tolerance for drama. Alaska in summer was a revelation: sunny, warm-ish, with that midnight sun phenomenon that drove my boy a little delirious, but the girls found it magical.

Aaron took us on a small cruise, weaving through waters where killer whales sliced across the surface. We visited the Alaska Zoo, hiked lush green trails, and rehashed old memories while Greg and the kids merged seamlessly into the group. My kids, whom I teasingly call my "Woo babies," seemed to shed the stress of the past year, playing with Aaron's children as though they'd known each other forever.

Meanwhile, Greg got along with Aaron in a way that left me blinking in pleasant surprise. I'd assumed it might be tense, that they'd be awkward. But illusions, for once, undersold things: They bonded over sports, technology, fatherhood philosophies, you name it.

By the time we left Alaska, I felt uncharacteristically optimistic. I caught glimpses of a new family dynamic that might actually work: Greg stepping into fatherly shoes Reginald had long abandoned. I remember thinking: *Maybe illusions can be good sometimes; illusions might pave the way for real changes.*

Then again, illusions are illusions.

Pole Dancing and Proposal

Back in Houston, as we settled into our new living situation, I introduced Greg to one of my major passions: pole aerobics. If any illusions about me had stuck around, they likely dissolved the moment he saw me spinning upside-down, applying insane core strength. He used to joke about how "Houston is the only place where you can be a stripper and a doctor," riffing on Katt Williams's comedy. But once he realized just how demanding it was, he dove right in. I'll never forget his face during his first real pole class—pure exhaustion.

Greg's the type who leans in when challenged. Within weeks, he was climbing and inverting better than some of my female classmates. We'd exchange playful critiques like, "Your invert's smoother now!" or "Try hooking your knee differently!" Then, we attended PoleCon together in Colorado. Once he saw the artistry on stage, he quickly asked, "Where do I sign up?" From that moment on, pole aerobics became our shared addiction. By mid-2019, it had truly become our ultimate pastime.

It's remarkable how a shared physical pursuit—especially one so unconventional—becomes a metaphor for building trust in a relationship. You literally learn to rely on each other's balance, to spot each other, and to push each other further. So, in July 2019, Greg proposed. One of those sweet, somewhat comedic proposals where he started a speech, and I interrupted with "Yes, yes, yes!" He still laughs that I didn't let him finish. But illusions aside, I saw the same synergy we had on the pole: learning to uplift each other. We told the kids. They squealed. I told basically everyone else: boss, nannies, random acquaintances.

And I'd never been more excited in my life.

Becky's "Congratulations"—and Sudden Departure

One of the first people I told was our longtime nanny, Becky—the same Becky who had seen me at my worst during Reginald's stealth move-out fiasco. She offered a stiff smile, and for a moment, I thought, *Okay, maybe she's not thrilled I found happiness.* Over the next month, she grew noticeably cold to Greg, dropping vague hints that he was "mean" and "always angry." The timeline was suspect: Greg had been around since December 2018 with no complaints from her. Suddenly, the minute we announce an engagement, he's the boogeyman?

In October 2019, Becky announced she was leaving us for a job with two doctors. She parted ways politely enough, though she asked if she might still visit the children. I shrugged a yes, though I found her request odd. That was Becky in a nutshell: warm and maternal at first, but once she felt overshadowed—maybe by Greg, maybe by my rising emotional stability—she turned cryptic, then jumped ship. She recommended her best friend, Ms. Elda, as her replacement. I only had faint recollections of Elda from a no-call, no-show fiasco, but illusions told me to give her a chance for the kids' sake.

Nanny Chaos and the Father's Flimsy Involvement

Elda was everything Becky was not: late, disheveled, erratic, prone to vanishing midweek on spontaneous road trips with boyfriends. Cooking dinner? Optional.

Actually feeding the kids? Not a priority. If Becky was borderline obsessive about punctuality and chores, Elda was borderline uninterested in them. Meanwhile, Greg insisted we keep giving her "one more chance," citing her possible low IQ or that maybe we "expected too much." In truth, we needed a nanny, and illusions told us we could shape Elda up. Ironically, the kids, still thrived because they had me, they had Greg, and their own resilience.

- Veronica soared academically: Gifted and Talented programs, blossoming artistry. Greg taped her sketches around the house.
- My son advanced in violin, joined the math team, and got popular enough to get endless invitations to classmates' parties.
- April, the youngest, excelled in daycare, gymnastics, and swimming. Greg started each day

> with her reciting: "I am beautiful, I am smart, I am the greatest."

Meanwhile, Reginald hovered in the margins, calling sporadically.

In the calls he did make, he'd ask the kids about me rather than them. "What's your mom doing? Where's she at?" My son sometimes hung up, thoroughly annoyed. Greg overheard one such conversation and spat, "Isn't he supposed to ask how they are?" Greg attempted to bridge the gap, messaging Reginald politely about picking them up or scheduling visits. Reginald either didn't respond or dropped cryptic lines.

The paternal black hole continued swirling, Veronica, in particular, feeling his absence. She wanted a father figure. Instead, she got a ghost who refused to show up consistently.

Stormy Rescue—and the Absent Father

One evening, a tropical storm hit. Roads flooded fast. I was at work, unable to leave immediately. Greg, unasked, jumped into his tiny Nissan Sentra and navigated terrifying floodwaters to grab my two older kids from their elementary school. He nearly spun out multiple times. My backup nanny, Andrea, snatched April from daycare. By the time we reassembled, soaked and anxious, Greg turned to me and asked if their father had so much as texted to check on them.

The answer, humiliatingly, was no. Greg just shook his head, baffled that a man so quick to claim paternal authority wasn't at all concerned for his kids' safety in a flash flood. The comedic vantage helped me shrug it off, but I saw Veronica's disappointment plainly. She realized Greg cared more in that moment than Reginald did.

Weddings, Ghana, and a Nanny Conspiracy

In November 2019, Greg and I had a small, spontaneous courthouse wedding. No fanfare, just an official vow in a cramped county office. Elda discovered it and, bizarrely, retaliated by hiding my son's glasses. She pouted that she wasn't invited. Truthfully, no one was invited. Even my parents were left out. We planned a bigger wedding for the next year.

Then, in December 2019, I traveled to Ghana with my oldest daughter, Liza, for my cousin's wedding. I left my mother with Greg to manage the kids. I was anxious because, historically, my mother had been wary about my new husband. But illusions guided me to hope she'd see Greg's heart. To my relief, she later told me over the phone that Greg was wonderful with them, though she was deeply concerned about Elda's *laziness*. My mother didn't drive, so Elda was still needed for school pick-ups. But Elda hated having an older adult around watching her every move.

Upon my return from Ghana, I saw the tension. My mother was frazzled. Elda had basically been AWOL half the time. Another nanny meltdown loomed. Then came the revelation that Elda had allied with Becky and possibly another nanny, Andrea. They schemed to *take the children away* from me and Reginald, claiming "neither parent has time." Becky boasted that she only dated Black men so the kids could *pass as hers* since she had no children of her own.

My mother overheard bits of this madness, panicked, and warned me. At first, I felt ridiculous even telling my lawyer, "The nannies want to kidnap my kids." She half-laughed. But illusions told me not to dismiss the possibility entirely: Something about Elda's posturing, her scowls, and her random phone calls spelled trouble.

Elda kept acting sweet in my presence—except she picked fights with Greg in subtle ways: passive aggression, sarcasm, and blaming him for minor annoyances. This was the same man who'd championed giving her repeated chances. Tensions were at a slow simmer. By illusions or comedic vantage, I tried to remain calm, ignoring the paternal black hole and the swirling nanny drama. The kids thrived, after all. But illusions don't shield you forever.

Elda's Telenovela Accusation

January 2020 came, and one cold evening, I arrived home around 7:30 p.m. to find Elda outside our house, standing in the driveway with an eerie calm. The instant I exited the car, she launched into an over-the-top meltdown, screaming, "He's beating the children! He's beating the children!" My mind reeled. If Greg had harmed them, I'd turn the entire house upside down. I demanded to know why Elda hadn't called 911 or pulled the kids away from an abuser. She just sobbed, "I'm scared," and told me to pack up and go back to the old Farland house. That was suspicious; the same property with leftover cameras Reginald could manipulate. Then Elda hopped in her car and sped off, leaving me to wonder if the children were inside, battered or traumatized. I rushed in, calling their names. Greg stood in the kitchen, casually stirring the pot with a dish rag over his shoulder, looking baffled as I glared at him. I snapped, "I'll deal with you in a minute," and dashed to the kids' rooms, expecting bruises or welts.

They giggled when I poked at their arms and asked if they were okay, confusion written on their faces. Not a scratch on them. Greg, oblivious, continued cooking dinner. Furious and embarrassed, I texted Elda that we were not fleeing to Farland. If she believed they were in mortal danger, she'd have called the cops. She offered no explanation. The next morning, she showed up to work as if nothing had happened.

Greg quietly insisted we keep her employed, seeing her meltdown as a *one-time outburst.* He wanted to show compassion. I found it idiotic, but illusions or not, we had few childcare options. So, on we trudged, my comedic vantage the only thing preventing me from firing Elda on the spot.

The Year Ends—and the Father Returns with New Schemes

Meanwhile, Reginald reappeared in random bursts. He'd skip scheduled visitation, then show up unannounced at the kids' school for a quick lunch cameo. He texted me about picking them up from time to time, only to cancel at the last second. I invited him to big events, hoping the presence of a crowd would quell tensions. The only event he attended was my son's First Holy Communion. He looked dramatically thinner, possibly from surgery or rigorous dieting. But that didn't stop him from proclaiming: "You were once my wife; you will always be my wife, no matter what." I nearly spat. I told Greg, who promptly texted Reginald to clarify boundaries. Reginald threatened legal measures, cryptic as ever. Greg, unshaken, reminded me that if Reginald threatened me, we'd escalate it legally. I nodded, though illusions told me Reginald's brand of threat was more psychological than direct.

In February 2020, Reginald contacted Greg out of the blue, requesting the kids for a random midweek overnight. Greg, eager to co-parent, said yes without checking with me. I hit the roof. Reginald rarely bothered with them on weekends; why this sudden interest in a school night overnight? My instincts screamed that something sinister was afoot, especially with Elda's meltdown and Becky's rumored conspiracies. I didn't yet realize how deeply the trifecta—Becky, Elda, and Andrea—might be working with Reginald to hatch new false accusations.

The House Finally Sells (June 2020)—A Reluctant Release

As the months marched on, illusions lulled me into a routine: I juggled kids, a stressful job, Elda's fiascos, Greg's fatherly attempts, and Reginald's halfhearted reappearances. Then came June 2020: out of nowhere, we got a buyer for the Farland property. At last, I sold it at a painful loss—thousands below what I owed.

Still, I felt a rush of relief. I'd been paying a steep mortgage on a place we'd vacated a year prior. I always half-suspected Reginald might show up unannounced to rummage around or remotely flick the lights. That house was haunted by illusions of a stable marriage that never truly existed. Now, signing it away felt like peeling off an exoskeleton, finalizing a piece of the past. Sure, it was depressing to lose money, but illusions told me the finality might be worth it.

We wouldn't be anchored by that monstrous property or subjected to Reginald's prying.

A comedic vantage told me I'd never have to mutter, "I'm paying $(X) for a 4,000-square-foot tomb." With the sale, I told the kids that one day, we'd buy a smaller place, truly ours. They nodded, unimpressed, probably more concerned about Elda skipping dinner again or Dad not calling. For me, though, it was a step forward: Another chain to Reginald's domain was severed; another dimension of illusions was dismantled. The comedic vantage also whispered, "We can't ever say we're stuck paying for that old tomb." Because illusions or not, I wouldn't willingly let him manipulate me through that property anymore.

Culminating Tensions—and a Frightening Next Chapter

By late June 2020, I had finally offloaded the Farland house—a tangible link to a painful past—and I exhaled in relief at finally parting with that burden. Yet that relief was laced with the bitter taste of unresolved tension. The drama had been brewing since earlier in the year: Elda's meltdown and the conspiracies swirling among family members in January and February had set the stage for the chaos that followed. Becky's departure hadn't silenced her jealous streak; Andrea—the second backup nanny—seemed to be in cahoots with them, and Reginald, threatened by Greg's presence, continued to play puppet master from the sidelines.

Every unwanted text from Reginald, every random midweek visit request, sent a shiver of foreboding down my spine. It felt like we were all dancing on a loaded stage, with the simmering tension of false accusations and petty grudges ready to boil over at any moment. There were moments when I fancied we'd already weathered the worst—forced vow fiascos, meltdown dinners, manipulative financial ruin, and even a monstrous vacant house—but I knew that calm was always fleeting. Elda's hysterical "He's beating them!" might have been a dress rehearsal for even graver allegations, and Greg's naive attempts at forging fatherly friendship did little to ease my apprehensions.

Even my father, who usually stayed out of day-to-day drama, reminded me that while we'd legally distanced ourselves from Reginald, the practical entanglements were far from over. The looming absence of the children's father threatened to pull us back into the chaos at any moment.

For now, I clung to the small victories—knowing we'd survived gas leaks, forced vow ceremonies, and sly fatherly sabotage before—and armed myself with the belief that truth and perseverance were our only real defenses.

I stared at the empty space in my finances once occupied by that 4,000-square-foot relic and whispered to myself, *Bring on the meltdown. We've survived worse.*

Though I had finally shed a painful link to my past, the seeds of discord planted in those earlier months still promised more turbulence ahead. As I closed this chapter of relative calm, I braced myself for the false accusations and escalating conflicts that were sure to follow. With my eyes on the children and my heart steeled by resilience, I knew the storm was only just beginning.

Chapter 8:

The Mental Toll on the Family

I parted ways with that towering house in June 2020, hoping to sever one more painful tie to my past. Yet the real strain had been mounting long before—stretching back to February when an unrelenting wave of stress, heartbreak, and legal battles began to wear us down.

I still recall those early February days vividly. On paper, things appeared manageable: I juggled a lingering mortgage on the large home while waiting for a buyer, and we were gradually settling into our new space. The children were adapting, and my husband, Greg, remained our steadfast protector.

Even as I balanced a demanding job in medicine—both a passion and a source of anxiety, especially given my ex's knack for abrupt legal bombshells—I couldn't have foreseen the hurricane that would strike on February 9, 2020.

That day, when Elda and Greg erupted into a fight that upended everything, our carefully constructed world was forever altered.

A Sudden Firing and a Storm of Threats

Elda had been part of the household for some time, albeit not a pleasant part. She was a nanny recommended by someone we once trusted, but her reliability was shaky; her moods were erratic. For reasons that still baffle me, Greg kept insisting we give her one more chance whenever I proposed letting her go. By early February, he had finally reached his limit. Their conflict on February 9 started as a spat over small housekeeping details—disrespectful words on her end and final warnings on his. Then, it blew up entirely.

I returned home to find Elda absolutely hysterical on the phone, telling me that Greg had fired her. I felt caught off guard. Greg usually conferred with me on important decisions, so having him dismiss her on the spot without a word was disconcerting. His explanation was brisk: He claimed she'd been disrespectful countless times, that they had verbally clashed that morning, and that he saw no reason to prolong the arrangement. I partly understood.

For months, Elda had tested our patience—arriving late, skipping tasks, vanishing mid-shift for personal errands. But I also resented Greg because, on so many occasions, I had wanted to fire her, and he had repeatedly talked me out of it. Now, he'd gone ahead and done it himself on a whim, leaving me to pick up the pieces. Once Elda calmed down enough to speak coherently, she demanded my reassurance.

She wanted me to overrule Greg's decision. I felt torn. My gut told me it was best to part ways, but I told her we'd keep her around for a few more days until she found something stable so there wouldn't be chaos in the children's routines. That choice triggered a bizarre fury. She accused Greg of abusing the children. She threatened to *sue both of us*. She ranted about having video footage—footage I instinctively knew did not exist. Then she stormed off.

Even as she left, heart pounding, I tried rationalizing her behavior as an impulsive tantrum—something that might blow over in a day. But deep down, I sensed that she would wreak havoc before she disappeared from our lives for good. The timing was ominous; she had just lost her job. She was furious at Greg and, by extension, me. And historically, she had connections to my ex, Reginald, who thrived on conflicts he could escalate. None of that spelled peace.

An Avalanche of False Allegations

On February 10, mere hours after Elda stormed out, chaos accelerated. Greg informed me that Reginald had somehow teamed up with Elda, and they were both at a Child Protective Services location, lodging accusations about ongoing abuse in our household. As if that weren't jarring enough, the police got involved. From what I heard later, Elda insisted she had witnessed *horrors* in the home for months, specifically since November—yet not once did she ever call the police or mention any of this to me in any coherent way. I found out that Reginald told the authorities he couldn't speak with me because we were "not on speaking terms." That claim alone felt surreal. Reginald was absolutely free to text or call me any day, yet he pretended we had a complete communication breakdown.

The police found the scenario peculiar. If Elda had known about the abuse since November, why wait three months, and why come forward the day after losing her job? The entire arrangement smelled rotten. Then, Reginald took things to a new level of cruelty.

That same day, he sent a text to Greg asking if he could get the kids for a surprise sleepover—and Greg had agreed. With that green light, he whisked the children off to Texas Children's Hospital under the pretense of a routine physical, or so he told them. But it wasn't routine at all. He insisted on invasive examinations, alleging everything from physical beatings to sexual abuse and neglect. My children were forced into humiliating, intimate medical procedures designed to investigate horrifying abuse claims that, so far, no one had verified.

I struggle to articulate my fury and anguish upon learning this. Any parent would cringe at the idea of their child undergoing invasive tests, especially for concocted reasons. I also knew Reginald had privileges at that particular hospital, which might have facilitated these hasty evaluations. The older kids, I later discovered, had to recite stories that kept changing with each retelling, resulting in contradictions so glaring that the hospital staff was reportedly perplexed. This was beyond petty sabotage; it was an outright assault on the kids' well-being. The damage inflicted by such a ruse—making them lie, subjecting them to invasive examinations—still makes my stomach churn.

On February 11, Reginald made his legal moves official. He filed a petition to Modify the Parent-Child

Relationship, with the request for a Temporary Restraining Order and so-called Emergency Temporary Orders.

Oddly, he filed this in Maverick County, a place neither he nor I resided in. Even the investigations were happening in Harold County, where I actually lived. I wondered if he believed that remote county was more likely to side with him. The affidavit, which I would eventually read, relied on blatant hearsay from Elda (and possibly other nannies).

It sketched cartoonish scenarios of Greg "picking the children up by their heads," "twisting their necks," "punching them," and other nonsense. I almost laughed at the absurdity, though the laughter caught in my throat each time I remembered these lies came at a grave cost to my kids.

The next day, after the hospital fiasco, Reginald dropped the children back at my home in silence. He didn't acknowledge the invasive procedures they had just endured. He didn't mention the new legal bombshell. He left them as though nothing had happened. The kids looked uneasy, unable to name why Dad had taken them to a hospital. They whispered about "private checks," uncertain if they'd done something wrong. My heartbreak felt physical.

A Few Days of Fragile Peace

From February 12 through the 17th, Elda was no longer around. We navigated drop-offs and pick-ups ourselves, with occasional help from our backup nanny, Andrea. It wasn't easy—my schedule remained demanding, and Greg had his job, too—but that small window of time was almost a reprieve. The children, momentarily free from

Elda's presence, returned to a routine that felt more stable, if tense.

On February 14, we traveled to Illinois as previously planned, a family trip we had been looking forward to. Of course, the minute Reginald realized I'd left Houston, he started frantically texting my oldest son, rummaging through phone numbers to figure out exactly where we were. My mother also got bombarded with calls from him, "Stop lying to me, Comfort; where are they?" she later recounted in a shaky voice. I remember looking around the airplane gate, feeling a pit in my stomach. It was Valentine's Day, of all days, and my ex was reasserting control, as he always managed to do, overshadowing any moment of calm.

Right then, my former divorce lawyer reached out with an alarming heads-up: She had glimpsed some new paperwork. She warned me that the charges were worse than I realized; allegations of abuse and rape not just against Greg but also me. She advised me, in a tone that was half-sympathetic, half-panicked, to leave Greg at once and retreat to the old Farland house. The logic made zero sense. If we were both indicted for monstrous crimes, how did my abandoning Greg fix anything? I refused. This ex-lawyer told me I was gambling with the possibility of losing custody forever. I recalled how Reginald had threatened, "I'll take the children away once I have enough money." And here we were, months after he'd signed a massive contract. The pieces fell into place in the ugliest possible way.

Daycare Standoff and Abrupt Paperwork

On February 17, after returning from Illinois, everything pivoted again. While I was at work, a process server supposedly tried to hand me some new legal documents but left them at the front desk. I never actually received them in person. This oversight was a technical detail, but it deprived me of time to prepare for what came next: Reginald, in a brazen move, arrived at my children's schools to remove them. The older two were apparently easy pickings because he convinced the staff that he had some urgent legal matter.

Then he tried to get April from her daycare, but the daycare called me in a panic: "He's here to collect your youngest child. Are you aware of this?" Bewildered, I told them I had no clue; no official order had come my way. My heart raced; I had no idea I was on the brink of losing them. I couldn't leave work that instant, so I called Greg. He rushed to the daycare to hold off the fiasco. Meanwhile, I finally read the paperwork I'd found at the front desk: a restraining order pinned on me, supervised visitation mandated, with Reginald claiming the children full-time. It was a gut punch. My own children would be snatched away, all because a man with an unscrupulous nanny had spun outlandish tales in a county we didn't reside in. By the time Greg reached the daycare, the police were called. The older kids looked at him with something bordering on hatred or confusion, possibly told by their father that Greg was the reason for the meltdown. My daughter, Veronica, sat on Reginald's lap as though he were physically shielding her from Greg's presence. Only April broke that tension by hugging Greg before leaving with her father.

I felt numb. My mind replayed each detail: the frantic call from the daycare, the police officer instructing that "the kids should go with their biological father." My maternal instincts screamed protest, but in that moment, there was no immediate legal defense. I needed a lawyer.

My first thought was Melissa—the attorney I had used previously—but she had insisted on *throwing Greg under the bus* at the onset of these abuse claims, which I refused to do. So, I called an attorney named Marty Murati. Over the phone, he cut straight to business: a $10,000 retainer for a case this complex. I told him I couldn't easily gather that sum, so I found a cheaper alternative online, a lawyer with sterling reviews who identified with NAACP activism. My naive hope was that she might champion me, a Black female physician, and my children.

That optimism would unravel quickly.

A Lawyer Who Did More Harm Than Good

On February 20, this new lawyer—let me call her *Alyssa*—filed a counterclaim and an interim "band-aid" order for supervised visitations. In effect, she was responding to Reginald's petition by somewhat conceding that I'd accept supervised visits, at least temporarily, while the dust settled. She did not, however, immediately file a motion to transfer the venue, even though we had every right to do so because Maverick County was an improper jurisdiction.

This omission would haunt me.

Melissa, the attorney I once worked with, was furious when she heard I'd hired someone else. She was certain that the first thing we should have done was challenge the venue—as Marty had suggested. But it was too late. Alyssa had locked me onto a path that felt disadvantageous from the start.

My heart sank as I realized I might be stuck with this approach. Yet I had no energy or finances to juggle multiple lawyers. I resigned myself to trusting Alyssa's process, at least for the short term, unaware of how deeply it would damage my position.

Heartbreak in a Monitored Room

Between February 22 and March 13, the supervised visits played out in these clinical, uncomfortable settings. Reginald rarely brought the children himself, instead delegating the job to none other than Elda—the nanny Greg'd fired, who had ranted about spurious abuse and threatened lawsuits. Now, she was re-hired. I had to pay for each hour I spent with my children, effectively renting time to see them.

On the first visit, they arrived under the weather, runny noses and all, but still excited to see me. It was a bittersweet reunion. The kids wondered why we couldn't just go home together. My heart clenched each time I had to remind them of the *rules we had to follow.* The supervisor took notes, ensuring I never said anything *inappropriate.* Reginald, from a distance, pestered the supervisor about whether Greg was present as if hoping to catch me defying an order.

Visit by visit, I observed subtle changes in my children's demeanor. They seemed more unruly as if living in an environment with no consistent discipline. One day, RJ complained that it burned when he pooped. He spent a long time in the restroom. Greg was so disturbed upon hearing that detail that he emailed Reginald, begging him to take RJ for a medical check-up. No response came. Another time, April physically hit the supervisor, and he didn't even attempt to correct her. Elda would show up late or not at all, claiming car troubles, so I had to miss my precious visitations with the kids. By March 13, COVID-19 closures were accelerating.

My last in-person supervised visit ended abruptly. The next hearing, set for March 23, got canceled, leaving me in a new purgatory: no possibility of seeing my children, no scheduled hearing, nothing.

COVID Purgatory and Relentless Panic

The world turned upside down that spring. My job as a family physician remained essential, so I was exposed daily to a virus that scorned any illusions of safety. Colleagues fell ill; patients struggled for oxygen; children sometimes manifested horrifying complications. Meanwhile, my personal crisis escalated quietly: the supervised visits had stopped, the courts were effectively on hold, and my children were living with a father who refused to let them call me or a nanny who actively despised me. Rare texts from my kids' phones (if they managed to hide somewhere to message) were the only sign they were still out there. I almost dreaded each day, waking to see if there was some new court motion or horrifying rumor.

In the background, Alyssa proposed we sign a Mediated Settlement Agreement to *cut losses*. She said it might be my only chance to avoid indefinite separation from the kids, especially in the chaos of pandemic-induced court delays. I hated the idea. A settlement offered from the vantage of fear rarely yields fairness, but she insisted it was the path forward. I felt cornered.

The Zoom Mediation That Shattered My Faith

On March 31, from 9 a.m. until 2 p.m., I endured a Zoom mediation. The mediator, a man who refused to call me by my professional title, seemed buddy-buddy with Reginald. He insisted on calling me by my first name, ignoring my credentials, while referencing "Dr. Woo" whenever possible. His approach was confrontational. Early on, he attacked my husband's credibility, citing some affidavit we'd never even seen. Alyssa seemed clueless or perhaps complicit.

He rattled off lines like, "All three nannies are willing to testify against you," or "You won't see your kids for months or years if you try to fight." My request to pause or consult someone else was brushed aside. Alyssa pressed me to just comply, reminding me that I hadn't physically seen my children since March 13. She hammered on the fear that resisting the mediator's offers would brand me as an uncooperative mother. My entire being revolted, but I felt paralyzed.

Then, ironically, news from CPS came mid-session: They found no evidence of abuse by me or Greg, only recommending some mild counseling. But the mediator sneered, "It doesn't matter what the CPS report says; we have got ways to get you, boy, this here is Family Court." He twisted the good news, claiming it indicated the children needed help and that the system could still keep them from me for ages. Every objective fact was turned upside down.

By midday, the mediator floated an outrageous sum: "Maybe Dr. Woo wants you to pay $5,000 a month in child support, or $50,000 lump sum. In exchange, you let him designate the children's primary residence, and we might allow your husband around them again." My husband was livid. He left the screen for a while, telling me privately, "This is extortion." The mediator overheard enough to get riled, ranting about text messages Greg had sent, referencing "penis size," calling it "micropenis." The entire fiasco degenerated into a personal vendetta. My own lawyer, Alyssa, sat there, urging me to "give up your principles," or else I'd be locked out of my children's lives. She insisted that "the kids won't understand your moral stance."

Meanwhile, we were in the middle of a pandemic that threatened everyone's safety; I was working in clinics, seeing patients' lungs collapse—daily reminders of mortality. My children were forcibly separated from me, and I was told a piece of paper could *fix* it if I just paid enough, compromised enough, or let them defame my husband.

Eventually, I caved. Under psychological duress, I signed that Mediated Settlement Agreement. My mind screamed that it was a betrayal of reason, that I should stand my ground, but I was terrified of indefinite separation from my kids. As soon as it was done, I felt sick. My lawyer phoned me that night, casually suggesting I might need to take out equity on my home to afford the ensuing legal war. She also made bizarre remarks about how *she typically only represents nurses and teachers, not doctors,* and how "being African is not the same as being Black in America."

Each comment piled on more confusion. Did she see me as some exotic paycheck or as a worthless mother? I realized, with a jolt, that she had no interest in championing me. She just wanted to churn a messy case for profit.

I fired her the next day, demanded a refund on the retainer, and received none of it. The damage, by then, was done. The MSA pinned me down to maximum child support, a mental health evaluation, restrictions on Greg's involvement with the children, and more. Even though a subsequent official report from CPS, the Children's Assessment Center, and HPD eventually cleared us entirely, the agreement was already locked in.

A Glimmer of Hope and More Legal Turmoil

Desperate, I went back to Melissa, the attorney I had once parted ways with, to see if she could salvage anything. She was visibly appalled at what Alyssa had done. She filed motions to set aside the MSA, highlighting that I'd been coerced, threatened, and misled. But Reginald's side contested everything. Meanwhile, I roped in attorney Marty again, this time focusing on the CPS portion. I remember walking into the CPS office with him, seeing his coffee-stained shirt, and feeling a small spark of hope. He calmly listened to Tabitha, the CPS worker assigned to investigate the repeated allegations.

Tabitha disclosed that they had over 25 calls from the same group of nannies, all spouting contradictory stories about the children being abused. She recognized these reports as suspect. She even laughed about how they tried to shame me for owning a *stripper pole*, only for her to mention that she, too, practiced aerial aerobics at home.

Around April, official documents arrived stating that every single abuse claim was unfounded. I should have felt jubilant. Instead, I stood amid the wreckage: the MSA was still in place, the children were living primarily with Reginald, and the pandemic kept the courts half-closed. Melissa tried vigorously to file a complaint with judicial boards, but these attempts rarely changed the outcome.

The system rarely indicted its own. Alyssa, determined to cover her tracks, filed motions to quash subpoenas or attacked me personally, disclosing privileged details she gleaned from me, all for vengeance. The entire spectacle was traumatizing, reinforcing that I had no stable ally in a legal system that let manipulative exes thrive.

An Activist or a Con Man

Out of desperation, Greg and I tried a different angle. Both of us had originally come from the Chicago area, where we'd seen activism yield real results for families. We met an individual called Zeke X, who claimed to be an activist or a journalist capable of exposing corruption in that remote county. We handed him $3,000 upfront, hoping he could shine a spotlight on these unethical tactics: the rigged jury panels, the judge who consistently favored local attorneys, and the mediator's threats. But soon after, Zeke vanished.

No calls, no updates, no coverage. We discovered he was known for milking desperate families and living comfortably off their fees. My illusions that activism might save me deflated, replaced by a bitter recognition that opportunists lurk everywhere, ready to exploit a mother in crisis.

I tried not to let rage or despair consume me, but I was exhausted. Each phone call or new acquaintance seemed like it might be a lifeline; each one ended up a flimsy rope. The children still faced irregular contact with me and unsupervised contact with Elda, ironically the biggest threat to them. Reginald relocated to California in June, leaving the kids behind with that nanny, which made zero sense.

They often visited me with rashes, fungal infections on their scalps, or unwashed clothing. They missed remote learning logins—no adult in Reginald's circle seemed interested in their academic progress. Heartache soared. I documented everything: pictures of their disheveled appearance, tardy records, random text pleas from them: "Mommy, can you come pick me up?" However, the MSA effectively barred me from any immediate rescue.

The Final Legal Hurdles

Reginald's new contract in California, ironically, was a driving force behind his aim to keep custody. He once wrote me a superficially *humble* letter, suggesting no child support from either side and an open relocation for him. He dangled $28,000 over four months in exchange for me to give him free rein with the children. My response was simple: I was not for sale. If we were going to resolve this, we'd do it lawfully. By late June, Melissa made a final attempt at transferring the case out of Maverick or appointing an amicus attorney for the children. Both motions were denied. Another hearing took place on July 28.

Melissa subpoenaed several people—CPS workers, even Reginald's parents—hoping to prove these allegations had been baseless. She pointed out Reginald worked 26 days per month, often up to 24 hours at a time, leaving the kids with nannies who had proven incompetent. Still, the judge refused to overturn the MSA or revert custody. The last blow was that we were slated for a full jury trial, but I faced an uphill battle in an environment that seemed stacked against me.

On July 22, Reginald began a formal mental health evaluation with Dr. Goldstein, further smearing my reputation. My volunteer efforts at my children's school—where teachers knew me by name and where I once got recognized for my engagement—seemed to vanish in the record. Greg's dark humor surfaced when he told me, "Now you see how they treat a Black man. They can twist your presence into absence in an instant." I couldn't help but nod. My husband's cynicism and sarcasm had become a coping mechanism for both of us.

Amid everything, Melissa's personal life took a downturn, leaving her with limited capacity to keep championing my cause. She proposed, multiple times, that I sign certain settlements if I wanted the children back in my arms—terms that either exiled Greg from their lives or demanded large sums of money. I could practically read between the lines: "Throw your husband under the bus to salvage your role as a mother." She was repeating that same ultimatum I had heard from multiple corners. I recognized the pattern.

It wasn't just about Greg; it was about subjugating me, ensuring I would fold under pressure. Each day, I asked myself: Could I push Greg aside to *win* my kids? And if I did, was that a real victory?

Ultimately, Melissa parted ways with me as well, urging me to consider arrangements that contradicted my ethics. I was left scrambling once more, recontacting Marty to represent me for the upcoming jury trial. By now, his retainer had soared to over $30,000, reflecting the near-impossible tangle we were in. The mental toll was staggering:

Day after day, I balanced a grueling medical job in the middle of a pandemic, worried if my children were being fed, if Elda left them alone, or if Reginald manipulated them anew. My finances were drained from unstoppable legal fees. My husband wrestled with guilt, feeling that if he'd never confronted Elda that fateful day in February, maybe we wouldn't be here.

My mother hovered in the background, outraged and powerless. My father, largely quiet, apologized for not stepping in more aggressively. Everyone felt battered.

Reflections on Emotional Damage

The downward spiral from February to July 2020 was unlike anything I'd experienced. I had faced heartbreak, betrayals, and divorces before, but this siege was of a different magnitude. My children found themselves subjected to terrifying medical procedures, indefinite supervised visitation, and no contact for months. Greg faced the possibility of criminal allegations that had no grounding in reality. I felt incompetent as a mother, stripped of both my authority and my ability to protect them. Each hearing or visitation carried a mixture of dread and relief: relief that I might see them for a moment, dread that some new fiasco would rob me of the next chance.

COVID-19 ravaged the broader world at the same time, an invisible plague that overshadowed any illusions of normalcy. I lost acquaintances to the virus, watched children in the hospital struggle to breathe, and then came home to documents claiming I was an unfit parent. Sleep became elusive; anxiety soared. Some nights, I'd slump against the kitchen counter, remembering the fiasco at the daycare where my baby clung to Greg but was forcibly taken by her father, how Veronica refused to leave Reginald's lap, how the older ones stared at Greg as though he were a monster.

I'd think about Elda and her vendetta, about how she manipulated the father's pockets, how Reginald capitalized on that manipulation to crush me in court. And I'd wonder: How does one survive such an onslaught?

Family, ironically, was my partial salvation. My mother, once lukewarm toward Greg, now recognized how fiercely he cared about the kids. My oldest daughter, Liza, wrote me messages of encouragement. Cousins pitched in with small financial help. A few dear friends, noticing my reclusiveness, urged me not to lose faith.

But the mental toll lingered: Each step forward revealed a booby trap, another unscrupulous legal tactic, or another monstrous fee. I lost my appetite. I cried spontaneously in the car after shifts. I missed the kids' daily giggles that used to fill the house. Greg tiptoed around me, trying to be supportive yet fighting his own frustration. We both dreaded the next attorney call or the next court date, which might vaporize more illusions of fairness.

Yet there was still a sliver of defiance in me. Even cornered by an MSA, with multiple attorneys giving contradictory advice, I managed to hold tight to some measure of integrity. I never sold out my husband nor accepted the brazen manipulations that demanded I erase him from the kids' lives entirely. I found doctors, activists, and attorneys who seemed sympathetic, though fleetingly. My children, no matter how distant, remained at the forefront of my prayers. If I had to endure the greatest mental toll to keep a door open for them, I would.

And that raw, unwavering love would be the only real anchor I had as the months trudged on, with the final showdown in a backwoods county looming.

And so I braced for the next phase, battered but resolved. My children deserved better than a father orchestrating invasive procedures, a nanny out for revenge, or a mother forced to settle for supervised visitation. The toll on me,

Greg, and the entire household was immense, but it had yet to break us fully. I clung to the hope that, eventually, the truth would stand taller than the lies. If that meant facing a jury, so be it. The mental toll, though severe, was a price I'd keep paying for as long as it took to reclaim my children's future.

Chapter 9:

Custody Battles and Modern-Day Lynching

I can pinpoint the exact moment I realized illusions wouldn't save me anymore: February 2021, when the official court notice arrived, declaring the custody modification trial would begin in July. After everything I'd survived—forced weddings, nanny conspiracies, remote camera sabotage—I genuinely thought we'd reached a plateau of calm. I clung to the hope that the worst was behind me. But such naïve beliefs hardly hold up in a Maverick County courtroom, especially when an ex is determined to brand you the unfit mother, worthy of being *lynched* by the system. That's precisely how it felt: a modern-day lynching, where every vulnerability, half-truth, or passing complaint from a disgruntled nanny morphed into a towering monolith of *evidence*. No matter that I never auditioned for this role—once the father, Reginald, decided to wage war, the trial overshadowed my entire existence from February to July.

Yet February didn't just bring that trial date; it unleashed new turmoil that obliterated any remaining hope for peace. That same month, another CPS case landed on Elda, the nanny who'd previously accused my husband and me of abuse. Reginald finally fired her but then, with alarming haste, replaced her by shipping our children off to two random retirees named Jewel (an Asian woman) and Benny (a White man)—if those were even their real names.

Meanwhile, my eldest son overheard the paternal grandmother declaring she'd "die" before letting her grandchildren be raised by two Black people. She vowed to do anything to keep them away from me now that I'd not only divorced her son but married a Black man.

A Demand for a Jury Trial

To truly understand how my hope shattered, I have to rewind to August 24, 2020, when the first ominous tremor shook the ground beneath me. That day, I learned Reginald wanted a jury trial in our custody modifications. Most states don't bother with jury trials for such disputes, so the idea conjured images of a theatrical showdown: ringmasters parading sob stories, sideshow acts spinning false narratives, a mother pinned as a villain if paternal theatrics overshadowed reason. I tried to keep day-to-day life steady, ignoring the underlying dread.

I had three kids—Veronica exploring her creative side, my son RJ devoted to violin, April proclaiming she was "beautiful and smart" daily—and a new husband, Greg, stepping up as a father figure. A half-lazy nanny, Elda, tested my patience, but we managed. Deep down, I convinced myself we'd be okay. But that hope couldn't silence the growing buzz of a psychological evaluation gathering steam.

Reginald demanded one, presumably to prove I was the unstable parent. This wasn't your average checkup: It meant rummaging through court records, medical files, teacher interviews, nanny gossip, anything to paint a picture of who truly *deserved* the kids. Meanwhile, Reginald offered security footage of my whereabouts, regardless of whether I had the children with me or not. The whole scenario felt like a *Big Brother* spinoff I never signed up for. Still, I believed we'd navigate it, thinking that once the father's side saw the real caretaker dynamic, the meltdown might recede.

They tried dragging Greg into it. "We need his background check, interviews, everything," they insisted, though Greg wasn't even a named party. Reginald's side wanted to depict him as a controlling figure who endangered the children. In reality, Greg was that sweet soul who had let a single mother of four move in, facing down all the chaos that entails. All major entities had cleared him, citing no wrongdoing. But I feared petty jealousy could be disguised as *child protection* in a custody fight. Reginald was prepping for a meltdown performance, eager to highlight any hint of *drama* around Greg.

By the end of 2020, the psychological evaluation was fully in swing. Dr. Goldstein interviewed teachers and coworkers and perhaps even rummaged through the catacombs of my life for more so-called dirt. Reginald rummaged, too, providing every snippet of my medical or educational records. He even produced a "confidential information" report showing Greg's clean criminal record—ironic that it proved Greg had no history, yet they pressed on. At this point, I thought perhaps they'd see there was nothing to uncover. But nothing could stop a determined father convinced I was a menace. He had an unwavering dedication, fueled by whatever meltdown synergy he'd planned for the jury trial.

The Psychological Evaluation

From August 2020 onward, Dr. Goldstein dug into the family. This process was designed to be thorough: background checks, psychological tests, multiple interviews, and *collateral* references. Teachers, nannies, and coworkers, everyone was on the table. Reginald kept pushing the narrative that I was unstable, that Greg was violent, and that the children lived under constant threat in my home.

Meanwhile, I watched Dr. Goldstein rummage through my medical records. He asked pointed questions about my history of abuse—traumas I'd tried to bury. Old hospital notes, diaries, and text messages from ages ago were laid bare, as if I were handing my entire life to a stranger with a notepad, hoping he wouldn't twist the details into a new brand of condemnation. They even scrutinized Greg's *confidential information.* Reginald insisted that if Greg had so much as a parking ticket on record, that might prove he was a monster lurking in the shadows. Of course, they found no skeletons; I believed that might help our case. I was painfully naive. As the weeks rolled on, Reginald's rhetoric became more aggressive.

He insisted Greg must be added as a party to the case or at least fully evaluated. My attorney, Marty Murati, tried to reason with the court: "Greg is not the biological father, not a named party, and every major agency has already cleared him." But the father's side wouldn't relent. They were determined to find some thread, some tiny scrap, that could paint Greg in a monstrous light.

Elda's Final Meltdown and the New Cycle of Abuse

Before Dr. Goldstein's report even hit the courts in May, we'd endured an incident that should have shattered all illusions. On January 12, 2021, Elda's meltdown reached its climax. Already notorious for her instability—hospitalized multiple times for chest pains, rumored heart attacks, and breakdowns—she had long been a volatile presence in our home. Yet Reginald kept employing her, or even her daughters. That day, everything unraveled when she snapped at my nine-year-old son, RJ. In a furious outburst, she beat him with a slipper (*chancla*), struck his head and stomach, hurled his phone, and wrestled him in *judo style*.

Elda then called the police—a rare display of agency on her part—and they arrived to find RJ battered and distraught. They restrained him, placed him in the back of a police car, and rushed him to the hospital. By the time I arrived, RJ was strapped in four-point restraints—subdued and terrified—with staff explaining that Reginald had given permission to *sedate him as much as needed*. My heart broke as I pleaded with the hospital staff to keep Elda away from my child, but in that institution—still beholden to Reginald's influence because he once held privileges there—my concerns were dismissed.

CPS was soon involved. Although their findings on Elda's alleged abuse were ultimately inconclusive, they unequivocally declared her unfit to care for the Woo children. True to form, Reginald fired Elda. One might have thought that such a fiasco would end any lingering doubts about me as an abuser; even Reginald admitted he doubted Elda's claims about me during his interview with Dr. Goldstein. But instead of dropping the custody fight, he immediately found new caregivers—continuing the same vicious cycle of neglect and abuse.

As Dr. Goldstein's evaluation was still underway, February 2021 hit like a sledgehammer. Reginald pivoted swiftly to two retirees named Jewel and Benny—individuals he didn't even know personally. He simply found them online, dropped the children off, and then returned to California. My illusions about any semblance of paternal decency were utterly demolished.

Jewel and Benny wasted no time in subjecting the children to verbal abuse, hurling insults like "stupid," "retarded," and "animals." April clung to the affirmations Greg had taught her—"I am smart, I am beautiful, I am the greatest!"—repeating them defiantly each time Benny called her a "dumbass." The children were forced into grueling tasks—cleaning, hauling—with barely enough food, and they arrived for my limited visits starving. Veronica developed a spitting habit, a painful echo of my own childhood responses to trauma, and I couldn't shake the fear that something even more sinister was unfolding behind closed doors. When I sought a medical evaluation, a female doctor brushed off my concerns; the children, for their part, shrank inward, traumatized and silent. It is rare for children who are truly traumatized to sing like canaries about their abuse, that I know firsthand.

Then, as if the cruelty weren't enough, the Texas winter storm of mid-February crushed the state's power grid. Temperatures plummeted to subzero, and my children ended up in a dark, unheated room under a single blanket. They huddled together in that frozen misery while their father lounged in sunny San Diego—shirtless, with a pregnant nanny by his side, or so the rumors went. Meanwhile, Greg and I braved our own powerless tundra, praying for the Woo children and mourning the collapse of any paternal illusion that had once given me hope.

It was the ultimate heartbreak: paternal neglect and abuse masked by a facade of control and indifference. This was Reginald's brand of fatherhood—never conceding, never reevaluating his approach, and always leaving us to pick up the shattered pieces.

The Motion to Compel and a Narrow Victory

By April 29, 2021, Reginald's side pushed the matter formally by filing a Motion to Compel the Completion of Child Custody Evaluation, specifically trying to force Greg's involvement in Dr. Goldstein's process. They wanted depositions, interviews, background checks—presumably searching for any sign that he'd ever so much as raised his voice at a child. In a small stroke of luck, on May 10, 2021, that motion was denied. The judge (one of the more reasonable ones, apparently) stated that Dr. Goldstein could go on without Greg's interview. This was a rare instance of sanity in a venue that would later prove lawless in many respects. Even so, they tacked on a note that I should "encourage" my husband to participate. However, it was ultimately up to Dr. Goldstein to decide if he wanted to finalize the evaluation without Greg's input.

Marty thought we should skip Greg's involvement altogether. "They'll just dig for drama," he said. "We've already had enough false allegations." I agreed; Greg had endured enough. He'd opened his home to me and four children. He'd been investigated for non-existent crimes and cleared by every entity imaginable. Why subject him to more?

I could almost taste Reginald's frustration. He wanted Greg in that hot seat, wanted to dredge up some sensational angle. But illusions told me maybe that small victory—denying the motion to compel—was a turning point. Perhaps not everything would break in Reginald's favor. Little did I know, we were simply collecting small, cosmetic wins before the avalanche.

Dr. Goldstein's Final Report

Shortly after the motion to compel was denied, Dr. Goldstein submitted his scathing final report on May 25, 2021.

It detailed Reginald's grand scheme in ways that I found both validating and disheartening:

- **Reginald's Reluctance to Stay in Houston:** He admitted Houston wasn't his top choice for building a career. He preferred California, planning for the children to fly back and forth. In truth, he'd already spent most of his time in California *acclimating* to a new job while the kids stayed with a nanny in Texas. So much for paternal devotion.
- **My *Hypervigilant* Parenting:** The report homed in on my history of abuse. It posited that my traumatic past made me fiercely protective, especially of my eldest daughter, Liza. Yet it also questioned whether I trusted men at all, referencing Reginald's portrayal of me as *paranoid.*
- **Reginald's Physicality with Liza:** Reginald admitted having to "restrain and spank" Liza when she was defiant. That jarred me. He had always projected onto Greg an image of a violent disciplinarian, but this admission suggested maybe

he was worried about his own capacity for aggression. Karma is a powerful fear, I suppose.

- **RJ's Health and the Father's Indifference:** My son had developed chest pains during this ordeal. I took him to a doctor, got an EKG indicating LVH (left ventricular hypertrophy), and told Reginald to follow up. Dr. Goldstein's notes confirmed Reginald never took the child for an ultrasound or thorough cardiology check. He simply stated the symptoms "went away." It was mind-blowing that a cardiothoracic surgeon could dismiss potential heart issues in his own child.
- **Elda's Contradictions:** Elda's meltdown was a lynchpin of Reginald's argument. If the jury believed her claims—her laundry list of abuse allegations—then I was unfit, end of story. If they questioned her, though, maybe the meltdown would fall apart. The entire fate of custody hinged on whether or not Elda, the same woman who later physically attacked RJ, was seen as credible.

Dr. Goldstein's final conclusion? *If Elda is telling the truth about Greg's discipline, the children belong with the father. If she's lying, the children stay with the mother.* That was it, the black-and-white pivot. However, illusions told me that maybe a jury would see Elda for who she was: An unstable nanny who changed her stories constantly. Marty, oddly enough, advised that we do a jury trial. Rare in custody disputes, sure, but he insisted a judge might side with father-of-the-year outright. At least with a jury, we might have a shot at reason.

Greg sided with Marty's logic. "A jury might see right through them," he said. "We'll show them that the father's absent, he's out in California, the kids keep rotating nannies." But I, forever the pessimist, feared no such luck. I told him, "In that county, no way I get a jury of my peers." This was near Galveston, a region historically unkind to outspoken Black mothers. I felt the paternal theatrics, the father's wealth, and the subtle racism might overshadow even the best logic. But illusions or not, I had no real choice. Reginald was pushing for a meltdown showdown in court, and if I didn't fight, my kids would be lost in nanny purgatory forever.

Pretrial Motions, Last-Minute Exhibits, and Lost Files

The trial opened with a barrage of pretrial motions, witness testimonies, and exhibit stipulations that felt as weighty as physical bricks on my shoulders. From the outset, it was clear that we were in for a rough ride.

Reginald's lawyer—ever the last-minute magician—began producing exhibits that were, to put it mildly, egregious. Reginald unveiled a timeline stuffed with hearsay and leaned heavily on the so-called *temporary order* known as the MSA, which, as my lawyer Marty Murati reminded everyone, should never have been admitted (Rule 802 and Rule 605 of the Texas Rules of Evidence, along with Texas Civil Practice and Remedies Code 154.073(a), make that abundantly clear).

Marty's objections were rapid-fire, yet the judge seemed almost indifferent, even remarking that the whole presentation was ridiculous—as if we were in a circus where filling in the gaps was expected.

I vividly recall Marty scribbling a little post-it note—"We're going to have to appeal"—and giving me a look of resigned certainty that, with this judge, our chances were slim. Deep down, I'd always known that the venue was stacked against us; every document that could bolster my case was mysteriously *lost* by the other party.

Only materials from after my divorce were accepted, while their team somehow managed to get through evidence that benefited them—my counselor's notes among it. Then came those infamous 121 pages of text messages, where, according to their narrative, Greg took every opportunity to belittle Reginald. In their opening statements—a true battle of narratives—they reminded the jury (yes, those 12 strangers) that there are always two sides to every story.

The Jury and the Optics of Introductions

As if the courtroom antics weren't enough, the judge then turned his attention to the jury panel—a motley collection of 60 strangers from a remote, podunk part of Maverick County. I looked at those faces and instantly knew they were nothing like me. These were hard-working, uneducated souls who wouldn't understand what it meant to be a highly educated and dedicated working mother. At that moment, the horror set in: If they caught even a whiff of my background, I was doomed. I could almost hear their unspoken verdict: "She's too smart, too busy, too… different." And so, every time I caught a glimpse of that jury, I felt like I was walking to my own hanging. The voir dire process was a spectacle in itself. Karen, Reginald's attorney, masterfully removed any potential jurors who believed children should be raised primarily by their mothers—those unspeakably maternal types who might be inclined to sympathize with me. Meanwhile, Marty took a rather pointed detour by asking the panel how important it was that an ex-spouse get along with a new spouse. The result? We ended up with eight male jurors and only four females—a configuration that somehow made the atmosphere feel more like a boys' club than a deliberative panel. I couldn't help but think: "Great, I'm up against a jury that might have been assembled at a local bachelor party."

Then came one of the most mortifying moments of the day: the introductions. The judge, with an air of absolute authority, introduced Reginald as Dr. Woo and me as Ms. Adwoafuaa Nwokocha. Even Marty had to stand up and introduce me as "Dr. Nwokocha" in front of the potential jurors. I could see the discomfort on his face, and I felt a surge of humiliation, knowing that my professional credentials were being paraded like a badge of shame. The optics of it all were designed to reinforce a narrative: that I was somehow less of a *real* person than the esteemed doctor, Reginald Woo.

Opening Statements: A Battle of Narratives

The day officially kicked off with the opening statements—a verbal duel that set the stage for what was to come. Karen took the floor first. With the conviction of a seasoned orator, she painted a picture of the aftermath of our divorce: the mother (that's me) was awarded custody, while the father was relegated to mere visitation. She noted, quite matter-of-factly, that Reginald had been an absent father for 16 months of our children's lives, only making occasional visits to pick them up for lunch at school. I almost wanted to shout that I'd been the one carrying the load every single day, but the courtroom was no place for that kind of outburst.

She then delivered one of the most theatrical moments of her opening: Reginald, mid-open-heart surgery, allegedly had to rush out of the OR because the children's nanny had frantically called to report that the children were being abused by their stepfather. The way she told it, he heroically abandoned his patient—with their chest still open—to rush to the rescue of his own children. (I still can't decide whether that sounds noble or downright ridiculous.)

Then came the personal attacks. Karen claimed that I had invited Greg to move in immediately after my divorce, that he had taken over the discipline of the children, and that I had fired the nanny, who was supposedly the only person keeping things in check. She framed every decision I had made as negligent, implying that I'd carelessly handed over parental responsibilities to an unqualified man. And then there were the 121 pages of text messages—a carefully curated tool designed to reinforce their narrative. Karen presented them not as isolated incidents but as evidence of a continuous pattern: messages where Greg—allegedly—repeatedly belittled Reginald. By showcasing every instance in which these texts undermined the father, they aimed to prove that our household was a constant battleground, thereby painting me as an unfit, irresponsible parent. She recounted the numerous calls to CPS—made by Reginald's nannies, Andrea, Becky, and even Elda—accusing Greg of hitting, choking, and smoking marijuana in the house while the children were upstairs.

The jury listened intently, their faces unreadable.

Marty Takes the Floor: A Reality Check

Then came my turn—or rather, Marty's. My lawyer took the floor with measured confidence, his tone steady but sharp, cutting through Karen's sensationalism with precision. He reminded the jury—yes, those 12 strangers—that there are always two sides to every story.

He laid out the facts: Reginald had filed a motion to modify the decree, a motion he had been preparing since the divorce, and the abuse allegations were built entirely on hearsay. He emphasized that Reginald himself had no firsthand knowledge of anything he was claiming.

Instead, he had rushed to his lawyer's office, filing a lawsuit within 12 hours of reporting a case to the CPS about Greg. He had taken those accusations at face value, never once stopping to investigate them for himself.

Marty methodically walked the jury through the timeline, highlighting the absurdity of it all:

- Greg had been investigated extensively by the Houston Police Department, the Children's Assessment Center, and CPS. He had faced over 20 counts of alleged child, physical, and sexual abuse—all of which had been cleared.
- The entire case had been built on an affidavit Reginald filed based on third-hand gossip rather than direct evidence.
- Reginald, a man who worked 26 days a month, had hired a rotating door of nannies to watch the children while he was absent.

- The very nanny who had triggered the allegations, Elda, had been fired by Reginald himself months later because even he didn't believe her when she claimed his son had attacked her.
- Meanwhile, I had never once called CPS on Reginald. The only reason CPS had ever been involved was because Reginald had initiated everything based on false claims.

Then, Marty delivered one of his most damning points: Reginald had already signed a contract to work in San Diego for the next three years. He wasn't even present in Texas for the majority of the time he had visitation. Every summer, he sent the children away to his parents in Illinois while he stayed in California or Texas.

How, then, could he claim to be a stable, full-time parent? Karen, of course, objected frequently, but the damage was done.

This wasn't a simple case of *two good parents fighting for their children*. This was a manipulative power grab built on shaky testimony, a weaponized legal system, and a carefully curated narrative. And I sat there, absorbing every word, realizing I wasn't just fighting for custody; I was fighting for my credibility as a mother.

The opening statements were a masterclass in manipulation. They twisted everyday events into something sinister, casting me as reckless, my husband as dangerous, and Reginald as the wounded hero.

I wanted to stand up, to make them understand that they had no idea what it was like to be in my shoes. But I knew better.

The courtroom wasn't the place for truth.

It was a stage.

And I had to wait my turn to tell my side of the story.

Testimony: Andrea Enters the Spotlight

Early in the trial, Andrea took the stand. A part-time nanny with limited hours in our home, she presented herself as an all-seeing oracle of our household. Listening to her testimony—live or on the transcript—was equally surreal.

She spoke about "concerning changes" in the children's behavior since I had "married Greg," characterizing him as controlling and vaguely implying drug use. She made loaded statements about him "walking around in a robe" and painted a picture of a household in disarray. Her most damning claim? That my children, supposedly in fear, would hide under their beds for hours.

Karen guided Andrea gently, allowing her to build a narrative filled with just enough vagueness to sound believable. But when Marty cross-examined her, the cracks began to show. He pointed out that she only worked limited shifts and had no way of knowing what happened in the house outside of her designated hours.

Many of her claims, he got her to admit, were secondhand—regurgitated from Elda or Becky. When asked about direct evidence of beatings, she hesitated, shifting in her seat. She did admit that I was a good provider and that we always had food in the fridge, and she conceded that she had never seen Greg hurt the children; however, she noted that his habit of walking around his house with his shirt off made her uncomfortable. At that point, Marty exclaimed, "Have you ever been to a beach?"

But her words had already left an impression, and some jurors still clung to them, moved by her emotional delivery.

I wanted to scream about the day Greg braved the floodwaters to get the kids when Reginald never even called. But I knew illusions ruled this courtroom; I had to wait my turn on the stand. I had to trust that Marty would dismantle the lies, brick by brick.

Intermission: From the Opening Act to the Next Scene

I left Day 1 with my head spinning from all the pretrial motions, last-minute exhibits, and a barrage of rehearsed introductions. The courtroom had felt less like a place of justice and more like the opening act of a surreal performance—one where every document and witness seemed designed more to construct an illusion than to reveal the messy truth of my life as a mother.

As I stepped out into the June air, I couldn't shake the feeling that the real show was only just beginning. There was a distinct chill in my bones—not from the heat, but from the knowledge that everything we'd seen so far was just a preview. The judge's indifference, the meticulously curated optics, and even the bizarre way my professional identity was branded ("Dr. Nwokocha") all left me wondering how much more of this spectacle was to come.

I spent the hours between sessions replaying the day's events in my mind, each detail a mix of dark irony and quiet defiance. The stale, distant testimonies of the petitioner's witnesses and the calculated way in which every piece of evidence was introduced made it clear: Day 1 wasn't about the raw emotion of parenting; it was about optics and legal maneuvering designed to paint me as the absent, unfit mother. But even as I sat in my car afterward, a stubborn spark of determination kept me awake.

I realized that beneath all the rehearsed lines and cold legal jargon, my truth—my everyday sacrifices, my love, and my constant presence for my children—remained unassailable. I knew then that on Day 2, the next act of this bizarre trial would unfold. And while I braced myself for more sterile, robotic testimonies from experts and distant witnesses, I clung to the hope that something more human, more raw, would eventually break through the facade.

So, with that defiant thought in mind and a weary heart full of sorrow and a bitter kind of humor, I prepared to step back into the fray.

Chapter 10:
A Stage of Distant Witnesses and Stale Testimony

I swear, if I had a dollar for every time I thought, *this can't be real*, I'd be able to pay off all my child support and then some. But there I was on Day 2 of the trial, a day so heavy with cold, mechanical testimony that I half expected to see robots reading affidavits off cue. I want you to picture this with me: a courtroom stage set not for a dramatic, heart-wrenching performance but for a parade of distant, emotionless witnesses whose only job was to recite facts, figures, and fancy credentials designed to lend credibility to a narrative that wasn't mine at all.

The Opening Act: Witnesses Without Heart

The day began with the petitioner's witnesses—Reginald's people. And let me tell you, none of these witnesses were family members or even friends.

Every single one was either a colleague, a psychologist, a nanny, or some other so-called *expert* whose testimony was as stale and robotic as a pre-recorded message on hold. It was all about optics and illusions, about showing the jury that Reginald's side was professional, well-prepared, and detached from the messy realities of everyday parenting. I couldn't help but think that if emotions had any currency here, these witnesses were bankrupt.

First up were the psychologists and medical experts. They produced their resumes—thick, impressive stacks of paper that detailed decades of training and prestigious positions. One by one, they appeared on stage, mostly via Zoom (because even the surgeons couldn't be bothered to show up in person), as if technology itself could lend an air of impartiality. Their tone was measured and distant, devoid of any warmth or personal insight. It was as though they were reading from a script written by a legal clerk rather than speaking from genuine experience. Their testimony, though impressive on paper, felt eerily detached from the heart of the matter: the day-to-day reality of my children's lives and my struggle to care for them.

Dr. Mwangi, a trauma surgeon in Colorado, was one of the first to testify. He claimed to have known Reginald for over six years—since 2015—and even declared himself one of Reginald's closest friends despite never having met me. I was floored; I hadn't even heard of him until Dr. Goldstein's report mentioned his name. His testimony focused on how frequently Reginald was with the children, asserting that, despite his grueling schedule as a surgeon who worked 26 out of 30 days, sometimes for 15 to 24 hours at a stretch, Reginald still managed to see his kids multiple times per week. He tried to paint a picture of a devoted father who always made time for his children, even under extreme professional demands.

But it all sounded so weird to me! In my experience, when it truly mattered, Reginald was always absent, leaving the kids in the care of nannies while he juggled his high-pressure job and celebrated his astronomical salary jump from a measly $60,000 a year to a cool $650,000 a year. I couldn't help but note the absurdity: the only *father* I knew was one who spent more time on Zoom calls with colleagues than actually parenting.

Next came Dr. Hannah Pham, a cardiothoracic surgeon in Canada, who claimed she'd known Reginald for three years. Unlike Dr. Mwangi, she had a bit more of a personal anecdote: She recounted how Reginald and the children would hang out with her and her dogs and how he'd help them with their homework during those interminable COVID days.

It sounded almost heartwarming; if only it weren't so scripted. She even mentioned that she spoke to Reginald daily and that he would casually bring up Greg's text messages (yes, those infamous texts that seemed to become a running gag throughout the trial). But as I listened, I couldn't shake the feeling that these stories were curated for effect, meant to bolster Reginald's credentials while conveniently ignoring the reality that he was absent when I needed him the most. When questioned by Marty, Dr. Pham admitted that Reginald was in either Houston or San Diego while the kids spent their summers in Chicago.

So much for him being a present, involved parent. My friend Dr. Washington was ready and eager to testify, but since it was time for the respondent's witnesses, her testimony was dismissed outright. She had been interviewed by Dr. Goldstein and had even written a letter on my behalf. As someone deeply familiar with the children's circumstances, she could have spoken to the reality of their situation and the depth of the racism they endured, especially given that she is both Asian and

African. But the moment she appeared on the screen, Karen dismissed her without hesitation.

The Turning Point: Reginald's Testimony

Then came the moment I dreaded and dreaded in equal measure: Reginald's own testimony. Finally, the man himself took the stand. And oh, did he have a lot to say. He began by talking about the children, weaving in details about how Greg and I had moved in together immediately after the divorce. He accused me of calling CPS twice and reporting him for leaving the children alone—claims that were so outlandish that I could barely keep my composure. According to him, he found out about my marriage to Greg from one of the nannies—another twist in this convoluted tale. With an air of self-satisfaction, Reginald lied on the stand, stating that after Elda told him about the abuse (the abuse that no one could corroborate), he had called me immediately, only to find that my phone had gone to voicemail. Then, he claimed that Greg had called him afterward, asking, "What's up?" And so, he said, he called his lawyer and CPS. He even read aloud some information from a CPS worker, stating that RJ had claimed abuse by both Greg and me and that he (RJ) didn't feel safe in the home.

Reginald's testimony quickly became a litany of contradictions and grandiose claims. He bragged about spending eight years after high school in medical school and college, then went on to claim he'd spent twelve years in training, an impressive resume that, in his mind, should automatically make him the superior parent. He then proudly announced that he had signed a contract for three years, making $650,000 a year—a stark contrast to my modest income. He even admitted that he had contemplated dropping out of the program but instead took five weeks of leave to *get his head straight.* It all sounded like a boastful monologue designed to show that he had everything under control—except, of course, the custody of his own children.

He then shifted gears to talk about co-parenting with me, describing it as difficult. Initially, I was flexible—until Greg showed up, he said. He complained that it was hard to co-parent with someone who constantly asked him to relinquish his parental rights. And then, as if that weren't enough, he claimed I had refused to let the children go to counseling, forcing him to take them to a pediatrician instead. He even mentioned that he planned for the children to attend an Elementary School in the Potomac Unified School District, insisting that the kids loved the current nanny he had living in his home, Katherine Kay, who, by his account, would handle everything childcare-related. There was no cross-examination on his testimony at that moment because Karen took a recess after he got flustered—a temporary break that, while it gave me a moment's respite, only deepened my sense of betrayal.

It was then that I realized everything on this day was about optics. Reginald was painting himself as a man who, despite the impossibility of his schedule, managed to be with the children multiple times a week—even though, in reality, the kids were mostly with nannies. No one in the jury batted an eye to the absurdity that a man could relinquish all parental responsibilities to a nanny simply because he was a doctor and a surgeon. They swallowed his story whole, a narrative so tailored to perfection that it left no room for the messy truth of my day-to-day reality.

A New Twist: Dr. Friedman Enters the Scene

Before the recess, another witness popped up via Zoom: Dr. Friedman. Now, this was someone I had never even met, and yet here she was—an expert on behavior tasked with evaluating RJ's issues. Dr. Friedman focused on how RJ had behavioral problems and said it was a good decision that the "loving father" had brought him in for evaluation. She made a big show of saying that she didn't work with RJ on his phone addiction but would happily take the credit for any improvements. One of her more memorable comments was about how unusual it was for a nine-year-old to carry his panda around at all times—a bizarre but supposedly telling sign of insecurity.

She went on to describe how the change in conservatorship and the ongoing pandemic had affected RJ's behavior, noting that he was very protective of his sisters. According to her, RJ spoke in baby talk around older people—a defense mechanism, she claimed—but not around his sisters, which only made him more of a latchkey kid who was forced to fend for himself. Dr. Friedman even shared a picture—a drawing by Veronica—that depicted her family without including the half-sister or the stepfather but included the nanny, Katherine Kay. She argued that children should be able to adjust well if moved from their home in Texas to California, citing that children are resilient creatures who adapt to change.

However, Marty, ever the skeptic, pointed out that Dr. Friedman had only seen RJ five times and the girls three times—each visit lasting barely an hour. He pressed her on the fact that the nanny had been responsible for bringing them in for most of the visits, with the father only making appearances on the first and last visits.

Moreover, she admitted she was unaware that one of the nannies had abused RJ and called the police. Her testimony, while sprinkled with insights, felt more like a patchwork of observations that could have easily been different if she'd had any consistent, long-term contact with the children. In the end, Marty passed her off, and the witness was excused.

The Intermission: A Recess of Mixed Emotions

At that point, the opposing counsel admitted an exhibit that Marty had never even seen. The jury was excused for a recess, and I took a long, shuddering breath. I couldn't help but think how much of Day 2 was a series of carefully orchestrated optics and stale recitations of facts. All the witnesses on Reginald's side were distant and robotic—hardly the people who could speak to the true, messy emotion of parenting. They were more like background extras in a movie that had been scripted by lawyers and painted by expert testimony, none of which had any emotional connection to my life.

And while I sat there in the recess, I couldn't shake the dark humor of it all: Here I was, fighting for my children's future, while these so-called experts were performing a monotonous recitation of resumes and vague anecdotes. It was as if I'd accidentally wandered into a daytime soap opera, only to find that every line was designed to make me look like the villain.

Marty objected to the admission of a series of text messages—those infamous texts from Greg—which, according to him, lacked proper dates and a solid predicate. The focus, once again, was squarely on Greg and his texts. I remember feeling a bitter pang as I listened to them discuss these texts as if they were the cornerstone of the entire case. (I mean, really? 121 pages of texts? As if a series of jokes could encapsulate the entirety of my struggles.)

Marty's objections were met with the judge's curt dismissal, and the focus remained on the optics rather than the substance of the accusations.

Enter Dr. Goldstein: The Zoom Revelation

Once everyone returned from recess, Dr. Goldstein appeared via Zoom. Now, Dr. Goldstein is a man with a 40-year resume and a plethora of credentials that would make any legal team blush. He began by recounting his extensive experience and said he would have liked to interview Greg and even Liza because, in his view, it was extremely unusual for a stepfather not to participate in the evaluation process. He stressed that in the 550 evaluations he had done over the years, this was only the second time he'd encountered such a scenario. But I couldn't help but wonder how many of those evaluations involved Black families—and especially Black men.

Then came a series of questions from Karen that felt like a barrage aimed to break me down. She started with the number of hours I worked—65 to 75 hours per week, she claimed—and then pivoted to a scandalous assertion that I had called Liza's father a pedophile because he cheated with a 16-year-old girl who, according to her, bore an uncanny resemblance to Liza when she was two. It was as if they were trying to rehash every sordid detail of my past to paint a picture of a reckless, irresponsible mother. Next, the focus shifted to Greg's text messages. Karen characterized them as derogatory, demeaning, and antagonistic—again, playing the same old tune. She suggested that I had even spoken to Greg about those messages, but he'd brushed them off, insisting that they were simply *funny jokes.* They claimed that Greg had also remarked that I was too nice to the children, that I coddled my son, and that I was essentially a pushover. Then came a discussion of a failed interview with RJ: when I brought him in, he was kicking and screaming, but when the father brought him in, he was an angel. The contradictions were dizzying.

Dr. Goldstein then turned his attention to Veronica. He reported that Veronica had said that Greg had choked her and that she had run into the bedroom and hidden under the bed. I nearly laughed—if I wasn't so enraged—because, physically, that was impossible. He also stated that he did not agree with my decision to allow the stepfather to be the primary disciplinarian and how Greg had unilaterally fired the nanny.

They added another bombshell: April allegedly said that Greg had spanked her and that "Daddy told the babysitters to kill Mommy, and Mommy did nothing." (I almost couldn't believe I was hearing this in a courtroom.) They proceeded to discuss hypothetical scenarios regarding a series of questions asked during the evaluation. Dr. Goldstein, for his part, said he didn't think that the texts necessarily impacted the way Adwoafuaa co-parented. Then came the personality testing—an area where Karen claimed I tested on a suspicious level, branding me as distrustful.

Dr. Goldstein, however, retorted that my close relationships and open willingness to discuss my distress painted a different picture: one of a woman who, though scarred by past trauma, was candid about her struggles. He mentioned that the testing had even rated me as overly virtuous and without fault, but in the interviews, I came across as vulnerable, as someone open to speaking about the negative emotions I had endured. When asked about the possibility of the children coming back home with me if Greg were still present—and whether the children would be comfortable given their fearfulness of him—Dr. Goldstein stated that it would be difficult.

At one point, the court played a series of voicemails that Greg had left for Reginald, which went something like this:

"By disrespecting Adwoafuaa the last time you spoke to her, you're disrespecting me. If you call her and curse her out, whatever you are doing to her, I'm doing to you. I would like for you to talk to her as if I am there at all times. We can have a good co-parenting relationship, but you have to understand—I am in control. I am in control. I am the king, I'm the God, and that's that. Good-bye."

Dated April 25, 2019, that message was one of many that painted Greg as a man who thought he ruled the roost. He insisted that, even though all the allegations had been ruled out, it didn't mean they hadn't happened—and that the nannies were lying. Dr. Goldstein and Karen tried to validate the inconsistencies in the children's stories, arguing that contradictions did not automatically invalidate anything. Another interview was reviewed in which the children said Greg would hit them, but they would hide under the bed. It was maddening.

Marty then cross-examined Dr. Goldstein, immediately zeroing in on a crucial fact: Reginald had admitted in his own report to being without the children from September 1, 2020, to May 15, 2021. In other words, Reginald had essentially abdicated his responsibilities as a parent, leaving the children to be raised primarily by nannies. Marty emphasized that, absent the concerns of Elda (one of the unreliable witnesses), there would be no reason to change the primary custody—that is, I was clearly the more involved parent both before and after the marital separation. He noted that all the children were functioning well with me as their primary caretaker, except for RJ, who had a few issues. Marty reminded the court that all allegations against Greg and me had been ruled out by March 31, 2020.

The other two nannies who worked for me didn't witness any abuse but did express discomfort with Greg. Marty then pointed out that Dr. Goldstein had verified, through a CPS interview conducted in November 2018, that Reginald had explicitly stated his intent to take the children away from me. He then drove home the point that Reginald had no interest in finding employment in Houston; he wanted a fresh start elsewhere. Dr. Goldstein pointed out that it was noteworthy that Reginald had told CPS back in November 2018 that he planned to take custody of the children, which only reinforced my concerns given the numerous threats he had made during our divorce. Dr. Goldstein also noted that these events, followed by Reginald's termination of the nanny, led Reginald to question whether Elda had been truthful about the abuse allegations involving me and Greg. He reminded the court of the incident when Elda accused RJ of attacking her with a knife—a claim Reginald himself didn't fully believe. He observed that Reginald had returned the children to me for an entire week at one point after making the allegations, suggesting that perhaps he had received some bad legal advice along the way.

Then, as if things couldn't get any more absurd, Karen jumped in to redirect the examination by stating that I was a bad co-parent for calling CPS five times and repeatedly asking Reginald to relinquish his parental rights. According to her, even without Greg, my inability to cooperate was glaringly apparent. She then tried to justify the purpose of imposing a domicile restriction so that both parents could contribute to the children's lives but claimed that Greg's presence only led to more animosity.

Finally, Reginald was called back to the stand. Karen pressed him to read notes from a supervised visit where RJ reportedly told me that April was talking back to Dad, and I allegedly responded, "That was not nice, and you need to be nice to your dad; they don't see him a lot, so they need to listen to him." The prosecution twisted that moment into evidence of derogatory talk in front of the children. Karen noted that I had arrived 20 minutes late for one of the visits and recalled an instance when a nanny showed up early (despite instructions that no one should arrive early) and texted the supervisor that she was scared of me.

And that, dear friend, is where Day 2 ended—a day of stale, distant testimony, full of numbers and empty credentials, all carefully orchestrated to build the illusion that I was an absent parent. I left the courtroom that day feeling like I'd just witnessed a bizarre, cold parade of expert witnesses who had no heart, no connection, and no understanding of what it meant to truly care for one's children. The entire process was about optics, about painting a picture of a perfect, unemotional petitioner whose every fact was supported by resumes and Zoom calls rather than the messy, unpredictable reality of parenting.

I couldn't shake the feeling that everything was staged for the jury, that the witnesses were mere props in a play designed to distract from the undeniable truth of my daily sacrifices. As I sat alone during recess, I thought about how these robotic testimonies—lacking any warmth or personal connection—only deepened the isolation I already felt. I wondered what Day 3 would bring and hoped that somehow the human element, the raw emotion of my lived experience, would finally burst through the sterile façade.

Now What?

Day 2 had been a masterclass in how the prosecution could assemble a team of distant, detached witnesses who recited their rehearsed lines with zero emotional connection. Their testimonies—replete with references to long hours, empty schedules, and unsupported claims—had been designed solely for optics. They were meant to create an illusion that I was somehow not present enough in my children's lives, that I was an absentee mother whose responsibilities were outsourced to unfeeling experts.

And yet, even as I listened to the cold, mechanical recitations of Dr. Mwangi, Dr. Pham, and the others, I couldn't help but feel a spark of defiance. Deep down, I knew that no resume or Zoom meeting could capture the messy, beautiful truth of being a mother. I recalled the moments when I would tuck my kids in at night, when I'd cry silently after a grueling shift at the clinic, or when I'd pick up the phone to check on my children at odd hours. Those moments—filled with love, fear, and an unyielding determination—weren't in any expert's script.

As the day wound down, the weight of every distant testimony pressed on me like a lead blanket. I was left with more questions than answers: How could a man like Reginald, who had been absent for so long, claim to be the devoted parent he professed to be? How could experts who had never met me truly understand the chaos and the care that defined my everyday life? And, most hauntingly, how could the jury be so easily swayed by a series of rehearsed statements and stale facts?

I knew that Day 3 loomed ahead like the next act in this dark, twisted play—a day when the circus of cold, impersonal testimony would give way to something, I hoped, more human; something that might finally let my truth shine through the cracks of this manufactured narrative. I resolved, in that quiet moment during recess, that I would face Day 3 with every ounce of courage I had left, clinging to the hope that the emotional, messy reality of being a mother would eventually break through all the sterile, calculated optics of this trial.

So, as I gathered my scattered thoughts and prepared for the next round, I couldn't help but feel both a deep sense of disillusionment and a spark of dark, defiant humor because if you're going to be dragged through the mud by a courtroom full of detached experts, sometimes the only thing you can do is laugh at the absurdity of it all.

And with that, I stepped out of the courtroom at the close of Day 2, not knowing what the next day would bring, but determined to fight on.

Chapter 11:

When the Circus Went on Tour

You know that feeling when you step into a place expecting a bit of organized chaos, and then, suddenly, you realize the entire circus has come to town? That was Day 3 of my trial—an entire parade of witnesses, conflicting stories, and enough dark humor to make a jaded comedian weep. I'll try to walk you through it as if we're chatting over a long, late-night call. Buckle up.

The Opening Act: Becky Takes the Stand

The day began with the first witness, Becky. Now, Becky wasn't originally involved in the mental health evaluation; oh no, she was dragged into court via subpoena. I still can't believe they made her request a Spanish interpreter, even though she used to speak perfect English. Maybe they thought her accent was *exotic* enough to add another layer to our twisted play. Becky, with all her disarming honesty, recounted that on certain evenings when she'd come home with the kids, she'd catch a whiff of marijuana smoke from the master bedroom. "It was like a haze that clung to the room," she said as if describing a particularly potent perfume. Then she mentioned that after she put the children down to bed, Greg would sneak into the bedroom. Becky said she was so unsettled by this that she parked her car outside and sat there for 15 minutes, waiting for an explanation from me.

At one point, I spoke to her—trying to sound as casual as possible—and asked if she thought my husband was, well, a pedophile. (I can't believe I said that out loud; I was so desperate for clarity!) Becky, clearly not in the mood for my twisted sense of humor, snapped back that I shouldn't put words in her mouth. And then, in a moment that still makes my blood boil, she recalled how I told her that I was going to get married to Greg. She even remembered a call three weeks later when I reached out because she was talking to my mother about how much she missed the kids. Her voice, laced with anger, still rings in my ears: "You just said you were going to marry him, you showed me the ring, and you put it right in front of my face!"

Becky ended her testimony with a shocker: She recalled a time when Greg locked April in the room for 15 minutes, and when he finally let her out, she emerged wearing nothing but her panties and a choking necklace, a detail that made my stomach turn even as I tried to process it. And yet, in her recounting, she never told me about it until now. Marty, my attorney, wasn't letting anything slide; he grilled Becky on whether she was single, whether she had any children of her own—she said no—and on the whole issue of Greg opening doors uninvited and whether she'd ever contacted my mother about me not having time for the children. Becky, like our other former nannies, admitted she hadn't worked for Reginald after the divorce. To our surprise, she mentioned how poorly the children looked when they returned from summers with the Woo family—their hair a tangled mess, uncombed and unclean.

In her eyes, I was not a good mother because I *never had time* for the kids.

As I listened to Becky's testimony, I couldn't help but feel as though I was watching a train wreck in slow motion—each detail more disturbing than the last.

Act Two: Greg's Turn at the Mic

Next up was Greg, my husband—the man who, at every other moment, had been my rock. Karen, the defense attorney, wasted no time in questioning him. She started off by asking if he had attended any of our children's birthday parties. With a half-smile, he admitted that he had been to April's birthday party back in November 2018. (I used to think that was sweet until I realized how much that tiny smile now felt like an ironic memory of better days.)

Then she hit him with the big one: Why did he refuse to complete Dr. Goldstein's mental health evaluation? Greg's answer was curt and measured: He said he hadn't seen the children since February 2018—well, to be precise, he clarified it was until February 2020—and he was heavily investigated by both the Houston Police Department and CPS. That was the extent of his involvement, according to him. Karen, however, wasn't satisfied with that. She tried to push an illegal, unproven document into evidence, a move that Marty objected to, and, surprisingly, the judge sustained the objection. Karen then charged that Greg didn't want his stepchildren to live with him, which was why he wouldn't participate in the mental health evaluation.

I could see the tension in the room as Greg admitted that he had spanked April one time—after she hit an adult.

Nothing major, just a moment of misjudgment in an otherwise careful man. But Karen wasn't done; she produced voicemails, demanding that Greg explain them. Greg stated that the voicemails were left because Reginald had threatened his wife, and he felt compelled to make it clear that you do not threaten a woman. When Karen asked him about his infamous text messages—where he called Reginald "Napoleon shrimp" and made other crass jokes about his anatomy—Greg explained that he handled Reginald with jokes rather than physical or threatening behavior. He even mentioned a cease-and-desist document he sent to Reginald and his lawyer, demanding $10,000 if they didn't stop slandering his name by calling him an abuser.

Karen then inquired how he felt about me asking Reginald to relinquish his parental rights. Greg said he understood my position because I supposedly didn't need Reginald's money. He admitted that he didn't see the children more than three times per year, that he focused on work while the kids were left depressed for not seeing him, and that the entire situation was far from ideal.

It was clear that, in his own way, he felt trapped in a role that was being unfairly twisted by the opposing side.

Act Three: The Entrance of Elda

Then came our third witness of the day: Elda Chavira. Now, if you remember, Elda was the very same nanny whose testimony had been a cornerstone of the prosecution's case. She entered the courtroom with a sort of swagger, even though she had her arm in a cast and had hobbled to the stand after Reginald patted her on the back.

(I still can't decide if that pat was a friendly gesture or something more sinister—especially considering that the children had once celebrated the fact that "Daddy saved them from the crazy nanny" when she was fired. Oh, the irony!)

Elda launched into her testimony with a dramatic flair. She claimed that she left her employment because of Greg—that he was beating up the children so badly that she had no choice but to warn me. According to her, she was terrified that Greg was going to hurt them "really, really bad." I almost laughed at the absurdity—if only I could cry.

She mentioned a text from January 2020, where she said she waited outside the home for 30 minutes and texted me about Greg beating the kids, adding that she had informed me. I recalled that night vividly; I'd confronted Greg, demanding an explanation for Miss Elda's tears and her presence outside our home.

In my anger, I had cursed him, declaring that anyone who put a hand on my children would be struck down by God. Yet, Greg remained clueless, and I wonder if that night's chaos is why Elda later said that Greg had "locked April in the room" and even recounted that she'd come out of the room with her underwear and a choking necklace—eerily similar to what Becky attested to on the stand. Were these events happening simultaneously that day, or had they occurred on multiple occasions? After hearing this, Greg later asked me, "What is a choking necklace?"

Karen pressed Elda further, asking her about a time when she witnessed Greg pushing her aside and running into the playroom to choke Veronica, exclaiming, "We don't slam doors in this house." Elda testified that Greg had indeed behaved in such a manner and that he fired her because she kept informing me of these incidents. As if to bolster her testimony, Karen produced an exhibit—a series of texts that, if nothing else, painted a picture of a chaotic household.

When cross-examined by Marty, he asked Elda when she first noticed any abuse beyond vague text messages. She claimed the abuse had started in December 2019, though she admitted she never reported it to the police because she wanted to talk it over with the mother first.

Marty then reminded her, with a touch of dry humor and legal precision, that under Section 261.109 of the law, she was supposed to report child abuse immediately. Elda shrugged off that reminder, saying she wasn't aware of the requirement.

In another moment of dark irony, she stated that I was always up-to-date on the children's activities and that I was a good provider—a statement that, coming from someone with her patchy memory, felt like a cruel twist of fate. Marty made Elda read a statement about how the children claimed the nanny, Ms. Katherine, was the best babysitter. He also pointed out the fact that both April and RJ had accused Elda of hitting them on multiple occasions.

When Marty pressed her on whether she was aware that RJ said she had hit him, she hesitated before admitting that she had, indeed, heard it. She then shifted the narrative, recounting an incident where RJ had become aggressive, grabbed scissors, and threatened his sisters.

In a bid to control the situation, she claimed she grabbed him around his waistline, insisting she was saving the day.

At one point, she even mentioned that RJ had tried to stab her with a knife—an accusation that sent shivers down my spine. Marty then asked her about another incident: when she admitted in October 2020 that she'd called the police on Liza because the children said Liza had hit them. Elda had called the police on RJ and Liza, but didn't call the police on Greg.

In her defense, Elda boasted about her long-standing judo training, claiming she had been a black belt for over 30 years, though I always wondered if that was just another embellishment in her increasingly unreliable testimony.

Act Four: Reginald's Return for Cross-Examination

Just when I thought the witnesses might start to line up in my favor, Reginald Woo took the stand again for cross-examination by Mr. Murati. Now, Reginald's testimony was a labyrinth of contradictions—a tangled web of assertions about where the children had been, which parent had raised them, and how often he had visited. Marty pressed him about the children being sent to his parents for the summer while he was busy juggling his two residences in Texas and California. (I remember feeling a surge of anger as he casually mentioned that the kids were in Chicago while he was in San Diego—like a minor footnote in his life story.)

Marty then questioned Reginald on whether he truly lived in California or Texas, to which Reginald mumbled something about residing in both. Eventually, under persistent questioning, he had to clarify that, for tax purposes, he resided in California—a detail that only further complicated the narrative.

Marty pointed out that within 24 hours of Elda first mentioning the abuse to him, Reginald had been at his lawyer's office. He then queried Reginald about his claim that the children only had cereal in their lunchboxes when going to school—an absurdity since they received free breakfast and lunch at Houston schools. The conversation turned to the more outlandish claims: that the children had been kept under a bed for 14 hours without food or that the nannies had witnessed Greg picking the children up by the head and twisting their necks. Marty methodically dismantled these allegations, showing that none of the nannies who testified had ever mentioned such details.

Then came the notorious winter freeze, a moment when the children were supposedly stuck in a cold, cramped space while Reginald, comfortably ensconced in California, was nowhere to be seen. Reginald became visibly flustered when Marty asked if he was upset that I had divorced him and then gotten remarried. He denied it at first but then, with a sudden burst of anger, clarified that he was indeed upset that I had remarried without telling him. (I never notified him, not even a courtesy call.) Marty then forced Reginald to read an excerpt from his own affidavit that indicated he had planned to modify the custody arrangement. It was as if his every word was designed to paint me as the unfit parent while exonerating him—an elaborate narrative that, in the end, proved to be as hollow as it was overblown.

Act Five: Nannies, Friends, and Family Testimonies

Just when I thought the witness list might offer a sliver of hope, the next witness was my personal nanny named Phyllis—my longtime aide in managing drop-offs. Phyllis started by describing each of the children's unique qualities and, with a kind of resigned fondness, outlined what kind of mother I was. She painted a picture of the kids that was both heartwarming and heartbreaking, highlighting their quirks and reminding the jury of the times I'd been there for them. Yet, when asked by Karen whether I could handle the children on my own, Phyllis's answer was laced with subtle criticism. She admitted that I needed to spoil the kids a little because I wasn't there as often as I should be—an observation that stung, even if I tried to laugh it off later.

Karen, never one to let a detail slip, pressed Phyllis on why she was needed for drop-offs if I was supposedly present most of the time. Marty stepped in to clarify that Phyllis's role was simply to ensure that the children were safe when someone unfamiliar was picking them up—a role she had willingly taken on because I was, by necessity, working long hours. Although her role for drop offs were mainly to avoid meeting with Reginald or Elda due to safety concerns. Phyllis then explained that while I was indeed a pushover sometimes, I always made sure that every minute of my allotted time with the children was devoted to their well-being.

Next up was Denise, a friend of mine from Chicago whom I've known for over 35 years. Denise described me as not only a dedicated mother but as someone who had received numerous awards for my involvement in the children's schools. She recalled how I volunteered for every field trip, how I chaperoned events, and how I even donated supplies when schools ran out of Kleenex boxes and extra pencils. Denise was especially effusive when talking about Greg's interactions with the children, noting that he always showed nothing but love—a stark contrast to the defense's portrayal of him as a dangerous influence. In a particularly moving moment, she said that my greatest strength was that, despite everything, I was always present for my children.

Then came Comfort Osei, my mother, who described me as her "sunshine" and her best friend—a woman who, despite the many miles between us, still managed to come to Texas whenever she could. My mother recounted how, in her eyes, I balanced school, medical school, residency, and motherhood with the grace of an octopus with eight hands. (I still chuckle at that image—if only I could see it from a distance.) But Comfort also recalled the dark moments: how the children would come back from summers in Chicago with dirty hair and dandruff and how she'd frantically try to book them a special salon appointment just to fix the mess. When it came to Greg, my mother simply said, "To know him is to love him." She swore that he had never physically struck the children and that he was a true blessing—a statement that, coming from her, carried more weight than any testimony in that courtroom.

Next was Paul Osei, my father, who spoke proudly of the woman I had become. He reminded everyone that I was named after his own mother, that I had given up a promising opportunity in neurosurgery to become a family physician so I could care for my children, and that Greg had always treated them as if they were his own. My father's words were both gentle and poignant, a reminder of the roots I had, the legacy of care I was born into, and the sacrifices I had made for my children's sake. He also mentioned that even though the children did get to speak to us when they were at their grandparents' houses, the arrangement was far from ideal—a subtle dig at the systemic failure that had led to this entire debacle.

Act Six: My Own Testimony and the Final Push

Finally, it was my turn to take the stand. I stepped up, not as the defiant, combative adversary that the opposing counsel tried to portray me as, but as a tired, determined mother with a lot to say. Marty asked me to identify myself—as if that were the beginning of a novel—and I confirmed that I was indeed Adwoafuaa Nwokocha, a family practitioner, a mother, and someone who had been battling for her children since the day I became their primary caregiver.

Marty dove into the January 2020 text messages with the former nanny Elda—those infamous messages where I confronted Greg after Miss Elda was seen crying outside our home. I recounted the night in vivid detail: I had stormed up to Greg, demanded to know why Miss Elda was crying, and how I had angrily shouted, "Whoever puts a hand on my children, I pray to God to strike you dead!" I was furious, and I was clueless about how to make him understand that my wrath wasn't empty; it was a promise of protection for my kids. Marty pressed further, asking me to explain why I had cursed him so vehemently that night and what I thought of the text messages that Greg was sending afterward. I explained that I was trying to coordinate a flexible visitation schedule with Reginald over the phone when he began spamming text messages; his frustration was palpable, as he insisted that I was "difficult" and even went as far as saying things would be easier if I were dead.

I also spoke about the constant threat of termination of parental rights that Reginald had dangled over my head. I explained that I requested a termination of parental rights because he kept threatening me with taking away the children, stating that I would not get a dime of his money. I explained that I had never called CPS on Reginald after the divorce because, in my heart, I believed that my children deserved stability, not endless turmoil. I recounted the photos that had been shown in court: images of the children with fungal infections, dirt under their nails, and even a permanent bald spot on April's head—a haunting reminder of the neglect they had suffered. I argued, with every ounce of pain in my voice, that the children were born and bred in Texas.

This was their home, where their friends, their school, and their extracurricular activities had all been carefully woven into the fabric of their lives. Uprooting them, I warned, would be nothing short of a catastrophe.

Karen, in her final rounds of questioning, pressed me on why I had seemingly moved the children's school after the nanny plot to kidnap them and why I had lost three nannies in the process. I admitted that the chaos forced me to make difficult decisions in the interest of protecting the kids. I explained that, as much as I hated to admit it, the drop-offs and pickups had become a full-time job in themselves—a never-ending cycle of ensuring that no random stranger could get close to my children. I told the jury that I had even removed the names of the unreliable nannies from the school pickup lists to safeguard my children. I recounted the moment I received disturbing news that the very nanny I'd fired in February 2020—hired by Reginald—was still watching the children. That, I argued, was not just negligence; it was an outright threat to their safety.

There were moments when the courtroom fell silent as if the weight of my words had finally broken through the carefully constructed narrative of the opposition. I described how I had been named Parent-Teacher of the Year for RJ's class two years in a row, awards that were a testament to my dedication, not just as a busy doctor but as a mother who had given her all to the children. I explained how I volunteered on school field trips and how I even donated supplies to schools that desperately needed Kleenex boxes and extra pencils. Every detail, every award, was proof that I had been there for my children, that I had been their rock in a storm of neglect and mismanagement.

Marty then brought up the numerous investigations that had cleared both Greg and me of any wrongdoing, emphasizing that even though there were charges and allegations, everything had been debunked by CPS, the Children's Assessment Center, and the Houston Police Department. I pointed out that the only evidence the prosecution had ever produced was a series of text messages and a hodgepodge of testimonies that contradicted one another. I tried to remind the jury that the truth of my daily sacrifices—late nights at the clinic, early mornings packing lunches, and the endless calls to ensure that the children were safe—was not something that could be captured by a few out-of-context texts or manipulated photographs.

As I continued, the tension in the courtroom was palpable. I felt as though I were standing on a tightrope, balancing between bitter despair and a flicker of hope that the truth might yet prevail. I spoke with a raw, unfiltered honesty that I rarely allowed myself in public—about the way I had sometimes cried myself to sleep, about the long nights when the only thing keeping me going was the thought of my children's smiles. I told them that while I might not be perfect, I was the one who had been there day in and day out, who had never abandoned my children even when the world around me was falling apart.

Then came the moment when Karen, with all the subtlety of a sledgehammer, made me read a paper, a document that included an email in which the nannies apparently expressed a desire to "plot" to kidnap the children and take them to Mexico because neither my ex-husband nor I had time for them. I was flabbergasted. I had never, ever said such a thing. My voice trembled as I tried to explain that the paper was a gross misrepresentation of my words and that it was taken completely out of context. But the damage was done, and it seemed that the prosecution had no intention of letting up.

Karen then shifted her focus to Greg once more, bombarding me with questions about how much younger he was, how we met, and how soon he began sleeping over at our house. It became painfully clear that their strategy was to tear down not just my credibility but to defame Greg's very character. I noticed as I sat there that the judge's eyes occasionally darted toward him—almost as if to remind us both that even our physical presence in that courtroom could be weaponized against us.

Then, Karen's line of questioning even touched on my exercise stripper pole (yes, the one in my bedroom that I proudly use for aerial aerobics), a detail that was meant to paint me as frivolous and unfit as a parent. I had to laugh bitterly at the absurdity of it all; I couldn't even mention that Reginald had actually bought me a pole for one Christmas because it was before the divorce.

Meanwhile, the judge's behavior toward me while I was on the stand was anything but neutral. Typically, judges maintain a hands-off approach during jury trials, but he made it abundantly clear that he viewed Greg and me as the bad guys, with Reginald cast as the virtuous party. It reminded me of that Netflix show, *Your Honor*, where the judge wields such influence that he can let a murderer off with just a slap on the wrist.

In my case, the judge jumped in while Karen was examining me, saying, "You're having a problem understanding her standing right in front of you? Is that what you're telling me!" When I asked, "May you repeat the question?" he retorted, "No, she doesn't need to repeat the question; listen the first time. You want to add all this other stuff rather than answer the question, and then when she asks it again—boom, you answer it real quick. So, listen to the question the first time; it's real simple." I asked again if she could repeat the question, and he responded, "You've already asked her that; Karen is going to do whatever she needs to do." I simply replied, "Okay."

Then, there was a debacle about Greg being on the fourth floor, lingering by the door despite being told to stay put. The judge charged at Marty, insisting the issue was on him. When Marty tried to explain, the judge dismissed him outright and continued, "I don't care what happened. I made specific instructions for none of the witnesses to be on the fourth floor. They've been in front of the jury hugging each other; it's not appropriate. When your client leaves, she can hit that stair right there, but instead, she went in front of the jury." In doing so, he tried to depict Greg and me as menacing threats to the jury—as if we were trying to intimidate them—and he did all of this in full view of everyone.

Karen then pressed hard on whether it was healthy for the children to have only two weeks with Reginald. I explained, with a mixture of exasperation and sorrow, that, in the past, the children had been returned to me after four to six weeks—often unbathed, with hair unwashed or uncombed, teeth unbrushed, suffering from fungal infections, nosebleeds, and even hospitalizations for asthma attacks. I had nothing but the stark truth: My children needed stability, not the chaos that had become their routine. I admitted that I had once wished that Reginald would terminate his parental rights because, when he took the children to his parents' house during summer visitation, it was clear he didn't want to spend time with them.

I explained that I did not file the lawsuit because I had no desire to tear my family apart further, even if the system forced my hand.

Almost There

As the final bell of Day 3 echoed in the corridors of the courthouse, I felt as though my heart had been torn out and replaced with ice. Every detail—from Becky's shaky testimony to Greg's resigned explanations, from Elda's dramatic claims to Reginald's contradictory assertions—had been laid bare for all to see.

I stepped out of the courtroom feeling numb, my mind a whirlwind of conflicting emotions. I couldn't help but think of the judge's final, scathing remarks about Greg, his incessant jabs, his dismissal of my every defense, and his cruel insistence that I was somehow to blame for everything. It was a modern-day lynching in a sterile, bureaucratic form, where the evidence had been manipulated, the truth distorted, and my very identity as a mother attacked with ruthless precision.

As I sat in the hushed, empty hallway afterward—trying to process the cacophony of voices and the relentless bombardment of text messages—I knew this was not the end of the story. Day 3 had been a hellish performance, a twisted carnival of lies and half-truths that had left me battered and alone. Yet, deep in the recesses of my heart, a spark of determination remained.

I resolved that no matter how dark the courtroom drama became, I would continue to fight for my children and for the truth that only I knew. That determination would carry me into Day 4—the final day of trial—where the full weight of the verdict would be delivered and where I would finally have to face the consequences of this modern-day lynching.

Chapter 12:

When Everything Came Crashing Down

June 24, 2021. I'll never forget that day; it hit me like the final day of a countdown, the day that would decide if I could still be the mother I'd fought tooth and nail to be. The trial had dragged on for days—testimony, evidence, cross-examinations, and enough emotional whiplash to last a lifetime. And then, on the last morning, I walked back into that courtroom with my attorney, Marty Murati, steeling myself for a battle I wasn't entirely sure I could win.

The judge, a formidable presence behind the bench, started things off by laying down the law for the jury. "Do not let bias, prejudice, or sympathy play any part in your deliberation," he said, his gaze sweeping over the 12 jurors like he was silently interrogating their ability to follow simple instructions. His tone wasn't exactly inspiring; it came off more as a stark warning than a gentle reminder.

He went on to remind everyone that the jurors' conduct would be reviewed just as closely as that of the witnesses, the parties, or even his own. "If it is found that you have disregarded any of these instructions," he emphasized, "it may lead to jury misconduct, necessitating another trial by another jury, thus wasting all of our time." I got the principle: If the jury wasn't totally impartial and solely guided by the *preponderance of evidence*, then the whole legal machine would just grind to a halt. But as I looked at these eight men and four women—some wide-eyed with curiosity, others clearly battling polite boredom—I couldn't help but feel my heart pounding. These strangers had the power to decide my children's future, and that thought alone was almost too much to bear.

The courtroom was charged, like it was a tinderbox waiting for the spark of closing arguments to set it off. On one side of the aisle, Reginald sat stiffly, sneaking the occasional glance at me while mostly huddled with his attorney, Karen. On my side, Marty maintained a calm demeanor, even though we both knew how high the stakes were. A heavy hush fell over the gallery, the kind that only comes when a verdict is teetering on the edge of reality.

Karen's Closing Argument: A Relentless Siege

At the judge's signal, Karen stood up and launched into her closing argument with the confidence of someone who'd rehearsed every biting word. She started off all polite, talking about *healing processes*, but that was just the calm before the storm:

"It's time for them to move on with their lives and begin the healing process, but I'm afraid Reginald has to keep dealing with Greg's unhealthy behavior—and with Adwoafuaa wanting to erase him from the children's lives."

I braced myself at that line because I knew all too well that her plan was to paint me as someone who systematically marginalized Reginald from day one. And trust me, that couldn't have been further from the truth. Karen didn't hold back. She went on to list every supposed failing in my parenting:

- alleged refusal to co-parent with Reginald and ignoring counseling for the kids
- the various trips to Tulum, Colorado, Ghana, and Hawaii—portraying me as an absentee parent with no regard for my children
- accusations that my kids were just *latchkey kids*, forced to fend for themselves while contrasting that with Reginald's supposed self-sacrificing devotion

Her words hit me like a series of stabs, each one twisting something I'd done or not done into a narrative that just wasn't true. "April is 5," she reminded the jury, "and there are 13 more years to operate on the verdict you return. These children, if awarded to Adwoafuaa, may go home tomorrow, but are they going to be stable, grounded, well-rounded citizens?" It was a rhetorical flourish designed to convince everyone that I was some chaotic force incapable of creating a secure home.

Then she turned her fury on Greg—my husband:

- claiming he was "unhealthy," "disrespectful to his mother-in-law," and a "clear and present danger" to my children
- accusing him of finding humor in the infamous *121 pages of texts*
- asserting that he had "exacerbated the situation even prior to CPS being called"

At one point, she hammered on the fact that Greg hadn't helped me secure custody. "He has done nothing," she said, "to ensure these children are in a safe environment. Even before CPS got involved, he was ridiculing Reginald. He told her she was sticking up for her ex-husband. He doesn't have respect for anyone!"

And then, as if that wasn't enough, she wrapped up by suggesting that I'd asked Reginald to terminate his parental rights three times. "What mother does that?" she exclaimed as if the raw frustration and tension behind that decision could be summed up in one dismissive question.

Her final flourish was to remind the jury that Reginald was a cardiac surgeon, a man who'd sacrificed two decades of his life in medical training, now earning $650,000 instead of $60,000. "He saves lives," she insisted, "so do not hold it against him that he moved to San Diego. The medical field demands 12, 14, and 18-hour days. He should be able to take the children anywhere—he's in San Diego, Mom's in Houston, grandparents in Chicago—he needs that flexibility." In her narrative, Reginald was the hero, I was the villain, and Greg? Just a warped, uncontrollable force. Then she sat down, a smug sense of triumph radiating from her as if she'd just wrapped a neat little noose around my custody hopes.

Marty's Counterargument: Shining Light on Hearsay

Then it was my turn. Marty, my attorney, rose for our closing argument. He didn't put on any theatrics—just a cool, measured "The truth is out there," which set the stage for his methodical dissection of Karen's claims.

He pointed out the glaring holes in Reginald's affidavit, noting that Reginald "had no direct knowledge of anything," he claimed. According to Marty, the entire case was built on hearsay: "He says he heard it from someone else, which he filed one day after hearing it, without any verification." In contrast, when I first received Elda's complaint, I took it upon myself to investigate personally.

Marty went over the absurd allegations—like children being "picked up by their heads and twisted" or one child being "under the bed for 14 hours without food." He even brought up the photos that clearly showed all the beds in our home that were only six inches off the ground, not a hiding place for a child. "These accusations," he said, "might catch the court's attention for a moment, but beyond the initial shock, there's no evidence to support them." He recapped how Reginald had been angling to change the custody arrangement since 2018, using any excuse he could muster—be it a false affidavit or complaints from disgruntled nannies. Marty reminded everyone that Reginald himself admitted to Dr. Goldstein that Houston was only his "third choice" for a job. Meanwhile, both CPS and the Houston Police Department had cleared Greg and me of any wrongdoing. He then posed a rhetorical question: How could a father-of-the-year candidate be so absent that he had to rely on nannies—sometimes questionable ones—to raise the children?

Then came the saga of the nanny fiascos:

- Becky and Andrea never witnessed Greg striking the kids.
- Elda, the nanny who screamed abuse, had also once claimed that RJ pulled a knife on her, even though, as a supposed black belt, she couldn't handle a nine-year-old.

- The contradictions were endless: Elda said the abuse started in November but didn't call the police until after she was fired. Then, conveniently, Reginald hired her.

Marty's words painted a clear pattern: Every nanny's story crumbled under scrutiny, yet Reginald clung to them because they supported his bid for custody. He also addressed the infamous texts from Greg. Sure, some of them were inappropriate, but let's be real; Greg had been under fire with accusations ranging from child molester to neglecter and abuser. "He was cleared, and so were the children," Marty explained. "But if you're accused of molesting your stepchildren, you might send some heated text messages, too."

He wrapped it all up by highlighting the stark differences: "Reginald works a lot; she works a lot. But she lives in Houston, near the children's school, while he moved 1,500 miles away. They see a counselor a few times, mostly brought in by a nanny. Dr. Goldstein's own report notes that, absent the concerns of these nannies, there's no reason to change the primary residence and Reginald abdicated his rights as a parent when he chose to move to California. So why are we here?"

That rhetorical question hung in the air like a challenge: Why change custody if the father had been so uninvolved and was living across the country? Then Marty took his seat, and I swear the tension in the room multiplied tenfold.

The Bombshell Verdict and Judge's Tirade

After the arguments, the jury took a mere five minutes to deliberate—barely enough time to flip through reams of texts, exhibits, and conflicting nanny testimonies.

We were called back, and my stomach did a complete somersault. The foreperson—a biracial African American woman—stood up, and I couldn't help but recall my father's ominous warning: "The minute they see Greg, you lose."

Her words were crisp and final:

Should the existing order naming me as the primary conservator be modified?

Yes.

- Which conservator should have the exclusive right to designate the children's residence?

  Dr. Woo.

- With or without a geographic restriction?

  Restricted.

- Area?
- Continental United States.

Each "Yes" struck like a blow. I sat there, numb, as the judge announced the new orders:

- I would pay maximum child support starting July 1st; Reginald no longer had to pay a dime.
- Reginald would cover health insurance, but I'd be responsible for paying it.
- Reginald had exclusive rights to decisions about the

children's medical, psychiatric, and educational needs, with communication limited to a parenting app.

- The visitation schedule would be the standard long-distance variety.
- The first right of refusal was eliminated.
- Dr. Goldstein's fees were to be split between us.
- And, in a final twist, Reginald, riding the wave of the verdict, declared: "After hearing all this testimony, I realize she's been nonresponsive, unremorseful. She insists nothing happened to the kids; no change is needed. So, I request the court for 100% decision-making for medical reasons, and I'm also asking that the children not be in Greg's presence at any time, including phone, social media, or video conferences like Skype or FaceTime."

Karen then jumped in, "If she stays married to Greg, is it possible to allow supervised or counselor-managed access to the children?" Reginald fired back, "That's a hard question. The family unit is fractured. He needs to acknowledge what he did, the demeaning text messages. I'd defer to a mental health specialist on how to integrate this family back together."

Deep down, I realized that everything I'd fought for was slipping away. The judge then zeroed in on Greg, repeating that if I insisted on remaining married, it might hamper my ability to see the children. Ironically, he even demanded that my older daughter, Liza, remain out of sight—though when reminded that it wasn't relevant, the judge's fixation cooled only slightly.

The final blow came with the judge's tirade against Greg, invoking Dr. Woo's requests. He declared that if I truly believed my children were my world, I'd "make some serious decisions." The subtext was clear: Divorce Greg, and maybe I'd be viewed more favorably.

Karen then cross-examined me in a last-ditch attempt to paint me as irresponsible: "Is it healthy for the kids to have only two weeks with Reginald?" I explained that, historically, the kids came back from his home unbathed, hair a mess, sometimes even with fungal infections or after being hospitalized for asthma. She pressed further, asking if I'd ever asked Reginald to terminate his parental rights; I admitted I had, yes, because he threatened to snatch the children away from me altogether. "I wanted to protect them from someone who didn't want to be truly present," I said, my voice trembling with a mix of anger and heartbreak.

Then came the final hammer: The jury, it seemed, had spoken unequivocally: I lost custody. The judge delivered the official rulings, and as if to rub salt in the wound, he addressed me as "Dr. Nwokocha"—a title that felt less like an honor and more like a cruel twist of fate.

What followed was an all-out tirade aimed at Greg. The judge recounted how people can do extraordinary things when threatened, but for Greg to claim that his behavior was "comedic" was, in his eyes, an insult. He called Greg "a sick individual in every sense of the word." He even went so far as to ridicule Greg's height—labeling him a "Napoleon shrimp"—and psychoanalyzing his text messages as if they signaled an unhealthy obsession with Reginald.

"Who appointed him king and god over Reginald?" the judge demanded, concluding that Greg was ill beyond belief, essentially branding him a stalker or even a potential felon.

I tried to speak, to protest that it was too far, but the judge cut me off: "That's your husband, and here's what I want you to understand. All those insults, that 46/48 waist, all that bull corn? He's talking about the father of your children." He insisted that by not stopping Greg, I was implicitly endorsing him. Then he shared an anecdote about a young man forced to hammer nails into a fence—an illustration of how words, once spoken, can't be taken back.

Throughout this diatribe, he maintained that Greg had no place around my kids, that I, as a doctor, should be more mindful, and that Greg was "sick" and in dire need of serious mental health work. He repeated that Reginald's fatherly patience was exemplary, while Greg was a clear danger. Finally, he granted an injunction against Greg's contact with the children but conveniently refused to impose a $1,000 per-communication penalty, arguing that would "bankrupt" me within six months.

The judge wrapped up with a paternalistic note: "You said your children are your world. You need to make serious decisions. Am I saying divorce Greg? I wouldn't wish that on anyone. But if he does this again—makes a tweet or a Facebook post—he's a danger to the children." The judge went on further to add, "We'd rather have your children raised by nannies than by you!"

At that moment, it was unmistakably clear: In the eyes of the court, my children were no longer mine. Everything about that day screamed injustice. Reginald theatrically sobbed in the hallway, clinging to sympathetic jurors, and I couldn't even bring myself to look at him. Deep down, I knew it wasn't really about the children; it was all about his wounded pride, his vendetta after suspecting I'd called CPS on him, and his jealousy of Greg.

The Aftermath and My Internal Resolve

Once the judge's gavel came down, reality set in like a bad hangover. The jury's decision, the judge's monologue, the father's public meltdown, it all felt wildly detached from the everyday truth I knew about my kids' lives. Later, Marty confided in me that some jurors admitted they'd have let me keep custody if not for Greg. Others dismissed the nannies' testimonies as worthless but said, "Greg cinched it." I couldn't shake my father's old warning: "The minute they see Greg—young, healthy, attractive, muscular, tall, a confident Nigerian man—the optics in that county will kill your case."

I was stunned by how easily that prejudice had woven itself into the whole proceeding. My father even offhandedly remarked that it wouldn't look good for me, a Black woman, to leave an Asian man for a Black man. I found that logic twisted, but it was a stark reminder of how deep racial prejudices run—even among people who supposedly share a common heritage. Meanwhile, Reginald's meltdown in the hallway—sobbing and clinging to jurors like a bad soap opera—made me feel sick. It all seemed so orchestrated, more a final act in his theatrical performance than genuine fatherly love.

Reginald's parting words echoed in my mind: "Adwoafuaa has no remorse." Remorse for what, exactly? Even Marty found that statement bizarre. The whole experience felt like a modern-day lynching of my maternal rights: a public condemnation, a humiliating final takedown, and a neat legal package that awarded father-of-the-year control.

Yet, in the midst of that heartbreak, I clung to one small ray of hope: at least my children were *freed* from the nanny purgatory. The judge's final orders—despite all their cruelty—at least ensured they wouldn't end up with incompetent caretakers. Perhaps Reginald will step up as a better father now, though I'm not holding my breath.

As I walked out of the 300th Judicial District Court of Maverick County that day, all illusions about paternal theatrics overshadowing the truth were shattered. The father might think he'd won, the system might have labeled Greg a "Napoleon shrimp" menace, and the judge might see me as some irresponsible mother who asked for the father's rights to be terminated—but I know my truth. And one day, I believe, the children will see it too.

That's how June 24, 2021, ended: a day when every carefully orchestrated piece of evidence coalesced into a verdict that felt like an out-of-body condemnation. I lost—thoroughly and publicly. But even as I left that courthouse, battered by the system's decisions, I felt a small, stubborn flame of defiance. The father's meltdown, the judge's venomous tirade about Greg, and the swift jury decision: they all belonged to that day, in that courtroom. Outside, my life, my love for my children, and my unwavering determination to keep fighting remained mine.

So, my friend, while that day may have stripped me of the right to shape my children's daily lives in the eyes of the law, it didn't strip me of my truth or my resolve to keep going, no matter how absurd and unjust the system may be.

Chapter 13:

Resilience and Survival

People often imagine that a courtroom showdown ends neatly with a judge's gavel, the tension dissolving instantly, and everyone simply packing up their baggage to move on with their lives. Cue the triumphant music, the slow fade to black, and a final sense of closure.

Except that's a fairy tale. Real trials—especially custody battles—never end with the final clang of a gavel. They merely shift to another stage, and the conflict picks right back up with renewed energy.

I learned this the hard way. After our final day in court, you'd think we could at least catch our breath. But no. The ink on the verdict wasn't even dry before Reginald decided to tighten the screws further. The man had won custody—he had *won* in the eyes of the law, in front of our kids, in front of the entire county—and that victory was apparently not enough.

Let me back up and provide some context. Reginald made about four times more than I did; his $650,000 a year dwarfed my physician's salary. But that little detail didn't stop him from getting the maximum child support out of me, plus an additional $1,000 a month for the kids' health insurance. He wasted zero time garnishing my wages as soon as the judge signed on the dotted line.

And somehow, this development wasn't just a legal reality; it became office gossip. My boss approached me one day, grinning like he had a joke locked and loaded. Then, right there in front of everyone, he started doing *the* Matthew

McConaughey *Wolf of Wall Street* money chant, thumping his chest with exaggerated enthusiasm. I raised an eyebrow. "What's that about?" I asked, already bracing for whatever nonsense was coming next.

He smirked. "You're one of us now," he said, nodding as if welcoming me into some exclusive club. "One of the guys."

I stared, waiting for an explanation.

"The child support crew," he clarified as if this was an honor. Then, in the same breath, he added that he actually respected me more now, so much so that he decided to give me a promotion and a $10/hr raise. In his own absurdly misogynistic way, he explained that this was why men got paid more. "You've got responsibilities now," he said as if I hadn't been raising children this entire time. The whole moment would have been laughable if it weren't laced with irony. Sure, a bump in pay was nice, but it still paled in comparison to what Reginald made.

But while my wages were being garnished and my financial stability squeezed, Reginald made sure to celebrate his victory in a far more personal way. He literally gathered our three children around, like a middle-school basketball team after a big championship, and proclaimed with glee, "I won!" Then he went on, "And now, I'm going to make sure your mother is bankrupt."

If you've never felt your stomach drop to your ankles, I can sum it up: it's part shock, part heartbreak, and part suppressed volcanic rage. You want to appear strong for your kids, so you swallow all of it and manage something like, "Kids, it'll be okay." But inside, you're half convinced that you're witnessing your life unravel, thread by thread.

Then, as if the universe decided to toss me a lifeline in the middle of all the absurdity, I discovered I was pregnant. In mid-December, my cycle went AWOL, and the test was undeniably positive—a brilliant, unexpected twist in a year that had already taken enough dark turns. I shared the news with Greg on Christmas. And while that might sound like a scene from a feel-good holiday rom-com, it was pure, unadulterated good news. Of course, the kids were with their "super stable" parent (yes, I'm being sarcastic) because it was an odd year—and I'd get them for New Year's instead. We had our own private celebration over dinner, and we planned to share the news with the kids later.

A Flicker of Hope: Filing for a Retrial

While all of this was happening, I held onto the faint belief that maybe, just maybe, we could fix this if we had a second chance to present our case. After all, the trial had felt more like a reality show in a county that often seemed determined to see me fail. So, I asked for a retrial. Denied.

That's it. One-word conclusion: *Denied.* There was no further explanation—just a neat little stamp on a piece of paper. People assume justice is blind, but sometimes, it feels more like justice is selectively ignorant. So, I decided to keep going. My next step was to file with the Court of Appeals.

Now, have you ever tried to juggle legal appeals with zero money for an attorney, all while continuing to work as a physician? It's up there with the world's most grueling triathlons, minus the cheering crowds. But hey, I didn't have a choice. I had to do something; the alternative was just sitting still while Reginald steamrolled my entire existence.

So, I filed my appeal *pro se*—meaning I prepared and submitted all the legal documents myself. In my dining room, no less. My belly was expanding daily with this new life I was carrying, and my stress levels were climbing right along with it. My phone was always an inch away, stuffed with online legal resources and sample appellate briefs I'd found. Meanwhile, I had to keep working shifts at my clinic. Necessity is the mother of invention, and it's also the mother of "holy crap, I might actually lose my mind."

Eventually, though, the legal complexities outgrew my amateur skill set. I mean, yes, I'm a doctor. I can handle a complicated diagnosis, but arcane points of law are an entirely different beast. Enter Joseph Rosenthal, an appellate lawyer with an exhaustive over 40-year resume that includes multiple leadership roles, numerous professional honors, and a wealth of professional activities, publications, presentations, and speeches. He recognized that I was in over my head—and I sure knew it, too. That didn't magically solve everything, but at least I could lean on someone who'd done more than watch an episode of *Law & Order*.

Reginald's Next Move: The Custody War Continues

Of course, Reginald wasn't exactly taking a break. In January 2022—while all this "appeal" mania swirled—he was back in court, filing a new lawsuit for enforcement. Let's all take a moment to admire how a man who loves to claim he's the busier, more important parent still finds the free time to orchestrate a legal blitzkrieg. He's a surgeon, a single father (by his own definition), and apparently a part-time private investigator, lawyer, and financial assassin. Impressive multitasking.

Let me clarify the custody arrangement we ended up with: on paper, it was "joint custody," which is basically a label that sounds nice but was overshadowed by the fact that Reginald was named the primary custodian. I was *allowed* first, third, and fifth weekends. The heartbreak of losing daily contact with my children was already heavy but then came the question of summer. Typically, the non-custodial parent (yours truly) gets an extended summer visitation.

Reginald decided he was going to interpret that rule in his own special way, specifically by shipping the kids off to Chicago to stay with his parents. They were already in Chicago during the jury trial because he already somehow knew he was going to win.

Let me remind you of some math: I had the right to see my kids during the summer. He was ignoring a court order by sending them states away. So, my mother and I decided that enough was enough; we weren't going to let him do this quietly. We drove over to his parent's house to insist the kids come with me. It seemed straightforward: I show up, wave the custody order, pick up my kids, and drive home for some well-deserved time together.

Ha! Nothing was ever that simple with Reginald. As soon as we got there, it erupted into a legal circus. Lawyers were called, phone arguments commenced, and I found myself in a bizarre standoff. Reginald's attorney, Karen, repeated one of her trademark lines, "The judge ruled that the children belong with Reginald." So I asked the obvious question: "Where exactly *is* Reginald?" Because the kids weren't with him, they were cooped up with his parents in Chicago while he was in San Diego performing surgeries and posting triumphant photos of himself in scrubs.

To call it hypocritical is an understatement. But guess who *won* that day? Not me. Not the kids. They had a police officer on their side—one who seemed more like an old family friend than a neutral officer of the law. He basically told me to step away from the property, refusing to read or honor the visitation order I had in hand. So I had to leave without my children, with them standing there looking disheveled and sunburned, RJ's glasses askew and taped, their hair matted. My heart cracked into a thousand tiny pieces, but there was nothing more I could do at that moment.

Private Investigators in the Shadows

At this point, Reginald's capacity to micromanage and stalk my every move didn't really shock me anymore. He had already proven he was the guy who would find the time and money to track me down for a petty advantage. So, when I learned that he'd hired private investigators to follow me around—whether I was alone, with my kids, or with my husband, Greg—I was mostly just annoyed, not surprised. But I'd be lying if I said it didn't stir up some anxiety. Picture driving to the grocery store, glancing in your rearview mirror, and wondering if the random sedan behind you is another paid lackey snapping photos. The man took *trust issues* to a whole new level.

And sure enough, he eventually *caught* me in December 2021 for something that, by normal human standards, is unbelievably trivial: The children saw Greg. He had been labeled by Reginald's side as some monstrous boogeyman, despite the court *itself* eventually concluding there was no evidence of wrongdoing on Greg's part.

Let me set the scene: It had been nearly two years since the kids laid eyes on Greg—two long years of them hopping between nannies, complaining of neglect, sunburns, missing extracurriculars, and living in an environment that felt like a revolving door. When they finally saw him, they ran into his arms. There was no fear, no trembling, just pure, unfiltered joy.

It's a surreal moment to watch if you've spent months hearing the other side paint your husband as Public Enemy Number One. The kids were excited to share every detail of their difficult experiences with the rotating nannies in San Diego. They told us about "mean old Elda" and the questionable babysitters in Houston and California, how many nannies had come and gone, and how some even left without saying goodbye. Meanwhile, their father was often away, doing his own thing.

For one night, we all sat down like the family we once were; Greg made his famous baked macaroni and cheese, I put together some delicious jollof rice, and my mother and my adult daughter, Liza, joined in the laughter. We decided to go see *Sing 2* because the kids wanted a movie outing with Greg like old times. It was all so normal, so *ordinary* in the best possible way.

Cue the private investigator. We were blissfully unaware that someone was likely in the shadows, snapping photographs, maybe filming us munching on popcorn.

Because when it comes to Reginald, you can bet that if you step one toe outside his rigid plan, he'll have a camera crew ready to document your every move. It wasn't enough for him to keep the children away; he needed proof that if I spent three minutes of joy with them and Greg, I would *pay*.

Served... at My Own Clinic

By January 2022, Reginald was itching to serve me legal papers for yet another enforcement lawsuit. My boss, fully aware of the harassment, was kind enough to move me around to different clinic sites so I could avoid the humiliating scenario of a process server barging into my workspace. But, eventually, they found me.

The server's strategy was almost clever in a comedic, manipulative way—like a cheap detective novel. A man and woman strolled into my clinic, raving about how they'd heard such amazing things about me, how they absolutely insisted that only *I* could treat them. I should have known something was off, but I was used to the occasional glowing reviews from patients. Plus, my front-desk staff never wanted to turn away potential patients, so they scheduled them without a second thought.

I took their vitals, asked about their symptoms—none of which made any medical sense—and tried to come up with a polite way to say, "Well, there's actually nothing wrong with you." Then came the moment of truth.

"Are you Dr. Nwokocha?"

I nodded. "Yes, I am."

"You've been served."

They didn't even have the decency to look sheepish. They seemed almost proud like they'd just pulled off the heist of the century. I managed to keep my composure. I even shrugged and said, "Thanks. My ex has been harassing me for months. You should've led with that."

They left, job done. My front-desk person looked at me, horrified, while I tried to process a wave of nausea. Whether from pregnancy hormones or raw stress, I nearly gagged on the spot. In the back of my mind, I kept thinking: *If these had been hitmen, I'd be dead. I literally invited them into my clinic.* There was no limit to Reginald's willingness to cross personal and professional boundaries.

Battling the Legal System… Again

When the dust settled, I dialed up Marty, my regular family-law attorney, to let him know about the new legal ambush. "We're doing this again," I said in lieu of a greeting. Marty sounded more tired than me, which was saying something.

He asked me point-blank if I had broken the judge's order by letting the kids see Greg. I told the truth: "Yes, I did." It was the truth, after all, and lying to my own lawyer wouldn't help. Marty groaned, but I could sense his wheels turning. He found a strategy, a motion to transfer the case from Maverick County to Harold County, a jurisdiction that might actually follow the law as written rather than old backroom alliances.

Imagine my giddy relief when the junior judge, Judge Bailey, actually read the statute and granted the transfer. My heart soared. For a single bright, shining moment, I thought we were free—free from the courthouse that had delivered so many questionable rulings, free from the shadow of old alliances and nepotism. I might have done a small victory dance in my living room when I got the news.

But my euphoria was short-lived because Reginald's side caught wind of it and was not about to let me slip out of the Maverick black hole. They hustled to the senior judge—Judge Falkenhausen, who had presided over the original fiasco—and he swiftly overturned Bailey's order. Like a door slamming in my face, we were right back to square one.

Now, I may not be a legal scholar, but everything about that reversal smelled like corruption. In fairness, it might also be just garden-variety judicial arrogance; *how dare a junior judge disagree with me?* But the result was the same: We were stuck in Maverick County again.

I phoned Joseph Rosenthal. "What can we do?" He filed motion after motion, appealing, requesting a stay, challenging the denial of the transfer, basically throwing every legal tactic at the wall. But the Court of Appeals dismissed them all, sometimes within days, sometimes without any explanation. It felt suspiciously like they weren't even reading them.

Around that time, I discovered that the senior judge came from a powerful Republican family, and his father had once been mayor of a nearby city. The entire Maverick courthouse was embroiled in a scandal involving a district clerk who had been accused of rigging jury panels based on race and region. The clerk conveniently retired to avoid formal repercussions, but the rot in the system was clear as day.

The Courtroom Ambush: July 2022

By July 2022, I was seven months pregnant. Anyone who's been pregnant in the heat of a Texas summer might empathize with how physically draining that can be. Add to it the looming pressure of a hearing where your freedom, finances, and relationship with your children all hang in the balance, and you get a swirling vortex of anxiety that's enough to keep you awake for weeks.

Marty urged me to take a deal. This deal meant I would only see my children *once a month in San Diego.* Gone were even the meager first, third, and fifth weekends. Gone was any semblance of normalcy. Just one weekend a month, across the country, at my own expense, subject to constant constraints.

I balked. I had already been bullied into signing an MSA (Mediated Settlement Agreement) in the past, and it led me directly to this monstrous outcome. My instincts screamed: "Don't sign anything else. They'll slip in something horrifying, and you'll be stuck again."

Against my lawyer's advice, I refused to take the deal. In the back of my mind, I told myself, *They can't possibly punish me that severely for letting the kids see Greg one time, especially when there's no evidence of harm or danger.* My husband, Greg, reassured me in that same vein: "This is your first offense. They can't be that extreme, right?"

Wrong. *So very wrong.*

From the moment I walked into that courtroom, I could sense the hostility radiating like a heatwave. The judge wasn't hiding his bias. It was almost comical. The opposing counsel, Karen, arrived with a stack of *evidence* the size of a phone book. They had photos from the private investigator, flight itineraries from Southwest Airlines, random social media comments from a private "women only" physician group I belonged to, and more. It was an ambush.

They started by calling Greg's name, claiming that he'd been served (he never received any valid service, by the way) and was required to be there in person. They *sounded* his name three times in the hallway, a formality that allowed them to declare him a no-show, and then they promptly issued a *capias* (basically a warrant) for his arrest. That alone was surreal enough to make me question my reality.

Then came the flight itineraries. Southwest Airlines, in an epic meltdown of scheduling, had delayed or canceled multiple flights the children were booked on. I tried to explain that, as a mere mortal, I do not control airline delays, COVID-19 travel policies, or bizarre weather patterns. The judge and Karen looked at me like I was claiming aliens had abducted the plane. Karen zeroed in on the issue of Greg seeing the kids. She all but hissed the words, like letting your stepfather see you for one evening was a mortal sin.

"You broke the order," she repeated ad nauseam. And yes, she was right—I had. But it wasn't like I'd taken them to a crack den. It was a movie theater, for crying out loud.

A Ruling That Defies Logic

And so, the judge lowered the boom. The list of punishments was so extensive I could hardly keep up.

He fined me $21,228. He suspended my summer possession permanently. He declared that for each of the six counts of violating the order, I would serve 150 days—totaling 900 days—*in the Maverick County Detention Center.*

This sentence was suspended, but it would hang over my head like a guillotine. If I so much as sneezed in the wrong direction, they could lock me up.

Oh, and I needed to pay a $20,000 bond to Reginald by August 15th at 5:00 p.m. sharp. Happy summer to you, too.

The judge's specific findings of contempt included

1. making airline reservations that required the children to arrive at the airport at 10:55 p.m. (counted as multiple violations)
2. making airline reservations that required the children to arrive at 3:30 a.m.
3. failing to return the children at 6:00 p.m. on January 2nd, 2022—they arrived on January 4th and missed school on January 3rd and 4th
4. allowing the children to be in the presence of Greg on December 30th, 2021

What set me off more than the official bullet points, though, was the judge's little speech after Reginald finished his testimony. "You don't care about court orders," he told me, practically spitting the words. "You do what you want. And I don't see any remorse on your face. You blame

Southwest Airlines for flight delays. You live in a different universe; maybe you took a spaceship here from Mars."

I remember standing there, seven months pregnant, sweaty palms pressed against the table, trying not to let my rage or tears bubble over. He forced me to look at Reginald and went on this bizarre diatribe:

"Look at him! This man you're carrying a child for hates that man at the end of the table. If he hates *him*, he hates *your children*, too, because they're part of him. You looked at your children and said, 'Screw you, I'm picking this man over you.'"

The logic was cartoonish, the insults stung like acid, and the entire scenario felt orchestrated to shame me, degrade me, and punish me for daring to build a life with someone other than Reginald.

Next, the judge read out loud some random social media comments where people speculated the judge had been "paid off" or that he planned to retire soon. He glared at me, demanding to know who these commenters were as if I'd personally recruited them. I tried to explain that social media is—shockingly—public and chaotic, and I don't personally vet or even know most of the people in these private groups. He scolded me for *validating* the idea that he'd been paid off as if I was personally responsible for every rumor that surfaced on the internet.

The comedic highlight was when he declared, "Reginald can't be racist. He married you and had three kids with you," as if that's the gold standard of non-racism. He concluded with a flourish: "He's raising your kids best he knows how in spite of the nonsense you bring, with this cat you're married to."

At that point, the only *cat* I was ready to reference was the one who had apparently scratched his face because he was red with anger. I stayed silent. I had learned by now that speaking up only led to more punishment. I had seen him tear down witnesses in the original trial, run roughshod over attorneys, and override that junior judge's ruling. This was his kingdom, and I was a trespasser.

The Cost of Survival

I was numb. Later, when I sat down with my teenage daughter Liza and recounted the ordeal, she looked at me with a knowing expression and reminded me, "Mom, Grandma once told me that on Day One of your trial, the judge said he didn't care about the law."

I could only shrug and reply, "None of that matters." My so-called crime was violating a visitation order: letting the kids see Greg once and dealing with flight delays and cancellations. For that, I now faced 900 days of potential jail time, a massive fine, no chance at a peaceful summer with my children, and a $20,000 bond—payable to the same man who made four times my income. But I didn't crumble. Even with my unborn child flipping inside me, I refused to show defeat. Liza gave me a fierce hug and said, "He wanted you to cry, Mom. He wanted you to lose it. But you didn't." It was a small victory in a sea of defeats, but at that moment, it felt like the only victory I had.

The following months turned into a marathon of survival tactics: scraping together money to pay the bond before August 15th, juggling my prenatal appointments around mandatory court dates, and watching my appeals get dismissed with disturbing regularity. Still, I found glimmers of joy. I painted the baby's room in bright, cheerful colors, reminding myself that not everything had to be overshadowed by gloom. Greg worked overtime to keep my spirits high, turning our nights into comedic therapy: We'd watch stand-up specials or roast s'mores in our backyard while sarcastically joking about the private investigators—"Surely they're documenting my grocery list, too: *Breaking news: She buys kale. Must be criminal intent!*"

Dark humor aside, there was an unshakable truth in all of this: I refused to be silenced by injustice. Legally, I had to comply with every order, but my determination and my voice remained my own. Yes, the trial ended, but the war raged on.

The courthouse ambushes, process servers, and mounting legal motions were all part of Reginald's campaign to break me down—financially, emotionally, and spiritually. Yet, I wouldn't label myself defeated. I stayed focused on mothering my children in whatever way I could. This reality wasn't what I envisioned when I said "I do" or first held my babies, but it was mine to survive.

If you came looking for a neat bow on this story, think again. There's no tidy conclusion, no final fade-out. I'm not done fighting—and that's the point. Sometimes, survival doesn't look like a triumph; it's just waking up, showing up, and refusing to stay down. That's resilience. And right now, I'll treasure every small sliver of light in this never-ending storm.

Chapter 14:
Finding Strength in Vulnerability

Sometimes, you can physically feel your life unravel in real time. You sense your body screaming, *Enough!*—even if your mind hasn't caught on yet. That's precisely how I found out I was about to become a mother for the fifth time, a month earlier than expected.

I had strolled into my OB-GYN's office for a routine checkup, mentally cataloging all the to-dos I had yet to complete: finishing touches on the nursery, double-checking the baby shower guest list, and—oh, yes—filing yet another response to Reginald's latest legal ambush. My anxiety soared every time I stepped foot in a medical setting, courtesy of the stress swirling around me. But that day, it wasn't just intangible tension. It was bright red blood, a *lot* of it. One minute, I was sitting in a chair fiddling with a two-year-old magazine; the next, I was on a gurney, hearing the urgent shuffle of nurses and seeing the stern, worried face of my doctor.

"Ambulance! Call an ambulance," my doctor announced, her voice slicing through the room like a scalpel.

The next few hours blurred into frantic lights, paramedics calling out numbers, and my heart thrashing against my rib cage. I remember thinking, *But I'm not ready. There's so much left to do.* Never mind that this was baby number five; it felt as if I were a first-timer all over again. Stress. Fear. Disbelief. And the strangest, darkest comedy of them all:

having the baby early because my ex-husband had turned my entire world into a legal carnival. *It's official*, I mused in a haze of morphine and worry; *Court fights can literally rip you open—who knew?*

A Daughter Arrives Early

She was supposed to arrive in September 2022. That was the plan. I would elegantly waddle through late summer, survive the occasional Texas heat wave, and eventually hold my newborn on a crisp fall morning. But life had other ideas. After the ambulance ride and an emergency C-section, my baby girl made her debut a full month earlier, sometime in August. She entered the world tiny, fierce, and perfect as if to say, "Stress may have yanked me out early, but here I am; deal with it."

I named her without hesitation, wanting something that symbolized strength. Because if this child's birth was any indicator, she had more guts in her tiny body than some grown adults I knew. She let out a wail the moment the doctors lifted her into the cold air, and I instantly burst into tears of relief. Preterm or not, she was alive, breathing, and letting everyone know it.

Meanwhile, I had just experienced my first-ever C-section. Let me tell you: It's not the same as a standard delivery. My body felt like it had been hit by a Mack truck, reversed over, then set on fire for good measure. Every muscle burned. My mind was a jumble of contradictory emotions—gratitude that the baby was safe, but also anger at the circumstances that had forced my pregnancy into crisis. I blame the unrelenting legal harassment from Reginald. I'd read somewhere that stress can induce premature labor. Well, let's just say I had enough stress to spark three births.

A Baby Shower, Post-Baby

If you think it's weird to throw a baby shower after you've already had the baby, you're not alone. It was downright surreal. Initially, the plan was to have the event in late August, but clearly, my daughter had other plans. By the time I was discharged, I was supposed to be home, preparing final decorations for the big day. Instead, I was gingerly shuffling around my living room, stitches burning at my abdomen, cradling my sweet newborn—who was already here, very much in the flesh.

Still, my mother, Liza, and I had already paid for this baby shower. The venue, the caterer, the invitations—everything was lined up. Canceling would have felt like letting the stress beast claim yet another victory. So, with a combination of stubbornness and comedic resignation, I slapped on some mascara, wore the loosest, flowiest dress I could find, and went. I left my brand-new baby girl at home with Greg's mom, the other Grandma, telling myself she'd be fine for a couple of hours. I think I half expected everyone to say, *Um, why are we having a baby shower? The baby's here.*

To my surprise, it was actually lovely. Friends and family who arrived were relieved I was okay, thrilled to meet the baby in pictures (since she wasn't physically present), and cheerfully teased me about how I always have to do things the "dramatic way." I slapped on a smile, partly out of sheer exhaustion, partly out of a sense of triumph that I could still celebrate amid chaos.

My incision throbbed with every step, reminding me that I was still healing from major surgery. But I forced myself to enjoy the moment. Even if I couldn't stay for the entire event, those few hours were a defiant statement: The stress might have forced my baby out early, but it hadn't entirely robbed me of joy.

September Visitation: A Whirlwind Weekend

Soon after the baby shower, my daily life morphed into a frenzied dance of newborn care, postpartum recovery, and the never-ending custody saga. The exhaustion from the C-section lingered, but I refused to let it stop me from seeing my older children. Under the custody arrangement from the last fiasco, I was entitled to a weekend visit in early September—September 2nd to 4th, 2022, to be exact. I could practically hear Reginald's eyes rolling from a distance, as though any time with my kids was an insult to his victory parade. My mother and Liza rallied around me, helping me juggle feedings and diaper changes for the newborn while the older kids complained about homework, rummaged through the fridge, and occasionally rolled their eyes at me. In other words, it was blissfully normal. For 72 hours, I got to experience the everyday chaos of motherhood that I'd once taken for granted. My older kids met their baby sister, my mother held the tiny one while my son recounted some new video game, and my daughter April raved about some K-pop group. We tried to pretend we were an ordinary family, as though some black cloud of litigation wasn't perpetually hovering overhead. For a moment, it worked.

Return of the Process Server

That fleeting normalcy lasted until September 14, 2022. I'd barely caught my breath after the two-day visitation with my children (September 2nd to 4th) when I discovered there was yet another post-judgment enforcement on the docket. In plain English, that meant Reginald was once again hauling me into court for supposedly violating orders despite my having just paid the bond, abided by every line of the custody agreement, and managed a short but sweet weekend visit.

So there I was on a Saturday, running on four hours of sleep thanks to my nocturnal newborn, picking up the kids from the airport for the next round of scheduled parenting time. They hopped off the plane, backpacks in tow, yawning from the flight. I gave them tired smiles and half-hugs, mentally ticking off what needed to happen next: feed them dinner, check their homework, and try to preserve at least a sliver of normal family life. Just as I was about to steer them toward the baggage claim, an airport worker approached me with a furrowed brow, glancing over my shoulder at a man in the distance.

"Ma'am, that man's been watching you ever since you got here," she said, her tone urgent. "He's been following you. We think he might be a trafficker."

My heart jolted into my throat. Human trafficking? That's not something you brush off. I gripped my kids' hands a little tighter. The worker's colleagues were eyeing the man, ready to step in if he made a move. Then, to my complete astonishment, he walked straight up to me—stopping only a few feet away.

The airport workers tensed, half-expecting a confrontation. But this wasn't a scene from an action movie. The man thrust an envelope in my direction. "You've been served," he said, looking bored. Then he turned around and left, like a pizza delivery guy who'd just fulfilled his shift's final order.

I probably stood there like a statue for a good 30 seconds. My older kids stared at me, then at the envelope, then back at me. My middle daughter Veronica, newly seven, shrank behind me, confused. *Served again?* The last time had been in front of patients at my clinic. Now, it was in front of half an airport terminal.

"Mom, what does that mean?" one of them asked. I swallowed, trying not to sound as exasperated as I felt. "It means your father is taking me to court. Again."

As if that wasn't enough, it was Veronica's birthday weekend. I had illusions of a small party—cake, balloons, maybe a trip to Main Event. *Because that's what normal families do*, right? They celebrate birthdays, eat pizza, and play arcade games. They don't get served legal papers in airports like characters in a cheap detective novel. But normalcy, it seemed, wasn't in the cards for us.

Accusations on Repeat

When I tore open the envelope later that evening, it felt like a cruel joke. The allegations mirrored everything we had already *resolved* in court, or so I thought. According to Reginald and his attorney, Karen, I had failed to pay fees (never mind the $20,000 bond I'd just forked over), exposed the kids to Greg (never mind that I'd been too busy recovering from a C-section to risk *any* drama), and in general, *violated* the court order in ways that were infuriatingly vague.

It was like a rerun of a bad sitcom with the same tired script. I would talk to Marty and Joseph, my lawyers, and they'd remind me we had receipts—literal *receipts*—proving I had paid the required bond. Private investigators had not caught me anywhere near Greg because Greg and I were basically living in separate orbits these days, thanks to the swirling chaos.

Yet here we were. Another post-judgment enforcement, another chance for the court to sock me with fines, jail time, or both.

Veronica's Birthday Party That Wasn't

The timing couldn't have been more malicious. Veronica's birthday weekend was overshadowed by the new hearing and the storm clouds it brought. We'd planned a party at Main Event—an arcade, bowling alley, and a general playground of neon lights and overpriced pizza. She had been talking about it for weeks, excited to invite her classmates and to revel in the attention that's the birthright of any child turning seven. My mother and Liza had organized invites, decorations, and a lovely cake with Veronica's favorite cartoon characters. We even had little goodie bags for the kids.

No one showed up.

Word got out that Reginald had me served again and was hiring PIs to follow my every move, so nobody wanted to get caught up in his paranoid drama. One by one,

Veronica's little circle backed out: *We can't go; something came up.* So, there I was, sitting under the garish fluorescent lights, a half-eaten pizza in front of me and a perpetually refreshing phone that refused to display any *We're on our way!* messages. Veronica stared at the door, her big eyes brimming with disappointment when it dawned on her that no one was coming.

You'd think that heartbreak would be enough drama for the day, but there was more. That evening, my kids told me what had really been going on whenever they returned to Reginald's house. He would interrogate them relentlessly. "Did you see Greg? Did he pick you up? Did you talk to him?" April and RJ knew the script by now. They would calmly tell him no, that they hadn't seen Greg. Because they truly hadn't, my newborn and I were mostly stuck at home, exhausted. The last thing I was doing was orchestrating secret rendezvous.

But Veronica was seven. She had no idea how to navigate an interrogation. She saw her father's frustration and wanted to please him, so one day, when he refused to accept "no" from her, she finally broke down and said, "Yes, I saw Greg in the hotel parking lot." Instantly, Reginald switched from frustration to triumph. He patted her on the head, presumably telling her she was being truthful, that she was a good girl. She didn't understand that a single lie—born out of a child's desire to make her father happy—could send me right back into the legal inferno.

Stolen Funds: The $400 Heist

Two weeks later, on September 28, 2022, I woke up bleary-eyed, checked my phone, and nearly dropped the device. There was a transaction to an American Express account for $400, listed under Reginald's name. My immediate reaction was disbelief. *Surely, it's some random glitch.* Then I realized it wasn't an error. He had siphoned money directly from my bank account to pay his own credit card bill. Not $500—because that might have been a felony—but $400, presumably to keep it neatly in the misdemeanor zone.

My anger ignited like a match. Up until that point, Reginald's manipulations, while horrifying, had mostly occurred in the courtroom. This was different—he was literally dipping his hand into my pocket, no better than a petty thief. Shaking, I ran to Greg and my mother, showed them the banking app, and spilled out my growing fear. "If you lie, you cheat. If you cheat, you steal. If you steal, you kill," I muttered.

It felt melodramatic but also painfully true. Reginald had grown so emboldened by the courts letting him push me around that now he felt he could do anything—even commit theft—without consequences.

I filed a police report with the Houston Police Department, categorizing it under cyber fraud or bank fraud. I also contacted Bank of America and explained the situation. The investigators discovered he had used my account and routing numbers to make a payment over the phone, something that typically requires verifying personal details. Where did he get that info?

Probably from an old check. Back when we were married, or even after, because my bank account had remained the same since I was 16 years old. In the chaos of divorce, I'd changed door locks, security alarms, and even my email addresses. But the bank account that had been around forever? I naively assumed it was safe.

With the bank's help, I recovered the $400, and they took official note of Reginald's fraud. Yet, in the back of my mind, I knew the odds of him facing legal repercussions for this theft were slim to none. Why?

Because the family court system had already shown that they'd let him bend or outright break the rules without consequence. He'd gotten away with so much that, by now, brazenly stealing from me must have seemed like child's play.

Another Round of Legal Maneuvers

In the midst of postpartum hormonal storms, stolen funds, and a newborn who needed my constant attention, Joseph Rosenthal leapt back into action, filing any motion or appeal he could conceive of.

The Court of Appeals, however, had about as much sympathy for me as a cat has for a mouse. On September 30, 2022, they summarily denied our petition for a writ of mandamus and any emergent relief.

The message was clear: *We don't want to hear your sob story.*

Meanwhile, I was on a leave of absence from work; my body was not ready to handle a 12-hour shift on my feet as a physician. But the mounting bills and the incessant demands of legal fees loomed large, so I decided to head out of town briefly, flying to Illinois for stronger family support.

My mother came too, carrying my newborn's supplies as though we were a traveling circus. I had to come back by October 3 for yet another enforcement hearing because, apparently, postpartum recovery was an inconvenience to the court schedule.

October 3, 2022: A Day of Strange Twists

The day of the enforcement hearing arrived, and I braced myself like I was walking into a lion's den—again. Marty, my family-law attorney, was there, bleary-eyed but determined. Joseph Rosenthal was prepared to keep fighting, though we both knew the track record of the Court of Appeals. My biggest fear was that they'd decide I had *violated* the orders one too many times and hit the nuclear button: jail time. I pictured myself in a bright orange jumpsuit, recovering from a C-section behind bars, all because one side of this insane conflict had the money and connections to keep me in a perpetual corner.

Just as the hearing started, Karen—Reginald's attorney—made a surprise announcement: She was retiring. Out of the blue. No pomp, no explanation, just a casual "I have two more cases, then I'm done." Marty turned to me, his eyebrows practically reaching his hairline. "What? That's random." In the back of my mind, I wondered if she was jumping ship before the tidal wave of corruption allegations or drama could swamp her.

Despite the unexpected news, the hearing pressed on. Reginald's side was still forging ahead, accusing me of the same old laundry list: exposing the kids to Greg (which I hadn't done) and failing to pay the required fees (which I had). The tension in the room felt like a coiled spring. I was half expecting the judge to lay into me the way he had before, delivering some outraged monologue about how I lived in another universe and made flight reservations that arrived at impossible hours.

Marty glanced my way, looking pained. "Just take the deal," he whispered urgently. "Whatever they're offering, just take it." The memory of the last time I refused his advice loomed large. Back then, I thought I had logic, fairness, and common sense on my side, only to be slammed with a suspended jail sentence, hefty fines, and humiliating scoldings from the bench. Now, I had a newborn who wasn't even two months old, plus three other kids caught in the crossfire. I was tired. No, not just tired, *exhausted* on every level: physically, emotionally, spiritually, and financially.

So, I sighed, swallowed my pride, and told Marty, "I'll take it." I didn't even know the specifics, but I knew it would be something restricting my visitation, forcing me to jump through more hoops and effectively giving Reginald the victory he craved. But the alternative—continuing to fight—seemed like a guaranteed way to wind up behind bars or deeper in a hole of legal debt. I was so numb, so battered, that I no longer had the energy to stand on principle.

The Deal

"All right," Karen declared. "Here's the deal." She was finalizing her retirement with a flourish, it seemed. The agreement: If I wanted to see my children, it had to be in San Diego. I had to do it alone, without Greg anywhere near me, and the visits had to occur in Reginald's home. No more free-form visits where I could have them stay in a hotel with me, rent an Airbnb, or even stay at my own place. No argument, no appeals. Comply or risk the suspended 900-day jail sentence snapping into effect.

Marty put a supportive hand on my shoulder as I nodded. "Also," he whispered, "You're going to want an iPhone. You'll need FaceTime. Android to iPhone calls can be complicated in this context." It was almost comical. My immediate reaction was, "They're forcing me into the Apple cult, too?" But I got it. FaceTime was the simplest way for me to see my children's faces. I needed an easy, frictionless method to connect with them, especially given the new limitations.

A few hours later, I walked out of the courthouse, holding an official piece of paper that effectively ended any illusions of a fair arrangement. I had *won* a monthly or occasional visitation in a city hundreds of miles away, in my ex-husband's domain, with no right to bring my husband or the rest of my life along. *Congratulations, you've lost—again.* But at least I wasn't in handcuffs, right?

Living in Limbo

I spent the months after the final hearing in a strange state of suspended animation like the world had pressed the "pause" button on my life. Even though I had a legal agreement, it was an arrangement that demanded I visit my children only on Reginald's turf and on his terms. The very thought of flying to San Diego, subjecting myself to his gloating presence under his roof, and pretending everything was fine while I snatched fleeting moments with my own kids felt like psychological torture. My newborn needed me at home, and every day of extended leave added to my financial strain. But how could I leave a baby who was just a few weeks old, prematurely born because of all this stress, to make a trip that would shred my nerves and my dignity?

So I did the only thing I could: I stayed put, kept my sanity in check, and relied on FaceTime. Each morning, I propped my phone against a pillow, dimly aware of how my reflection looked half-dead from lack of sleep, and dialed my older children. It became a routine as predictable as the sunrise.

Sometimes, they wouldn't answer; maybe they were in the middle of breakfast or simply too tired themselves. Other times, they picked up, wearing that *just-rolled-out-of-bed* look that used to greet me in person every day. RJ would barrage me with terrible puns that made me cringe, Veronica would roll her eyes in classic teenage form, and April—on good days—would launch into a breathless recap of her latest favorite cartoon or a dream she had the night before. All the while, my newborn would coo in the background, a sweet, tangible reminder that life hadn't entirely ground to a halt.

Those calls were a soothing balm, but they also underscored the miles between us. I couldn't cook them breakfast, check their math homework at the kitchen table, or fix their hair before school. Instead, I played the role of a digital presence, a pixelated figure who popped in to ask if they slept well and whether RJ had any new jokes he was ready to torment us with. After all the court battles, the unending swirl of appeals, and that final arrangement forcing me to bow to Reginald's demands, there wasn't much else I could do. I hated it, but I knew fighting the same losing fight could land me in jail for *violations*. I'd learned that lesson the hard way.

In the year that followed, I poured whatever energy I had left into rebuilding my life—starting with my own body. A C-section, unexpected and urgent, had taken a physical toll I never saw coming. I tried to regain my professional footing, returning to my job as a physician when the postpartum fog began to lift. My patients would complain about unfair bosses or noisy neighbors, and I'd nod with empathy, biting my tongue against the urge to say, "Believe me, if you heard my story, you'd feel lucky by comparison." My coworkers knew bits of it.

They noticed the days I had to swap shifts to accommodate a hearing or a court-mandated call. But the details were so convoluted—private investigators, missing nannies, shady judges, stolen bank funds—that it sounded like an overblown soap opera. I sometimes caught a flicker of disbelief in their eyes as though they suspected I was weaving half-truths. It was easier not to dwell on it.

Financially, I felt like a tightrope walker with no safety net. The legal fees never really ended; even though Reginald had supposedly *won*, that didn't stop the constant trickle of new motions, new administrative costs, and new attempts to corner me into paying for something else. Greg and I became experts at dissecting our budget, finessing every line item, and scouring secondhand stores for baby clothes and supplies. My mother, bless her, stepped in wherever she could, rearranging her own life to help me stay afloat. I'll never forget how she'd hand me a pot of jollof at nine o'clock at night, saying, "There are enough leftovers for tomorrow," as though I were still a teenager at home—

only now, I was a mother of five, legally battered, but still determined to stand.

Despite the exhaustion, there were bright pockets. My newborn quickly proved she was a fighter in every sense. Each day, she grew a little stronger, and each milestone—her first gummy smile, her first clumsy reach for a toy—reminded me that new life continues to bloom in the most desolate places. When I was up at three in the morning, rocking her to sleep in the dark, I sometimes let the tears flow. They weren't just tears of fatigue; they were a release of pent-up anger, relief, sorrow, and hope all rolled into one. Because if there's one thing this rollercoaster taught me, it's that vulnerability is not a sign of defeat. It's a measure of humanity.

In January 2023, a final blow arrived in the form of a brief letter from the Supreme Court. They basically said, "We don't get how the jury reached its decision, but it's not our place to question them." That's it. Case closed. No deeper explanations. It was like a cosmic shrug. All the illusions I had that maybe, just maybe, a higher authority would see the glaring inconsistencies disappeared in a puff of resigned disappointment. By that point, I'd already cried all the tears I could for our legal system, so I read the letter, set it down on the kitchen counter, and stared at the clock. In the next room, my baby fussed in her bassinet—oblivious to the fact that her mother had officially lost the last Hail Mary pass. Funny how life refuses to pause for our heartbreaks.

Still, there's a kind of strange relief in knowing the road has reached its end. No more appeals, no more endless motions. No more illusions that a single new hearing will magically fix everything. Yes, I was stuck with an arrangement that made me jump through hoops just to see my children. Yes, Reginald had *won* the battle on paper, stolen money from my account, and hammered my finances. But I was still here, still standing, and still connected to my kids, even if half our relationship was built on FaceTime calls that occasionally got dropped mid-sentence.

People sometimes ask if I regret fighting so hard and wonder if maybe I should've saved my resources and my sanity. But regrets aren't that simple. The fights I waged were for my children's well-being and for my right to be their mother without intrusive bullying constraints.

Even when I lost, I took comfort in knowing I did everything possible. Because one day, when RJ, Veronica, and April are older, they'll remember I didn't simply vanish or rollover. They'll piece together the times they were shuffled between nannies or asked leading questions about Greg.

They'll see patterns that aren't so clear to them now. And eventually, they'll understand just how hard I tried.

That's the truth I cling to whenever the weight of it all threatens to crush me. Surviving isn't always about a triumphant court victory or a vindication letter stamped "Approved." Sometimes, it's scraping together a shred of laughter when everything seems hopeless—like cackling at RJ's corny jokes or reveling in the squeals of a baby who has no clue her arrival disrupted a carefully orchestrated custody war. Survival is hearing Veronica ask, "When can I come see you, Mommy?" and answering, "Soon, baby," even when I'm not entirely sure how or when I'll make it happen.

So, no, I haven't emerged from this with a Hollywood-style happy ending. But I have emerged. That's more than some people can say after years of being ground down by a system they naively believed would protect them. I still have a family to nurture, and I still have a life that deserves living, even if it's under the shadow of constant vigilance. If anything, I've learned to appreciate the moments of reprieve—those exhalations of peace before the next wave of chaos hits.

And as I look ahead, I realize I'm not shouldering this alone. My support system is an odd mosaic of friends, family, and even the occasional stranger who offered a helping hand or a kind word at exactly the right time.

My mother's unwavering presence, Greg's steadfast commitment, and the attorneys and colleagues who stood by me longer than I expected—each one formed a crucial strand in the net that kept me from falling into an abyss of despair.

In the next chapter of my journey, I want to shine a spotlight on that collective force, the unsung heroes who refused to let me drown. Because behind every story of personal resilience, there's always a chorus of people who buoyed you up when you thought you had no fight left.

Chapter 15:

My Support System

After trudging through legal landmines, financial strain, and the heartache of being separated from my children, I finally reached the undeniable truth: I couldn't do it all alone. In the previous chapter, I discovered that even when life pins you down, the right people—and a steady dose of faith—can keep you standing. I've always believed that when life gears up to break you, there's a higher power and a ragtag crew of unwavering souls ready to catch you before you shatter. For me, that crew has been my faith, my parents, my friends, and especially my daughter, Liza.

This chapter is a heartfelt, sometimes wry, tribute to the village that refused to let me crumble under the weight of it all, even when the world seemed determined to do push-ups on my shoulders. They became the pillars that held me upright when everything else was collapsing.

Faith: The Anchor in the Storm

There's this little passage that's been my go-to mantra through the years—what started as a scribble on a sticky note morphed into my personal creed whenever life tried to knock me over. Proverbs 3:5–6 says (New International Version, 2011/1973):

"Trust in the Lord with all your heart and lean not on your own understanding; in all your ways acknowledge Him, and He shall direct your path."

I first crammed these words into my brain back in college. By the time I hit med school—with 24-hour shifts, sleep deprivation, and more medical puzzles than I care to count—I clung to that verse like it was my literal life vest.

When I was juggling custody battles, financial drain, and emotional rollercoasters, I realized that if I couldn't trust my own dim light, I could at least lean on something a little brighter. I trusted that the Lord had mapped out a path, even if I could only see two steps ahead (or sometimes less).

In med school, I stumbled on a fact: Black women have one of the lowest suicide rates across ethnic groups (Frakt, 2020). The reason? We're wired for community and a deep connection to something higher.

At first, it was just an interesting statistic, but over the years, I saw its truth manifest, especially when I was dealing with one legal curveball after another or when another nanny fiasco sent me spiraling. I always believed that God had strategically placed guardians in my path, and honestly, that's how I survived being told repeatedly that my kids weren't safe with me. It's also how I kept breathing when the phone never stopped buzzing with crises.

Faith, love, and a bit of divine guidance—that was the recipe that kept me from collapsing.

Allies Emerging From Unexpected Corners

Imagine my shock when I discovered that simply sharing my story unlocked a whole network of fellow survivors of legal nightmares. Take my boss, for example. He always struck me as calm, collected, and a bit mysterious until I learned that he'd once been caught in a custody battle so brutal it nearly cost him everything. He even sold his private practice to fight for his stepchild, and, like my husband, Greg, he'd faced a mental health evaluation after being falsely accused of something utterly absurd. When I nervously opened up about my own struggles, expecting harsh judgment, he surprised me by listening with genuine empathy. He even promoted me to his right-hand person as the area medical director for several urgent care facilities across Houston. At that moment, I realized I wasn't fighting this battle alone; if a seasoned physician like him could survive such chaos, then maybe I wasn't as powerless as I'd always feared.

A Colleague's Lifetime in Court

Not long after, another colleague shared her own nightmarish tale. Her ex—armed with resources that made her look like a mere mortal in comparison—took custody of her daughters, dragging her through the courts like it was a twisted game show. She even joked that she was on a first-name basis with half the courthouse staff. But when her daughters finally hit adulthood, she sighed in relief. Her story was both chilling and oddly comforting: It confirmed that many women face relentless legal battles, yet eventually, time grants a reprieve. My childhood best friend, Layla, would quip, "They're adults longer than they're children. Just keep that in mind." Sometimes, a dose of brutal reality is exactly what you need to remind you that these battles aren't forever. And yes, I've spent many a late night browsing Reddit and Quora, devouring stories from other parents wrestling with the same beastly system—a digital village of survivors that made me feel less alone.

From Trials to Triumph: Spiritual and Financial Support

My husband and I also had our own spiritual skirmishes. A dear friend invited us to her non-denominational church, and even though my husband grew up Seventh Day Adventist and I was a cradle Catholic, this neutral ground somehow soothed us. We prayed—sometimes loudly, sometimes in whispered desperation—for the kids' safety and for a guardian angel to swoop in when we couldn't be there.

It became our ritual: Sunday mornings, eyes half-closed from exhaustion, we drove to that church and let our tears flow during worship. We prayed for sanity, for a break from a system that seemed more interested in theatrics than genuine care, and for the strength to carry on. Each service was like a temporary band-aide on a deep wound—a small mercy in a chaotic world. Before I knew it, prayer became our background music, a constant reminder that hope and desperation could coexist in the most absurd of ways.

My Husband: Protector, Gemini, and Budget Coach

Through all the chaos, my husband proved to be my staunchest ally, quirks and all. Picture a man who defends women and children like a medieval knight; only his sword is a barrage of text messages that could give even President Trump, Kendrick Lamar, or Kanye West a run for their money. At first, I resented his biting texts (yes, I even questioned if I needed earplugs for his dramatic rants). But soon, I realized that his fierce, sometimes over-the-top reactions were his way of fighting back against Reginald's endless negligence. Apparently, Geminis keep quiet until someone pushes the wrong button, then, well, game on.

Simultaneously, my husband transformed into our household's CFO. With looming lawsuits, we held weekly "finance meetings" over coffee, scrutinizing every expense like we were preparing for a bank audit.

After selling the Farland property, we channeled every spare cent toward child support and lawyers. Greg took charge of the house bills, and I had to sacrifice my 401(k) contributions and those little luxuries. Our ride-sharing options downgraded to a 2012 Nissan for him and a trusty Honda for me, and we only traveled when absolutely necessary. Fortunately, the pandemic placed our school loans on deferment, which offered some relief for available funds. When our new baby arrived, Greg even ferried her to my job between shifts. Suffocating? Sure. Liberating? Absolutely. We were in this together, financially squeezed but bonded like a quirky, resilient team.

"A-List Status" Southwest Airlines: The Unexpected Lifeline

One of our secret weapons turned out to be Southwest Airlines Rapid Rewards Program. Every first, third, and fifth weekend, we'd fly the kids from California to Texas. True, Southwest cancellations nearly got me into a situation so absurd it could've landed me in a comedy sketch (seriously, don't ask for the details), but overall, it worked like a charm.

The kids racked up enough miles to hit "A-list status," and I saved a small fortune on nanny or daycare fees. Despite the occasional headache from delays, I've come to appreciate Southwest—especially in a world where Reginald's goal seemed to be my financial ruin. Those airline points became a literal lifeline, reconnecting me with my children's laughter.

Without the constant drain of pricey daycare and a revolving door of nannies (I lost count of how many had a suspiciously short tenure), our monthly expenses took a nosedive. "God's plan," I'd joke, was that we'd achieve "perpetual solvency"—at least enough to drive Reginald up the wall. We still had extracurriculars galore (music, gymnastics, soccer, swimming—you name it), but at least I wasn't hemorrhaging money on nannies who ghosted every other month.

The Village: Letters and Solidarity

The old African proverb—"It takes a village to raise a child"—never rang truer. My own village appeared in every form imaginable: in person, through heartfelt court letters, via calls, and through texts brimming with unwavering support. Even those who couldn't attend the hearings sent testimonials that celebrated my dedication and my character and exposed the toxicity of Reginald's environment. Gone were the chaotic nannies, Dr. Friedman, Dr. Goldstein, Dr. Pham, Dr. Mwangi, and my half-sarcastically dubbed "bat s*** crazy" crew.

In their place stood true allies, my steadfast nanny Phyllis, along with Denise, Comfort, Paul, and even Dr. Reina Washington, who, though her testimony on the first day was deferred since the respondent's witnesses went first, was reared and ready to speak on my behalf.

Dr. Reina Washington—one of my former resident physicians during my academic medicine days—recalled with admiration how I balanced an efficient work schedule with the constant care of my children. A nontraditional resident who already held a degree in business administration, Reina shared a personal story: Her parents separated when she was just three, and her father was a medical student who threatened to take the children away once he finished residency.

She declared that her mother's love was stronger than her father's anger—a truth that resonated with me deeply and affirmed that I had the emotional maturity to put my children's well-being first. Of African and Japanese descent, Reina proudly embraces both cultures—a heritage she inherited from her nurturing mother, who affectionately nicknamed her "chocolate babydoll." Her story reminded me why I insisted on keeping my children connected to their roots, even keeping them enrolled in Chinese Sunday School after my divorce.

Then there's my dear friend Dr. Elizabeth Acosta Flores, who met me as a Family Medicine resident in 2010 and quickly became a confidante. She'd witnessed firsthand how my children thrived under my care—cheerful, well-groomed, and happy despite my grueling schedule.

Yet she was always concerned about Reginald's glaring absence and the heavy reliance on nannies. As my best friend, she warned that my openness and genuine warmth—qualities that made me a great mother—could also be my Achilles' heel if I allowed those same nannies to become like family. She even discussed with Dr. Goldstein the devastating effects of neglect and adverse childhood experiences, especially as the Woo children suffered under their father's care.

Dr. Aaron Ito, who has known both Reginald and me for over 16 years, added his own colorful perspective. He remembered me as a determined medical student juggling single motherhood and tirelessly supporting Liza while Reginald was obsessively focused on his career.

Dr. Ito also shared a deeply personal sacrifice of his own: He gave up a fellowship in neurotology when his daughter no longer recognized him, choosing his family over a coveted career opportunity. He recalled Reginald's disparaging remarks about Japanese and Black people from his medical school days and recounted a memorable trip to Alaska, where he was surprised by how warmly the children bonded with Greg. He admired that I had figured out my priorities long before he did—ensuring that our children embraced their multicultural heritage without marginalizing their Chinese roots. He even confided that if anything were to happen to his own family, he would trust Greg and me to raise his children.

My trial lawyer, Marty Murati, provided a brutally honest account of the legal circus. He observed that, since the judge and Karen (who were once law school classmates) were so close, the trial was rigged from the start. Marty recalled that while the jury claimed they liked me, they were quick to condemn the way Greg treated the father. He suggested that without the nasty text messages sent to my ex, the case might have been winnable—but the judge's bias and even bizarre acts (like a District Clerk allegedly removing Democrats from jury panels) sealed our fate. Marty's unfiltered commentary reminded me how deeply flawed the system was, even though he joked that a new trial before a different judge was always a possibility.

Lisa Randall, my mentor-turned-friend since 1998 through Northwestern's alumni mentoring program, sent a letter that warmed my heart. She recounted the many times she'd seen me with my children—whether in Chicago or during her visits to Houston—and spoke of the joy and discipline I instilled in them. According to Lisa, the children were always happy, well-behaved, and filled with love—a testament to the nurturing home I worked so hard to create.

Dr. Boahemaa Boateng added her invaluable perspective. She attended my first wedding with Reginald and, after moving to Houston, saw me operating as a single mother even while still married. She emphasized that divorce was never taken lightly in our families, as both our parents had remained happily married for years. With Reginald often absent, I frequently called on my cousin to help pick up the children when nannies proved unreliable. She even attended my wedding with Greg, where the boundaries between the bride's and groom's sides blurred because everyone got along so well. Greg, sharing our West African family values, embraced my children with genuine care; once, after brunch, he immediately went over to comfort April when she bit her lip until she stopped crying. After the change in custody, my cousin continued helping with drop-offs, even as the children repeatedly asked, "Why can't we sleep at mommy's house?" RJ's tears at the last drop-off, when he refused to leave with his father, remain etched in her memory.

Even Dr. Juarez, a colleague from Oklahoma City, shared his own slice of chaos. A seasoned ER doc with a knack for Geriatric Medicine (and a wallet that could make you blush at $210–$250 per hour), he recounted his family's humble beginnings—from Dominican and Bolivian roots scraping by on WIC and school lunches to siblings who all became doctors.

His letter detailed the wreckage of a physician's divorce, where what might have been a civilized separation turned into a full-blown war. From forced temporary orders signed in the ER (because who has time for legal jargon when you're saving lives?) to a sudden $141,000 withdrawal by his ex, his tale echoed my own experiences. It wasn't about the money; it was about the sheer unfairness of a system that seemed hell-bent on breaking you. Dr. Juarez's reflections on finding solace in faith and perspective resonated with me deeply. After all, if I could survive a life in the ER, I could also stand firm in the courtroom defending my children. And, in the end, he found love again—with a partner willing to sign a prenup, no less.

Suckers No More

In Dr. Juarez's words, I heard a mirror of my own frustrations: the misuse of children as weapons in a bitter legal battle, the petty squabbles over custody details, and that gut-wrenching moment when you just want to scream at a rigged system. He realized that nothing could truly break him unless he let it—and neither would I. My battles with Reginald's threats and last-minute legal antics taught me that, sometimes, your best defense is simply refusing to be crushed. If I could stand in an ER saving lives, I could stand in a courtroom saving my children.

Dr. Juarez's mention of new love paralleled my own journey: I had Greg, and he had his own partner. We both learned that life doesn't end just because a spouse decides to leave the picture.

"Money doesn't last forever," he wrote, "but neither does heartbreak. In the end, we're blessed to have shelter, health, and a future." His words were like a warm blanket on a cold night, reminding me that eventually, even this madness will fade.

Liza's Love Letter

Even with every piece of support and every hard-won victory echoing around me, one voice always reminded me of what truly mattered. My daughter Liza's words stood out with clarity. I still remember the moment she spoke during my vow renewal with Greg in Aruba. In her clear, unfiltered tone, she said:

> Thank you everyone for coming out today. I stand before you with a heart overflowing with love and pride as I witness my mother's beautiful union. As her daughter, I am honored to share a few heartfelt words about the incredibly strong, intelligent woman she is.
>
> My mom has been there every step of the way. Her unwavering support and encouragement have shaped me into the person I am today. I cherish the countless memories we've created together, and I'm grateful for her love and guidance. My mother has shown me what true resilience looks

> like. Her patience, laughter, and boundless love have been a source of inspiration and encouragement. She has weathered life's storms with grace, standing tall in the face of hardships. My mom is not only hardworking but also incredibly loving and caring. Her selflessness knows no bounds, and she always puts others before herself. Her love is a constant presence in our lives.
>
> And thank you, Greg, for always providing unwavering support to my mother. Your laughter, love, and kindness have brought her immense happiness. I wish you guys the happiest forever!
>
> And now, as I witness her finding her own happy ending, my heart swells with joy. She deserves every ounce of happiness, every chapter of her story filled with love and fulfillment. Her journey has been one of courage, compassion, and unwavering faith.

Those words reminded me that even after everything, love still finds a way to shine through.

Moving Forward With Faith, Family, and Fierce Love

Looking back, I see how close I came to unraveling, and yet, I also see the threads that held me together: unshakeable faith, a husband who would go to absurd lengths (yes, even sending those merciless text messages) to protect us, and a community of bosses, colleagues, best friends, nannies, cousins, and even random supporters on social media who believed in me more than I sometimes believed in myself. That old African proverb about raising a child through a village wasn't just about child-rearing; it was about nurturing the mother, too. It reminded me that I didn't have to face every crisis alone.

Am I angry about what Reginald did? Sure, I am. Do I sometimes resent the court system? Occasionally. But I've learned to choose gratitude over bitterness. My husband, despite his Gemini flare, stands with me in unwavering devotion. My children know, without a doubt, that no matter what's said in some courtroom, they are deeply cherished. My father's old lesson about never settling for mediocrity—never coasting for B's and C's—reminds me that I refuse to be a victim. Instead, I choose growth, resilience, and to keep moving forward even when the road is steep. I cherish this odd, patchwork community that has rallied around me.

Now, having shared my side of the story—the frantic prayers, the court battles, and the heroic gestures from my village—I invite you to experience a different perspective. My mother, a pillar of strength as both a grandmother and a nurturer, has observed every twist of our journey with grace and wisdom. In the next chapter, she takes the mic to share her personal insights on everything we've endured. Her voice will reveal a perspective you won't want to miss.

Let's turn the page and listen to her story.

Chapter 16:
A Grandmother's Voice

They say that a grandmother's wisdom is timeless, etched into every wrinkle and every tear. For me, it is the raw, unfiltered voice of truth, echoing through the years, carrying the weight of our family's struggles and triumphs. This is my story. This is my heart.

A Promising Beginning

I remember the very first time I met Reginald after my daughter completed medical school. It was one of those days when an ordinary moment is transformed by the promise of a new beginning. Reginald came to our home with a humble request—to ask my husband, in a soft yet determined manner, for our daughter's hand in marriage.

I had long known that Reginald and my daughter had been dating off and on throughout their long, arduous days in medical school. Even then, my first impression of him was unmistakable: He was always smiling, a man of few words whose gentle, brief responses said more than a thousand sentences ever could. I still recall leaning in close to my daughter, Adwoafuaa, half-teasingly remarking, "Chinese men are good men, but they're so thrifty, you might end up with one shoe for a whole year!" I meant it affectionately—a playful warning about the cultural quirks that might come along with his practical nature. I had already witnessed success in our family when my eldest son married his wonderful Ghanaian wife—a union that has now flourished for over 10 years. I had hoped that my daughter, too, would find a partner whose quiet strength, practicality, and deep-rooted values would serve as a foundation for lasting happiness.

But, as life has often taught me, even the most promising beginnings can be shadowed by unforeseen heartache. Not long after that hopeful start, Reginald betrayed our trust by cheating on my daughter. In an effort to help her heal, I even tried setting her up with several Ghanaian men from our community—men who shared our proud, deep-rooted ancestry and cultural values.

Yet, despite my gentle urgings, my daughter insisted that she was still in love with Reginald and needed more time to mend her broken heart. I was deeply concerned about the cultural differences that might come between them—both families were forged in the crucible of immigrant sacrifice, and I feared that these barriers would only widen the gulf of misunderstanding.

Then, fate introduced me to the Woo family. I still remember the first time I met Reginald's parents; they welcomed me with warmth and genuine hospitality. They invited us to a famous Chinese restaurant in Woodridge, Illinois, renowned for its master chef and exceptional cuisine. We met without the distraction of children, for, at that time, both Adwoafuaa and Reginald were still in Houston.

Over a sumptuous meal, we spoke of our children, our struggles, and our hopes for the future. I mentioned that Adwoafuaa already had a child, and when I showed them a photograph of little Liza, their eyes lit up. They marveled at her innocence, exclaiming that she was the most adorable child they had ever seen. Their pure, unguarded admiration touched me deeply.

From that evening on, a strong bond grew between Reginald's mother and me. She confided in me as if I were the only friend she had, sharing intimate details about her other children—all of whom were physicians—and remarking that Reginald, like his father, was a man of few words. We bonded over our shared immigrant experiences, leaving our homelands, enduring hardships, and building a better life for our children. In that sacred space of shared sacrifice and hope, I began to believe that perhaps, together, our families could weather any storm.

The Wedding That Wasn't Hers

The joy of that promising beginning was soon marred by an event that left me with a heavy heart. Not long after my daughter announced her pregnancy—before the wedding was even official—the Woo family moved swiftly. In what I now refer to as a *kamikaze wedding*, they arranged a traditional Chinese ceremony followed by a courthouse wedding. There was no time for my daughter to grieve or plan the celebration she had always dreamed of; everything was decided for her in a flurry of formalities. The guest list was dictated solely by the Woo family; they only invited immediate family members. Reginald was allowed to bring a few of his friends, but my daughter's closest companions—Dr. Elizabeth Acosta Flores, Denise, Savannah, and Layla—were nowhere to be seen. Worse yet, my daughter had little say in the matter. I remember watching that day with a deep, lingering sorrow, knowing in my heart that she would have wished for so much more—a celebration filled with laughter, love, and the presence of those who understood her best. Instead, she was thrust into a ceremony that belonged more to family obligation than to her personal joy.

My husband, her brother, his wife, and I were there from our side of the family, offering our quiet support. But I could sense the disappointment that shrouded her spirit. It was as if, at that moment, her own identity was being swallowed by the rigid expectations of another family's traditions, a stark reminder that sometimes, even the most significant milestones can feel hollow when they are not truly one's own.

Cracks in the Foundation

Before the wedding, my daughter and Reginald moved to Houston—a city of promise but also one that would soon reveal its harsh realities. Not long after their arrival, they encountered unexpected fertility issues. Yet, as if defying the odds, my daughter began having children—one after another.

It was nothing short of miraculous to witness her balance the roles of wife, devoted mother, and brilliant physician. Even though she had graduated as a surgeon, she willingly traded that high-pressure life for one that allowed her to be present at home. Her priorities were as clear as they were unwavering—a stark contrast to Reginald, who seemed to drift away from responsibility.

In Houston, my daughter handled everything herself. She took charge of the household finances, cooked meals, fixed the lights, threw out the garbage, and even managed the mundane tasks of daily life, while Reginald and his mother shared control over their own accounts as if their money were more precious than our family's well-being. Every time I visited, I saw the toll this took on her, and I gently urged her, "You need help; hire a nanny. This isn't a luxury; it's a necessity." But she, with her steely determination, continued to shoulder every burden alone.

I remember the year 2013 vividly—a year that was meant to be filled with celebration. My husband finally graduated from deaconing school, a day when our family should have been united in joy. I had even invited the Woo family, hoping that maybe they might share in our happiness. But my daughter, heavily pregnant with baby Veronica, couldn't attend the ceremony. To make matters worse, none of the Woo family showed up either. I later learned that Reginald's mother had taken responsibility for her absence. It was a painful, one-sided reminder: Whenever there was a special event on their side—a dinner, an occasion, a family gathering—we were always expected to be there bright and early. Yet, when it came to celebrating our milestones, excuses abounded. In the seven years that the children were married, the Woo family visited our home only once or twice, leaving me with a sense of isolation and neglect that still stings today.

There were also moments when our two families seemed to come together, if only briefly. We traveled with the Woo family to Taiwan—a journey meant to be an exploration of culture and kinship. It was during that trip that we discovered it was the first time in 40 years that Reginald's father had ever traveled outside his home country. My daughter was pregnant with little April at the time and couldn't participate fully, but I soaked in every detail.

I remember how Dr. Woo Senior met Mr. Shen, Reginald's maternal grandfather; the two men embraced and wept together, their tears a testament to the weight of shared history. For a few shining days, our family was treated like royalty: We roamed bustling markets, visited the zoo (where school children eagerly lined up to take photos with us, having never seen Black people in real life, only on television), and stayed in the most comfortable hotels imaginable. A grand welcoming dinner was held in honor of Mr. Shen's birthday, and even though Reginald's maternal grandmother was frail, she made every effort to be there. We had our own personal guide who led us through the wonders of Asia. It was my first time in that part of the world, and I cherished every moment.

Yet, as with so many bright memories, there was a shadow. Soon after our return to the United States, we learned that Reginald's maternal grandmother had passed away. I can still hear Reginald's mother breaking down as she cried, "I married a man who doesn't travel, and it took 40 years for him to finally come with me to see my parents." I opened up to her then, sharing my own grief, and for a fleeting moment, I believed that our families might truly be united by our shared sorrow. But that fragile unity, like a delicate thread, could not hold for long.

The Tides of Betrayal and Neglect

The turning point—the moment that shattered what little remained of our fragile peace—came with Hurricane Harvey. I saw that storm as both the beginning and the downfall of my daughter's marriage.

When Hurricane Harvey struck, Reginald was completely consumed by his work. My daughter, desperate and terrified, pleaded with us to leave, to seek shelter from the storm's fury. I, perhaps misguided by loyalty or fear, sided with him, saying, "We will pray to God that everything will be alright." I clung to hope, even as I now know that hope alone could not save us.

The next day, as Reginald prepared to leave for work, he was met with flooded streets and utter devastation. His face fell, and he turned back home—ashamed and defeated, for he knew deep in his heart that my daughter had been right all along. My daughter's anger was palpable, and I found myself repeatedly trying to soothe her, to shield her from the full force of the betrayal. That day, the storm washed away any remaining illusions of stability, revealing deep cracks in our foundation that could no longer be mended. And then, as if to compound the pain, came the cruel refrain that would haunt our home for years. Whenever the children misbehaved, Reginald would announce in a tone so cold it cut through my very soul, "If you misbehave, you'll have to go to Black Grandma, and if you're good, you'll go to White Grandma!" I can still picture little Veronica's face, eyes wide with confusion and innocence, as she cried out, "I love my Black Grandma!"

In those words, I saw a perverse distortion—a painting of our heritage as something inferior, as if Black were bad and White were good. I have often wondered whether his words sprang from pure racism or from a bitter jealousy of the stability and love that our family so effortlessly provided. Whatever the reason, the venom in his tone was unmistakable, a clear sign of his utter disrespect for me, for our traditions, and for the legacy of our ancestors.

Every summer before the divorce, the children were forced to navigate this cruel dichotomy. I would welcome them with open arms during long, tender visits—bathing them, comforting them, and filling their days with love. But Reginald insisted that his own mother be the one present, despite her limitations as an office aide who could only offer brief, perfunctory visits. I had retired early so that I could be there for my daughter and her children, providing the care and stability they so desperately needed. Meanwhile, in Reginald's $2.5 million California home, I would hear of broken appliances—a dishwasher that never worked, a stove in constant disrepair, an air conditioner that barely functioned. It was as if Reginald had been raised to expect indulgence, to always be *baby last*, with every luxury handed to him on a silver platter. I often compared him to his sister—so humble, so grounded, so undeniably responsible—a stark contrast to the man he had become. I later discovered that the sister went to boarding school, which may have helped her to become the woman that she was.

At times, I even wondered if Reginald harbored jealousy toward my daughter. Here was a woman who had risen to become the medical director at a brand-new urgent care center in Houston—a shining beacon of hard work and brilliance—yet at her ribbon-cutting ceremony, he was conspicuously absent. It was as if he secretly craved the power to undermine her every success, to diminish her light. I don't believe he fully understood the magnitude of his actions, what he was doing not only to her but to the children who depended on her steadfast love.

I warned him repeatedly, with all the passion of a mother who had seen too much heartbreak, "Don't move out of the house. You will be abandoning your family." But his parents, clinging to their own rigid traditions, warned him that if he returned, he would be cut off from the inheritance. They had already arranged an apartment for him—a final, irrevocable severing of ties. Despite my desperate pleas, he chose to leave. I remember that moment vividly, my voice trembling with anger and despair as I told him it would all be over if he walked away. At that time, my own mother was frail, and in a touching act of love, my daughter surprised me with tickets to see my mother in Ghana for Mother's Day. Though my mother passed away shortly after that visit, I was blessed to see her one last time in May. I returned to Ghana in September to help prepare for my mother's funeral, and when I came back to the United States, I was met with the shocking news that my daughter and Reginald were divorced.

The divorce had happened so swiftly; I had never witnessed such a rapid unraveling, especially when Reginald didn't even show up in court because he was too busy with work. I wasn't sure if he thought he would finish his training and then return to reclaim his wife or if he simply no longer cared. In our culture, it is customary for both sides of the family to come together to mend broken bonds through counseling and heartfelt discussions.

But Reginald refused to attend any counseling sessions, and his family swiftly closed the door on reconciliation. My daughter's desperate calls to his mother went unanswered, and I couldn't shake the feeling that his family had played a role in hastening the end of their union. Meanwhile, my husband, our son, his wife, and I remained open to listening to any concerns he might have—even as his indifference grew.

That summer, Reginald was granted six weeks of visitation with the children, and it turned into a nightmare. He never told us where he was taking them; he simply dropped them off at his parents' house and vanished. We were forced to call child welfare and even the police to locate the children, only to discover that they had been taken as far away as Illinois while Reginald stayed in Houston. Their phones were cut off, leaving us unable to reach them.

When the children finally returned, they looked as if they'd been through a war zone: April's nose was bleeding, their hair was still styled exactly as my daughter had originally chosen for the Woo family, and fungal infections marred their delicate skin and scalp.

We rushed them to get groomed, to restore even a semblance of dignity. Yet, the neglect did not end there. When Reginald forcibly attempted to reclaim custody from my daughter, he sent me harsh, disrespectful messages, accusing me of taking too long to care for the children. It was then that I truly understood the extent of the abuse my daughter had endured—his inability to communicate with kindness, his relentless disrespect, and his callous disregard for the very children he was meant to nurture. His words—nasty, hateful words—still echo in my heart, and after that, I refused to speak with him any further, though his brother-in-law eventually intervened so that I could finish caring for the children in peace.

Resilience, Reflection, and a New Dawn

Even in all this pain, there were still moments—small, real moments—that kept our family together. I found some comfort in those who truly cared for my daughter's children. My favorite nanny, Becky, was one of those blessings. She was like our right hand—always on top of everything, caring, and dependable. Even when I wasn't in Houston, Becky and I kept in touch over WhatsApp. But for reasons I still can't explain, Becky eventually left for a better-paying job with two doctors. When she was with my daughter, she took pride in serving two physicians, seeing it as a mark of prestige. After my daughter divorced

Reginald and started a new life with someone who wasn't a doctor, Becky felt her role wasn't as important anymore and chose to leave. Before she went, she recommended another nanny, Elda. Elda, however, turned out to be a disaster—always late, careless, and more inclined to feed the children fast food than the homemade Ghanaian meals I worked so hard to prepare. Worse yet, Elda knew she was on thin ice and eventually decided to cry wolf about minor issues, further undermining her credibility. She would take the kids wherever she pleased but never where they truly needed to be.

Then there was Andrea, someone we only called on in emergencies. Although she was around my age, Andrea had never had grandchildren, and her awkward interactions with the Woo children led them to call her "nana," even when it never felt right. Andrea and Reginald rarely interacted; she would leave before he even got home, her mind foggy with forgetfulness.

Worse yet, some nannies began to side with Reginald. I received calls from them insisting that Greg—the man who would later bring a fresh start into our lives—was mistreating the children. They tried to get me to join their side, even though I never once saw Greg treat the kids badly. I remember spending an entire week with Greg and the Woo children while my daughter was in Ghana, celebrating her baby cousin's wedding. In that week, I saw a loving, protective, and gentle father, someone who cared deeply for the children. I dismissed those baseless accusations immediately and told my daughter about the nanny's misguided claims. Becky later told me plainly, "Adwoafuaa doesn't have time for the children, Reginald doesn't have time for the children, but I have time for the children." Becky, who never had children of her own and always dreamed of caring for mixed families, spoke with a raw honesty that reminded me real care isn't about titles; it's about simply being there.

I also remember when Reginald first proposed—back when little Liza was very young. At that time, he seemed to be a loving father. I recall a visit when my daughter was in Ghana and left Liza with him. To my surprise, he took really good care of her, disciplining her gently and nurturing her as if he meant it. Even his own family welcomed Liza with open arms. I remember our trip to Taiwan, when Reginald's mother was patient with Liza. His sister would play with her non-stop.

It filled me with pride to see that my daughter's child—born out of wedlock—was accepted so warmly by his family. My daughter later mentioned that some believed Liza's fair complexion and her ability to pass for white made her more acceptable to them. I never truly understood that, but I can't shake the feeling that once Reginald's own children arrived, his treatment of Liza changed completely. One day, with the honest frankness of a child, Liza asked him, "Why are you treating me this way?" And he answered flatly, "Because I have my own children now."

After my daughter divorced him, Reginald cut Liza off entirely. He removed her from the family's health insurance—a move that made no financial sense since the premium would have stayed the same regardless of the number of children. Liza was in the middle of expensive dental surgery when this happened, and, as always, my daughter ended up paying out of pocket.

Reginald continued to keep the insurance for the family, benefiting from a discounted rate as a resident. That was his way of saying he no longer felt responsible for Liza. My daughter told him, towards the end of their marriage, if she would have known that he would treat Liza this way, she would have never married him. I was left to wonder if he had ever truly loved her or if he was simply incapable of love.

Despite everything, my daughter's spirit never wavered. She's still full of life—a true force who drags me along to every event and trip, even at my age. We've been to Las Vegas, Aruba, Wisconsin Dells, and Dallas. No matter the occasion, she always plans something special—whether it's the Renaissance Festival, rodeos, water parks, or ice skating.

The girls even take horseback riding lessons, just as my daughter once did for Liza. I smile when I think of the day she took me and the Woo children to see Cirque du Soleil and Shen Yun and that unforgettable evening in Dallas when we all watched a total lunar eclipse together. Even with her busy schedule, she never loses her faith, keeping the children close to church and even volunteering in the church nursery when she can. It doesn't surprise me that she was named Physician of the Year—a title that only hints at the depth of her talent and strength. Every mother and grandmother dreams that her daughter will find a partner who will be the father of her children—a man who will stand by her through thick and thin. I clung to that hope, too, even as I watched my daughter's marriage fall apart. I tried to remind Reginald of the values my own mother taught me—a woman who, despite her own hardships, eventually found her way back to my father. I even gave Greg a hard time when he first started dating my daughter. I wanted her to hold onto something familiar, even though I saw the hurtful behavior in Reginald every day. It wasn't anything personal against Greg; I only wanted my daughter to be safe and happy.

Then came the day I found out that my daughter and Greg were married. I was shocked; I thought it was too soon. My daughter hadn't even invited me, my husband, or her siblings; only my dear sister, Aunty Amma, was there. At that moment, I finally realized what I'd known all along: Reginald was never the savior she needed. My daughter wasn't after fancy titles or what society expected; she just wanted to be happy. I remembered my own impulsive courthouse wedding to my husband after just three days of knowing him—a decision that, 50 years later, still proves the power of love. My daughter's happiness became her guiding light.

Later, my daughter and my son even threw us a magnificent 50th wedding anniversary bash—everyone came together in support. I've been through so much—especially losing my youngest, my *baby last*, to brain cancer—but I remain grateful for our journey as immigrants who managed to put the remaining children through medical school.

One day, I'll share my own story—raw, honest, and unfiltered. I have always been, and will always be, the maternal grandmother of these precious children. I was there from the very start; I stood in the birthing room holding the umbilical cord as Dr. Woo made that first decisive cut. I've bathed these babies, nurtured them, and stayed with my daughter until each child was strong enough for daycare. I retired early so I could be there whenever my family needed me. I admit I became a bit too friendly with the nannies at times. Reginald would push the children onto his parents, who accepted everything without question.

I've always believed that, during the summers, they treated the children poorly—punishing my daughter for divorcing their son, even though it was only the innocent little ones who suffered. I pleaded with the courts not to cut the grandparents out because California is too far for us to visit. Please, do not take these children away from the mother who nursed each one until they were nearly two—especially not during those crucial early years.

In short, if Dr. Woo has the right to decide where the children live, then know this: the Black maternal grandparents—myself included—will never be allowed to see our grandchildren or have any contact with them. That thought shatters my heart into pieces. Dr. Woo seems determined to do whatever it takes to hurt my daughter and her family just because she dared to divorce him. As I sit here reflecting on our long, winding journey—a tapestry of hope, heartbreak, betrayal, and raw resilience—I see that every tear and every smile has built the foundation of who we are.

I've seen Reginald's gentle smile on better days and felt the sting of his harsh words in our darkest hours. I've watched my daughter transform her pain into an unyielding determination to protect her children, and I've learned that true strength isn't measured by being unscarred but by the courage to keep moving forward despite the scars.

Now, as I close this chapter, I promise to remain a guardian of my grandchildren's hearts—a presence that will stand by them through every storm, every trial, and every moment of joy. I'll be there in every whispered prayer, every warm hug, and every meal made with love. My heart is stuck to theirs, and I will fight for the care and love they deserve.

Despite everything, my daughter's energy and determination have shone through. And now, after all the pain and heartbreak, a new dawn has come. My daughter has found love again, a real, honest love in Greg, whose kindness, protectiveness, and gentle nature have begun to fill the void Reginald left behind. I've shared every raw, painful detail of our past, and now, with a bruised yet hopeful heart, I pass this story on to Greg, the man who stepped in when another walked away.

Chapter 17:

From My Eyes—Greg's Perspective

I still remember the exact moment I first laid eyes on Adwoafuaa. She had this glow, like a vibrant aura that commanded every inch of the room, even though I later learned she was going through some pretty heavy situations. Her smile was warm, her laugh contagious, and her eyes held an intensity I couldn't quite place, as if she'd been braving storms but never lost sight of the lighthouse.

One random day, she crossed paths with me, and I thought: *Damn, this woman is absolutely gorgeous… an angel.* I joked to my buddies that if I ever saw a halo in real life, it'd probably be hovering above her head. They teased me right back, of course.

At that time, I had no clue—*no clue*—what she had endured with her ex-husband or how complicated her family dynamics actually were. She was always resilient, never once letting the pain or stress overshadow who she was. Now, looking back, I realize how truly extraordinary that is. Most people crumble under that level of tension or let cynicism eat them from the inside. Adwoafuaa? She stood strong, reared three kids (and an adult daughter!), and managed to hold down a full-time job as a physician.

And that was just the tip of the iceberg. Yet, the more I learned, the more I understood the massive load she was carrying. She tried to warn me about it—about him. In fact, I recall her once saying, "My ex is different. He's…

challenging." She didn't go into many details at first, but enough slipped through for me to see that he wasn't just your standard disagreeable ex-husband. He was something else. While it made me cautious, it also made me want to protect her—and the children—from anything that threatened their peace. Little did I know just how threatening the months and years to come would feel.

Discovering Adwoafuaa's World

Our initial dates were sweet and surprisingly normal. We went out to improv comedy clubs, dinners, and concerts and talked about life and dreams. It all felt so refreshing. But behind that refreshing surface, there were hints: cryptic references to child protective services (CPS) investigations, tension-filled phone calls, messy divorces, and a father who seemed to vanish and reappear like an unwanted phantom.

She told me she had three younger kids and an adult daughter, Liza. And yes, I braced myself. *Three children?* Not going to lie; my family freaked out when I told them. My mother put on her reading glasses, blinked, and said, "Are you sure about this, Greg? You know how that can be… baby-daddy drama, lots of bills, fewer romantic vacations…"

My dad, more measured, only asked, "Where is the father in all this?" and I told him that from what I could gather, the father was absent, which was pretty much true *at that time.*

Given the short glimpses Adwoafuaa offered, it sounded like he was barely involved. She had won some child support or something like that, but the father didn't seem to be making major appearances. So, I told my parents,

"Nah, it's probably not going to cause drama. He's out of the picture." We laugh about it now—like a cosmic joke. Because if only I'd known how deep in the picture he'd be, I might have paused or demanded a heads-up from the universe.

Still, whenever I worried about the possibilities, I remembered the shining grace Adwoafuaa showed. Moreover, I thought, *If she can handle it, I can handle it.* My family kept repeating, "Be careful, Greg," but eventually, they took my word that everything would be fine.

Wrestling with Prejudice

You know what was the strangest thing I learned? Adwoafuaa's three children had this odd preference for their father, which was apparently linked to race. It was more than them just liking Dad because he was *fun*, or had more money, or something typical. She told me that in their father's household and among his extended family, certain biases were openly or subtly taught: that White features, White skin, and White culture were *superior* to African ones.

Now, I'm not a saint, but racism or colorism makes me sick to my stomach. Hearing from Adwoafuaa that the kids sometimes repeated comments about "Black Grandma" or made disparaging remarks about African hair versus White hair left me speechless. I couldn't believe that in this day and age, her ex-husband's circle had hammered such garbage into their heads.

The children would come back from visits with Dad saying, "We don't like dark skin," or "We want to look more white." It was as if they'd internalized a hierarchy that put me, Adwoafuaa, or her side of the family at the bottom. I was appalled.

One day, I heard them use the phrase "Black Grandma," and from their tone, it wasn't just an identification of someone's race. It was an insult, an expression of negativity. It took a lot of willpower to remain calm. Adwoafuaa tried to correct them gently, to talk about how no one race is better and how we mustn't degrade or put down the beautiful parts of who we are. But I could sense how uncomfortable it was for her to see that in her own children.

For me, that was the first sign that something was deeply wrong with how Reginald and his side of the family approached the world. It also hinted at the possibility of bigger manipulations to come, especially around identity.

If the father taught them that white equals best, then it's not a stretch for him to also fill their heads with nonsense about Adwoafuaa, how she's an inferior mother, how she's incompetent, or anything else to control the narrative.

When Her Mom Disliked Me

It's funny how the biggest friction in the early months wasn't actually about Reginald or the kids. It was Adwoafuaa's own mother. She disliked me on sight. I couldn't figure out why. It got so intense that I considered ending things, not because I doubted Adwoafuaa, but because it's extremely stressful to enter a relationship knowing the potential mother-in-law is giving you the evil eye.

We had arguments about it, Adwoafuaa and I, because I kept feeling like, "Look, if your mom hates me this much, maybe we shouldn't do this." But she was resolute. She confronted her mother calmly, insisting that I was good for her, that the relationship was healthy, and that she wasn't going to let her family drive me away.

That moment was huge. It showed me Adwoafuaa wasn't a pushover; if she believed in something, she'd fight for it. Only later did I discover that her mother's hostility toward me was strategic: She still harbored a secret hope that Reginald and Adwoafuaa would reconcile. So, the mother tried to sabotage me.

When I learned that, I felt relief in a twisted way because it wasn't personal; her mother was just trying to push me out for the ex-husband. Once I got it, the tension made more sense. And fortunately, with time, her mother came around. She recognized my intentions were pure and that, no, Adwoafuaa wasn't about to jump back into Reginald's arms.

Chuck E. Cheese and the Unexpected Joy

One of my fondest memories from those early days was April's third birthday party at Chuck E. Cheese. I invited some of my nieces because I wanted them to meet Adwoafuaa's kids in a carefree, kid-centered environment. My sister-in-law came with her kids, too.

The moment the children started jumping, playing, and screaming at that arcade, I realized something magical: They got along brilliantly. You'd think they were old friends. April was laughing while running after my niece, who was squealing in delight.

The look on Adwoafuaa's face was pure joy. If you could freeze a moment in time that summed up what we wanted—a normal, happy, blended sense of family—that was it. For a moment, I let myself forget about exes and child support nightmares. We were just normal parents (and parent figures) celebrating a birthday.

Ironically, it was that memory that fueled me months later when everything started spiraling. I often reminded myself that the kids *could* be happy and that Adwoafuaa was an incredibly loving mom.

I saw it with my own eyes, so no court or slander could convince me otherwise.

Attempts at Warning

You might be wondering, "Greg, how much did you actually know about Reginald from the start?" Well, not much, if I'm honest. Adwoafuaa tried to mention certain *red flags*, as she called them.

She told me how they'd had repeated CPS visits, how he'd pulled stunts like leaving the gas stove on or refusing to help when Hurricane Harvey hit, and how he hoarded money into his 401k.

She also told me his father made her feel uncomfortable, creeping around the house or using little intimidation tactics.

One day, I told Adwoafuaa bluntly: "If this man had been Black, you'd have left him in the dust long ago." She paused, then admitted I was probably right—that she might have walked away sooner if the father was a Black man displaying that many deal-breakers.

But, for whatever reason—maybe the veneer of success, maybe cultural or personal illusions—she stayed longer, hoping to fix things.

I realized that her ex had issues that transcended just normal divorce bitterness. He was controlling, manipulative, and (from what I gleaned) had an outsized ego. But I still wasn't prepared for how that ego would lash out once he realized Adwoafuaa was truly moving on.

Meeting the *Lingering* Ex

It was around November 2018, I think, when one of the CPS encounters ended, and Reginald told the investigator he wanted to meet me. Seemed odd—why so soon? He and Adwoafuaa were separated. She finalized the divorce. The kids were adjusting. Yet he insisted. I was uncomfortable but figured maybe he wanted to talk like two adults. Possibly he wanted reassurance that I wasn't some abuser. Maybe he just wanted clarity.

In the days leading up to our meeting, though, Adwoafuaa kept telling me: "He's weird. He lingers around the house. He sets the thermostat to 99 degrees at night just to mess with me." That's exactly what she said. I almost laughed: Who sets a thermostat to 99? Is that even physically comfortable?

Turned out it was part of his plan to drive her crazy or sabotage daily routines. She'd come home late from work, find the house scorching hot, and realize the father had been in the house unannounced. That's not normal ex-behavior. That's twisted.

When we finally met in person, he extended his hand, and I immediately noticed his handshake was weak and delicate—an unexpected display of fragility that clashed with the cold intensity in his eyes. Then he told me, "I just want Adwoafuaa to be happy." On the surface, it sounded nice, but everything in his body language screamed the opposite. His eyes were cold; his posture rigid.

It felt like I was facing a predator, not a co-parent. I left that meeting feeling uneasy. My gut told me he was far from done meddling.

The Nanny Chronicles

Adwoafuaa and Reginald's children went through a series of nannies. I used to wonder, *Why so many?* Then I saw the environment. With the father sporadically in and out, Adwoafuaa working long hours as a doctor and the kids in constant flux, it was a tough job for any nanny. But some stuck out more than others.

Becky was, in my view, the all-star nanny. She had a professional demeanor and truly cared for the kids. She cooked real meals, cleaned diligently, engaged them in educational play, and seemed to love the job. I always told Adwoafuaa, "Becky might be the best caretaker you'll ever hire." And even now, I stand by that statement; Becky was wonderful *in terms of how she served the kids.* However, Becky had personal ups and downs.

When Adwoafuaa was happy, Becky would be moody; when Adwoafuaa was going through a tough time, Becky would be super nice. I found it bizarre that Becky's emotional state was inversely linked to Adwoafuaa's. She would talk about how her boyfriend was a 40-something year old still living with his mother and compare that to me, not realizing I owned my own house. Little jealous remarks would pop up. But overall, Becky was strong with the kids.

If she'd stuck around permanently, I suspect the children would've had a more stable environment.

Elda, on the other hand, was the nanny from hell. Slow, lazy, a compulsive liar, and exuding this weird negative energy. At first, Adwoafuaa wanted to fire her many times, but ironically, *I* was the one who told her, "Give her a chance. Let's not be too hasty." Looking back, I cringe because Elda caused repeated chaos.

There was a time in January 2020 when she made a *half-outcry* about something or other—some sort of false statement that threatened legal trouble for Adwoafuaa. Still, I hesitated to outright fire her, thinking she might shape up. That was a mistake. Elda was incompetent, and she also gave me that unsettling vibe that she enjoyed sowing discord.

One day, I overheard Elda telling Adwoafuaa, "You're always so happy, always smiling, always laughing." The tone wasn't admiration; it was resentment, like *How dare you be joyful?* It reminded me of Reginald's claim, "I just want Adwoafuaa to be happy," which had that same suspicious ring. It's as if certain people simply couldn't stand to see Adwoafuaa thriving.

On top of that, Becky was thrilled when Adwoafuaa was single, but the minute I came into the picture and Adwoafuaa seemed genuinely content, Becky's mood took a dive. I don't pretend to psychoanalyze them, but it's strange how Adwoafuaa's happiness seemed to irritate multiple people. I guess some folks only find satisfaction when others are struggling.

Falling in Love with Wonder Woman

Yes, I'm going to brag about my wife. Because if you'd seen her in action—balancing the kids' needs, her medical career, housekeeping, volunteering at the church, planning family trips—you'd be in awe, too.

She's like a circus performer, spinning five plates at once while tossing a ball in the air, and she rarely drops anything.

When we started dating seriously, I realized how hands-on she was with the children: reading them bedtime stories, helping with projects, taking them to Chinese school, or soccer. She rarely missed a beat. And she never looked for credit. She did it out of genuine love, working her 12-hour shift and then coming home to read Dr. Seuss or some elaborate fantasy story she'd make up on the spot. I've never seen so much energy in one person.

Sometimes, I'd wake up at six in the morning to find her already up, cooking or preparing school lunches. She told me she wanted them to have balanced meals—part Ghanaian cuisine, part American staples, part Chinese influences.

The kids thrived in that environment, it seemed to me. RJ tried out the violin, April enjoyed gymnastics, and Veronica was bounding around the soccer field. Seeing Adwoafuaa coordinate it all, I thought, *I want her to be the mother of my child one day.* And ironically, that dream came true in a timeline we never planned.

We used to do aerial aerobics together—something I never imagined in a million years. She introduced me to it, and I got so addicted I entered my first competition. If anyone were to ask me when I knew she was *the one*, it was the moment she not only coached me during practice but also choreographed my entire performance routine with endearing confidence. She was my personal cheerleader and coach all rolled into one, and I thought, *Man, she is unstoppable*. The synergy we had was effortless.

Then, the court drama escalated, and I watched a judge basically demonize Adwoafuaa—this same unstoppable mother and accomplished doctor. The judge tore her down as if she were incompetent or a danger to the kids. It enraged me to the point that, ironically, it confirmed my decision to marry her. If the legal system was going to treat her like some unworthy mother, then I wanted to stand by her, to show the world she was far from that.

Watching Reginald Become *Our Ex*

I often joke that I feel like Reginald is "our ex," because dealing with him was like an unwanted third party in our relationship. He'd pop up with malicious phone calls, would answer RJ's phone breathing heavily on the other line, send private investigators, and spread rumors. He left the family but then acted outraged that Adwoafuaa moved on.

The audacity was staggering.

Let me be clear: A man who abandons his family shouldn't expect the mother to stay single and grieving. Yet he would treat Adwoafuaa as if she were still his property. That's how it looked from my vantage point. He'd refer to her in ways that implied ownership, and it disgusted me. She was no one's property, certainly not the man who left them in the dust. I never minded co-parenting or the father stepping back in for the kids' sake, but this was different.

He wanted to sabotage her happiness, not be a father in good faith.

I saw him degrade her. I saw how the kids suffered neglect under his and his families watch. I saw how random nannies came and went, each more incompetent than the last—except for one or two who were decent. I can't imagine a father who truly loves his children, letting them roam around half-fed, half-bathed, or letting them get sunburned to the point of peeling. I recall Adwoafuaa telling me that when Reginald's older sister was younger they made her walk around in the summer with an umbrella to keep her fair skinned. Therefore, it seemed purposeful as to what they were doing to the Woo children, downright hateful even.

People say to me, "You must hate Reginald," but here's the thing: I don't know him enough to hate him. I just see him as an unfit father who's so obsessed with controlling Adwoafuaa that he's actually neglected the kids' well-being. If that's not twisted, I don't know what is. Meanwhile, the courts turned a blind eye. A judge even suggested that if I hated Reginald, I must hate the children. That's insane logic. Meanwhile, Reginald is the one letting them suffer. So, who truly hates them?

Then Reginald left them in the care of a nanny who abhors my wife and actually beat the children. I could never in a million years hate Reginald as much as Elda hated Adwoafuaa. In fact, I don't hate him at all. I just feel sorry for him. This is whom he left his own children with while he was living in California. Someone make it make sense!

The Last Meal with the Kids

The final time I saw the children was during that fateful visit when Adwoafuaa ended up getting charged with contempt for (supposedly) violating some court order. We had dinner together as a family. Despite the tension swirling around us, we tried to preserve a sense of normalcy.

I remember RJ playing a bit on his old violin, rummaging in a closet to find it, and April reciting affirmations she used to say in the car rides. Veronica showed me some drawings she'd left on the walls. It was bittersweet. *They recognized everything.* Our home still carried their footprints—old art, leftover toys, reminders of who they were before all this legal chaos.

But the kids themselves were different. Their eyes looked wary as if bracing for the next jolt. They told us stories about caretaker after caretaker, about bizarre punishments or neglect. April had gained a lot of weight; she had scalp lesions and thinning hair. RJ's spirit seemed dampened. Veronica, the once chatty little girl, was quieter, more subdued.

I recognized trauma in them. It killed me to see it. Their once bright shining light dimmed by their own father's need for vengeance.

That night, after dinner, Adwoafuaa and I cried in private. She said, "They're not the same. They've changed so much." And I agreed. It was as if we were seeing them after they'd survived a war zone. They tried to put on normal smiles, but behind those smiles was heartbreak. We promised we'd always be here for them, no matter the distance or the legal nonsense. Still, I felt powerless.

How do you protect children from their own biological father if he's the source of the harm?

Tangled in Courtroom Vendettas

So let's talk about the courtroom itself, where Karen, the father's attorney, and the judge seemed to have personal vendettas against us. I sat in that courtroom more than once, stunned at the animosity they threw our way. It wasn't just legal procedure; it was personal.

One time, I joked to Adwoafuaa, "Did you date the judge in college or something? Why does he hate you so much?" Adwoafuaa had no idea. Then I found an article about how the judge once wanted to be a physician but couldn't pass organic chemistry. A lightbulb went off in my head: *He can't stand that Adwoafuaa is Dr. N, that she accomplished something he wanted but failed at.*

If that sounds far-fetched, let me tell you, I watched him address Reginald as "Doctor" with so much deference, then turn around and talk down to Adwoafuaa as if she was a scolded child. It was night and day. He wouldn't call her "Doctor," even though she earned that title fair and square—busted her butt at Northwestern University, overcame massive hurdles, and probably soared through organic chemistry while he flunked. Did that fuel his anger? Who knows. But it sure explained the bitter tone.

Then there was Karen, Reginald's attorney, who seemed to personally relish making our lives hell. I learned early on about the illegality of improper service from two distinct incidents. In one, a process server dropped off paperwork at the front desk of Adwoafuaa's job with the receptionist, never truly serving her. In another, Karen left paperwork on my windshield and pretended that counted as valid service.

Little did she know, my house is rigged with cameras; I even have video of her process server creeping around, never actually handing me anything. Even after I sent her that footage, she still managed to convince the judge that I'd been served, which resulted in a bench warrant for me. Are you kidding?

That was the point where I decided *enough is enough.* I reported her to the Texas Bar Association and provided the emails, the video evidence, and everything. I said, "Here is an attorney knowingly misrepresenting facts to the court." The bar responded in that hush-hush Olivia Pope manner—like, "We're handling it." Soon after, Karen announced her *retirement.* She disappeared from practice, never to be heard from in any county. Coincidence? Possibly. But I like to believe that, for once, the system delivered a tiny scrap of accountability.

Claiming My Family

One day, I looked at Adwoafuaa and said, "No one can threaten my woman, my kids, or my future child and get away with it. Period." That's how I grew up. In my family, you protect your own. Sure, you try to solve things peacefully, but if push comes to shove, you don't stand by while someone bullies or terrorizes your spouse or children. I wanted to shield Adwoafuaa from Reginald's harassment, but the courts and the system made it nearly impossible. Each time we tried to shield ourselves, we'd be called "uncooperative" or "in contempt." It was maddening.

Still, we found solace in each other. The adversity convinced me I wanted to spend my life with this woman. I proposed in a quiet, intimate setting—no big fanfare, no fireworks. She said yes, and it felt like we were forging a union in the face of a hurricane. Then came the biggest surprise: *Adwoafuaa got pregnant.* We definitely didn't plan it, but after everything we'd lost—having the three kids physically taken from her, losing in court multiple times—here was a blessing. Another child that we could raise from the start in a stable environment with love and synergy.

It didn't diminish our grief for the older children, but it gave us hope. Our house, which had felt emptier after losing the kids, suddenly had a future occupant.

We started redecorating, painting a nursery, trying to find pockets of joy. Yet, I never once forgot about the older ones. I see them as precious souls who got caught in a crossfire they never asked for.

Beyond the Courtroom's Shadow

Watching the downfall of Karen was satisfying to a degree—*okay, maybe that's petty*, but it was. She had no business fabricating reasons to arrest me. That fiasco taught me to trust my instincts, keep evidence, and record everything. In a twisted sense, dealing with Reginald taught me to always be vigilant—cameras on, documents saved, phone calls recorded if needed. Because some people play dirty, and if you're naive, you'll get crushed.

I sometimes reflect on how all of this parallels a Greek tragedy: the *heroine* (Adwoafuaa) escapes a harmful marriage, finds new love (me), and tries to rebuild, only for the father figure to lash out with epic fury, aided by a biased judge and unscrupulous lawyer. The difference is that we haven't let the tragedy consume us. We're forging ahead, cherishing the baby we have, waiting for the day the older children might return or at least see the light.

Occasionally, I ask Adwoafuaa, "If you could go back, would you have done anything differently with Reginald?" She sighs, then says, "I'd have left earlier. I'd have walked away before it ever got to this." She regrets enabling him, perhaps out of love or fear.

I regret not stepping in more forcefully once I realized how malicious he was. But regrets are a dead end. We move forward.

A Love That Endures

I see a lot of jealousy aimed at Adwoafuaa: from Elda, from Becky, from certain colleagues, from the judge, from the ex himself. It might sound arrogant, but many women resent how she carries herself with confidence, good looks, and a thriving career. That positivity, that refusal to break, can either inspire people or provoke them. Clearly, it provoked quite a few.

Through it all, I've never questioned her ability as a mother. She is, hands down, the best mother I've seen.

She's not perfect—nobody is—but she's warm, present, creative, and protective. The kids from her first marriage were nurtured in a setting brimming with bedtime stories, extracurriculars, healthy meals, and big hugs. That can't just be erased by a single court order or a father's propaganda. The kids will remember who was there at 2 a.m. when they had nightmares, who taught them to tie their shoes, and who kissed their bruises. Adwoafuaa, that's who.

So yes, it boils my blood to see how the system can tear kids away from a mother like that. But that's the reality we ended up navigating. Now, the baby we share is living proof that we can still build something beautiful out of heartbreak. We vow to give this child every ounce of love and stability we can muster.

The Unfinished Chapter

I'm aware that, for now, the children remain largely in Reginald's custody. Adwoafuaa and I haven't seen them physically in a very long time. She relies on phone calls and short bursts of communication. Every once in a while, we see photos that break our hearts: the kids looking neglected, with worn-out clothes or unkempt hair. We see the light drained from their faces. And I rage quietly because there's only so much we can do from afar while the father stands behind ironclad legal rulings.

But I still have faith that one day, the children will grow up and form their own judgments. They'll remember the bedtime stories, the Chuck E. Cheese parties, the trips to the park, and the stable love that Adwoafuaa gave them. They'll realize who was using them as pawns and who truly cared for them. I look forward to the day April calls or texts to say, "Hey, I understand now. You guys were always on my side." Or RJ decides he wants to play his violin for me again. I am looking forward to the day Veronica asks if she can come to visit. And I'll say yes, absolutely, whenever they want, my door is wide open.

Until then, I stand by Adwoafuaa. She may have lost that court battle in a small county in Texas, but she wins daily in my eyes—wins by staying strong, forging new paths, and never letting the negativity kill her spirit. The father can claim monetary victories, manipulate the kids, or wave around court documents. But real victories—the intangible kind—belong to those who keep their integrity. And Adwoafuaa's integrity is unbreakable.

Aftermath: Reporting, Retiring, and Reclaiming Peace

People sometimes call me a protective bulldog because I vow that if you harm my wife or child, I'll push back. But ironically, in this entire fiasco, my hands have been tied by a legal labyrinth. You can't just go punch a man for forging checks or psychologically abusing children; that'll land you in jail, not him. So, I've learned to gather evidence, speak out, and use the law to fight back, though the law rarely fights fair. It's humbling.

At the end of the day, I see Adwoafuaa as my unicorn—rare, magical, and unstoppable in her own right. She overcame so many obstacles: a rocky divorce, a manipulative ex, biased courts, and monstrous legal fees. She never gave up on love, never gave up on mothering. When she calls me "her rock," I tell her, "I might be the rock, but you're the entire mountain range" because she stands tall through storms that would flatten most people.

Watching her do that taught me about patience, resilience, and grace in the face of cruelty. She taught me how to juggle tasks, how to be an even better father figure, and how to keep my own cynicism at bay. Most of all, she taught me that even when the world says you can't, or you won't, or you're not good enough: persevere. The truth eventually emerges. Is our story perfect? Hardly. We've got scars. We've lost precious years with those three beautiful children. But I'm determined to remain hopeful. We'll keep living in a way that if they knock on our door tomorrow, they'll find a stable, loving home—and new baby sibling—ready to welcome them.

Until then, Adwoafuaa and I hold on to each other and to the knowledge that no judge, no crooked attorney, and no ex-partner with a vendetta can extinguish the love we share.

Whenever I think of April, RJ, or Veronica, I whisper a prayer: that they stay safe, that they remember who truly cared for them, and that we'll reunite in a drama-free environment one day. Because these children are "souls from God," as Adwoafuaa puts it, they don't deserve the chaos thrust upon them. And I wish, more than anything, I could have protected them from it.

Until that day comes, I stand by Adwoafuaa—my wife, my Wonder Woman, the mother of our child, and the best partner I could ever ask for. That's the only way I know how to close this chapter: with untiring faith in her, in us, and in the possibility that truth and love can still triumph over manipulative chaos. If there's one thing I learned from Adwoafuaa, it's that even in the darkest storms, you can keep smiling.

And I'll do just that, for her and all our children, until the clouds finally break. In the pages that follow, you'll see the current state of our struggle: the hard-won victories, the ongoing challenges, and the fresh hope that still drives us forward.

Join us as we bring you up to speed on our latest battles and the steps we're taking to reclaim our lives from the shadow of injustice.

Turn the page, and let's face the future together.

Chapter 18:
California Dreams and Nightmares

After hearing from Greg and my mother, you might have thought their voices were the final notes in our symphony of struggle and survival—a bittersweet finale if you will. But hold on to your hats because it's my turn to step back into the spotlight. Yes, I'm back and ready to dish out where we stand with all the grit and gallows humor life has so generously provided.

I've heard it said that time flies when you're having fun, but apparently, it also zooms by when you're forced to parent three children through a phone screen. After I lost substantial visitation in Texas, the next 12 months morphed into a surreal stretch of FaceTime calls, text messages, and a relentless, gnawing hope that soon, *very soon*, I'd get to see my babies in person.

In some ways, FaceTime actually offered comedic relief. Veronica would prop up the phone, and I'd watch her roam the house, narrating every corner like a reality TV star: "This is the fridge, Mom; it's empty again." April would pop in occasionally, giggling at some silly filter that turned her face into a rainbow. RJ, in that classic pre-teenage way, mostly grunted while fighting off drowsiness at 9 p.m. But behind those small slices of normality, I felt the ache of distance.

A phone doesn't let you hug your child or wipe tears from their cheeks. It doesn't let you smell their hair after a shower or tuck them in with a kiss.

Throughout that year, Reginald appeared suspiciously calm—like a villain recharging off-stage, plotting his next big scene. I should have known the quiet wouldn't last. By the time we inched closer to me being *allowed* my rightful in-person visits, Reginald snapped into action as if someone pressed his "paranoia and litigation" button. Before I knew it, he'd discovered a brand-new battleground: California. Apparently, Texas wasn't giving him enough mileage on the sabotage front.

Madeleine Lewis: Reginald's California Clone of Karen

I'd gotten used to the name *Karen* rolling off my tongue with a mix of dread and exasperation. She was Reginald's ride-or-die attorney in Texas, orchestrating a buffet of motions and restraining orders that left me dizzy. But guess what? There was a new challenger entering the ring. Name: Madeleine Lewis. The location: San Diego. The assignment: continuing Reginald's unstoppable legal vendetta.

From the few glimpses I caught, Madeleine seemed like a carbon copy of Karen—unafraid to push ethical lines to their breaking point, indefatigable in her devotion to The Great Reginald. I found myself genuinely wondering if they were related. Same borderline reality-bending approach, the same brand of "rules don't apply to us." The only hiccup? The case hadn't even been formally transferred out of Texas yet. Usually, one waits for a court's official blessing. But Reginald, consistent in his disregard for normal procedures, jumped straight in, filing for a temporary restraining order in California—like a homeowner who storms onto a property that isn't even on the market yet, declaring, "It's mine!"

Thankfully, I wasn't caught entirely off-guard. Ever since the fiasco of the 2021 jury trial, I'd quietly hired a local attorney in San Diego, Nancy Barclay, just in case. The *case* being that I knew Reginald's brand of mania rarely stays put. He thrives on shifting courts, especially if he sniffs an advantage. So, I made sure Nancy kept an eye on developments in San Diego. I'd call her every month or so: "No big changes yet, but be on standby." And she'd sigh, telling me, "He'll come after you here eventually, trust me." Score one for self-fulfilling prophecies.

The Motion Marathon: UCCJEA, TROs, and the "Risk of Abduction" Charade

On May 9, 2023, Reginald flung his latest grenade: a motion to transfer UCCJEA jurisdiction from Texas to California and to hold a fancy judges' conference. Let me decode that: He wanted to haul the entire custody matter to California, presumably because he guessed it would be an easier stage to rehash the same old cry: *Greg is an evil abuser, and Adwoafuaa is a reckless mother who chooses her husband over the kids.* He tried that script in Texas so many times—

sometimes with success, sometimes not. Now, he was performing a spinoff in front of a fresh audience.

To justify switching states, he banged on the fact that I *hadn't physically visited since September 17, 2022.* Well, yeah, when you weaponized every single holiday so I can't see them, it's a bit tough to appear in person. Then he dove into the usual bullet points that made him feel triumphant:

1. **Greg, the monster**: He insisted that in a new venue, it'd be far simpler to brand Greg as a monstrous stepfather. (Never mind actual investigations found nothing. That's an inconvenient detail.)

2. **I'm not exercising visitation**: He spun it as if I'd *chosen* to forfeit contact, ignoring how systematically he blocked me.

3. **I live with *the abuser***: Always hammered that one in. Yes, I share a home with my husband who's never laid a hand on me or the children: the horror.

4. **My Supreme Court appeals were denied**: As if I'm a lost cause, someone whose pleas are worthless.

5. **He's *protecting* the kids**: By restricting me to FaceTime sessions or forcing me to travel to a place where he can monitor my every move.

He ended his motion, basically urging the court to *keep mother's visitation restricted until August 31, 2023, and beyond.* Because, obviously, so long as I "value my marriage more than my kids' safety," I shouldn't see them. You can't make this stuff up. When I read that line, I actually laughed—like a hollow, disbelieving laugh at the kind of hyperbole that belongs in a B-grade melodrama.

The saving grace: Judge Bailey—the reasonable one in Maverick County—denied the request, stating that as long as appeals were ongoing in Texas, they weren't relinquishing jurisdiction. Earlier, Joseph Rosenthal had attempted to appeal the Supreme Court's original denial we received in January 2023, telling the Supreme Court of Texas, "Hey, look, you got it wrong." It didn't bode well, but it unwittingly bought us some time to keep the case out of California.

Furious but undeterred, Reginald pressed on. On July 25, 2023, he filed another motion for a UCCJEA judges' conference, arguing that Texas was no longer a proper forum for the case. He claimed that recent changes in the local legal landscape—his preferred judges and their cozy alliances had long since retired—meant he could no longer rely on the system in Texas. If it wasn't so painful, it'd be comedic: Once upon a time, he insisted Texas was perfect for the case because, hey, that's where the kids originally lived, right? But times had changed, and now he contended that Texas was simply not the venue for his legal ambitions.

He demanded that all my visitation revolve around San Diego. No more kids flying out to see me, no more me daring to keep them in Houston. My lawyer, Nancy, once again marched into a legal battle and spiked his motion.

Then came August 25, 2023, and Reginald's ex parte application, another attempt at a temporary restraining order, complete with

- ***Talking Parents* messages** between him and me.
- **screenshots of text messages** between me and Veronica, my middle child.

He tried to paint me as the *aggressor* for doing outlandish things like… telling him the flight itinerary. Yes, apparently, providing logistics is *aggressive*. He included a conversation with Veronica about Christmas, where I explained to her that her father refused to let them travel; somehow, that's *manipulating the child*. Gotta love the spin.

He even spelled out his fear that I might *abduct the children* and not return them to California. Because, apparently, I'm some international fugitive, eager to vanish with three kids in a place where I can't even remain employed if I skip states. The list of accusations goes on:

1. **I violate court orders if I let Greg near them** (except no official evidence supports that).
2. **I'm an impossible co-parent** (the classic "angry Black woman" trope, I see you).
3. **I have no ties to California** (why would I tie myself to a place where he wields control?).

We launched a motion to quash on July 10, 2023, and ironically, the main reason we succeeded was that my Texas appeal remained pending—a bizarre instance of an ongoing legal headache acting as my shield.

Reunion and Reality Check: Seeing My Kids Again

Finally, after all that digital parenting, the day arrived when I could physically see them. I was practically trembling with excitement. But the emotional whiplash hit the moment I laid eyes on them.

April, my once-energetic little gymnast, had changed in ways that broke my heart. Once lean and full of boundless energy, she had ballooned from 44 pounds to nearly 100. After the doctors repeatedly warned about her weight gain, Reginald signed her up for tennis lessons—a move meant to get her moving and boost her confidence. Thankfully, she also found a passion for acting and joined a choir class at school. I like to think that Greg's daily affirmations helped April build the courage and confidence she needed to push through, even after the mishaps with the volatile nanny, Benny.

Despite everything, she's showing us that even when life gets a bit messy, a strong foundation can make all the difference.

RJ, my sweet mama's boy, had become distant—no longer the eager little fellow who once declared he wanted to live with me. He'd been coached, or perhaps slowly convinced, that coming back home was risky. I remember him mentioning that he disliked leaving his sisters alone with Dad, especially when Reginald would vanish for work overnight. It hurt to see him accept this twisted reality with such quiet resignation. He also mentioned that on some nights, when Dad left them completely on their own, he had to scrounge for dinner. I longed to ask why he never reached out for help, but I kept my questions to myself; the last thing I wanted was to add to his burden.

Veronica, my 10-year-old powerhouse, had grown into someone beyond what I could have imagined. Once the little helper of the house, she now fully embraced her Black identity with fierce pride. Just the other day, she looked me in the eye and said, "Thank you, Mommy, for making me Black." Hearing that warmed me in a way that no compliment ever could. Even with all the noise from outside influences, she hadn't internalized the negative messages. Instead, she's proudly celebrating her roots—so much so that her current playlist is all Kendrick Lamar and SZA. Of course, she still does her share of the work—laundry, dishes, and grumbling about the non-functioning stove—but even her complaints come with a maturity that surprises me.

Then, there was the final blow that drove me to pick up my pen and start writing this book. I later found out, indirectly as usual, that Reginald had had RJ labeled as *autistic* and placed on an IEP at his new school. I found this news out after the fact. And as if that wasn't enough, Reginald went ahead and bought a $2.5 million house, changed the kids' school district once again, and blocked me from visiting their schools.

That was the final straw—a clear signal that he was cooking up yet another one of his sneaky plans. My girlfriends had been telling me for years to write this book, saying I'd taken too long to share my story, and even my daughter Liza had urged me to get on TikTok and spill the tea, but I never did. Thankfully, a few staff members at the new school weren't comfortable with his threat for the school to call him and the police if I showed up, and they quietly tipped me off.

In the midst of all this, I also clung to a note RJ had written me on Mother's Day—a heartfelt letter filled with memories of our past. He reminisced about the time we took in a stray and named her "momma cat," the day he first got his pandas, and even the ridiculous moment when April and Veronica were taking a bath, and April ended up making a mess that left them both covered in, well, chaos. He wrapped it up by thanking me for all the *Roblox*, and, in a bittersweet tone, he said he hoped we could spend more time together when he returned to Houston. His words reminded me of the bond we shared—a bond I'm determined to rebuild, no matter how many obstacles lie ahead.

Every glance, every hesitant smile from my children told its own story. As I looked into April's determined eyes, RJ's quiet acceptance, and Veronica's fierce pride, I felt the heavy weight of reality but also a spark of hope. Despite the many changes and the harsh reality imposed by Reginald's schemes, there was a promise that maybe, just maybe, we could piece together something new from all these fragments.

The Great Shuffle: Texas, Harold County, Death of a Judge, and 666

While I reeled from the emotional chaos of that reunion, the legal saga marched on. On February 22, 2024, Reginald again tried to yank everything into California. With his beloved Judge Falkenhausen retired, and Karen apparently not in the foreground, he needed a new stage where he could flaunt his paternal hero act.

Me? I was filing motions to pull the case *out* of Maverick County into Harold County because at least Harold County's a step up from a place that once proudly declared it "didn't care about the law." My hope? Harold County might, just might, examine facts fairly, or at least more fairly than the old Maverick regime. Alternatively, if it ended up in California, I prayed a *blue state* might empathize with a mother's predicament. But the universe had other plans.

One day in March 2024, I got news from Joseph Rosenthal: Judge Falkenhausen, the very man who oversaw my trial, had died. Honestly, I felt more numb than celebratory. He'd inflicted a lot of damage, but his passing resolved nothing for me; the rulings he made lingered. The heartbreak was still real, and the system that enabled him was still intact.

On May 29, 2024, I officially requested that the case be removed from Maverick County. Reginald resisted, wanting to pivot everything into California or keep child support in Maverick County (why not keep me paying top dollar?). By June 3, the docket read: "Case moved to California," except for the part about child support, which is apparently still stuck in Maverick County. Lovely. The old docket number contains 666 in Maverick County, which felt ominous, like a cosmic nod that this county was the devil I could never quite escape.

July 22, 2024, introduced Family Court Services mediation in California. I gritted my teeth and tried optimism: Maybe a fresh mediator would see Reginald's nonsense. He demanded all visitation in San Diego, removing the fifth weekend entirely. My single request: Let my husband, Greg, be allowed contact with the children. Reginald rehashed his claims about inconclusive stepfather abuse, referencing the old 2021 fiasco. He complained I "exposed them to Greg" and that I sometimes stay in hotels with the kids. (Hello, if I came to San Diego, I'd need a place to sleep other than Reginald's lair, no?) He also fussed that I speak negatively about him.

I, in turn, raised genuine concerns:

- their skyrocketing weight and lack of outdoor activities
- the father's stalking tendencies and private investigators—evident in that bizarre Aruba fiasco, when he admitted to hiring a private investigator to follow me and the kids, as well as his unabashed habit of tracking their phones and broadcasting their whereabouts
- endless phone screens and no extracurricular structure

The mediator, to my relief, saw no reason to slash my time. She suggested maybe one visit to Texas so the kids could maintain ties. She even recommended supervised exchanges in neutral spots, given Reginald's proud admissions of PI hires and phone tracking. I saw her eyes practically roll at his spree of paranoia. I thought, *At last, a voice of reason!*

Come September 12, 2024, we had our official court date, and the new judge basically trashed the mediator's recommendations. She decreed that everything remain in San Diego, shaved my summer from six weeks to five, changed times from 6 p.m. to 7 p.m., and introduced a phone schedule from 5 p.m. to 7 p.m. daily. Then, in a final twist that might be comedic if it weren't so tragic, she never signed those orders.

So now I'm stuck in a bizarre limbo: one child's school enforces them, the other says they're not valid, and for child support, I'm still paying Maverick County. Yes, I left that county in 2019, but apparently, it refuses to let go.

Welcome to the Twilight Zone: A Life Between Two Courts (and Zero Closure)

So here I am, living a drama that feels like some Netflix series that got renewed against all odds. I have

1. **a partial *transfer*** to California for custody.
2. **unsigned orders** that might as well be scribbled on a napkin.
3. **Maverick County** still hanging on for dear life over child support, plus the stench of that old docket #666.
4. **Reginald** proclaiming himself champion father, all the while limiting my access to a handful of visits in San Diego, laced with the threat of more PIs and cryptic phone trackers.
5. **a shattered sense of finality** because how can anything be final when it's tangled in two jurisdictions?

Some days, I think the system's logic is: "We'll see if she breaks first." Because I can't fathom any other reason for the indefinite purgatory: My kids are aging day by day, forming new memories, stifling old ones, and potentially forgetting how life felt with me as a daily presence.

Meanwhile, I scramble to keep them in my orbit with phone calls, texts, and the occasional fleeting weekend.

- I dream of RJ reclaiming that easy closeness we once had.
- I picture April, healthy and bounding across a gymnastics mat like she used to.
- I imagine Veronica not having to be the house's mini-housekeeper or missing major milestones without me.

Of course, Reginald's dream is apparently me remaining locked out. The *California dream* he touts is a nightmare for me; he used it to brand me "inconvenient," ironically turning Texas into the lesser evil. I can't help but smirk at the cosmic irony:

Once, he championed Texas as the only appropriate jurisdiction. Now it's "inconvenient." If he found a way, he'd drag me to all 50 states, filing motions from Honolulu to Anchorage, as long as it keeps me off-balance.

Survival in this surreal blend of jurisdictions depends on micro-triumphs: an appeal that momentarily protects me from a forced venue change, a mediator who calls out Reginald's private investigators, a passing comment from the kids that they miss me, even if Dad's there glowering. Those slivers of hope stitch me together. I refuse to let the system's labyrinth and Reginald's obsession define me or my motherhood.

But is it draining? Absolutely. I dream of a day when a single, signed order emerges from a single, rational judge, clarifying that I can parent without enduring 100 legal hurdles every month. Meanwhile, I juggle full-time medical directorship, the heartbreak of absent children, a toddler in the terrific twos stage, and the knowledge that my older kids are halfway across the country, living under their father's curated narrative.

Will I keep fighting? Yes, but it's a strategic kind of fight now, picking battles that truly matter, avoiding the pitfalls of his endless litigation traps. I don't want my children to see an endless war. I want them to remember me as the mother who did everything possible within reason, not the mother who mirrored their father's scorched-earth tactics. So I hold the line, rely on lawyers like Nancy who remain vigilant, and pray that someday, the California *dream* transitions from a fiasco to something workable.

If you asked me what I learned from this chapter of my life, I'd say

1. **FaceTime parenting** is simultaneously a lifesaver and a heartbreak.
2. **A father bent on paranoia** can drag you to any corner of the legal map.
3. **Court systems** can overlap in baffling ways, leaving you suspended in two places at once.
4. **Judges** might ignore mediators or logic, flipping your carefully laid hopes upside down.
5. **Unsigned orders** can be even more torturous than horrible orders—because at least if they're signed, you know what to challenge.
6. **Children adapt** to insane circumstances, but it costs them pieces of their childhood they can't get back.

All that said, I end this chapter with a determined (if weary) spark. Because, for all the *California nightmares* swirling around, the dream remains that one day, my kids will thrive with me—no matter which state tries to stand in the way.

The road's long and the battle's ongoing, but I still have faith that truth and genuine love will outlast the never-ending flurry of motions. If this is the Twilight Zone, well, I'm forging my exit plan, one step at a time.

From Courtrooms to Acceptance

If I had known that simply divorcing a man would place me on a collision course with every brand of crazy—from unscrupulous lawyers to gossip-hungry judges—I might've paused for a second before signing that marriage certificate. But hindsight is a comedian with a dark sense of humor, and here I am, looking back at this entire fiasco. What started as standard *irreconcilable differences* turned into a full-blown soap opera starring my ex-husband, Reginald, in the role of Vengeful Surgeon Extraordinaire. And for anyone who thinks I'm exaggerating, trust me: You haven't seen a fraction of the pandemonium that's unspooled behind the scenes.

The Court's Bread and Butter: Men Like Reginald

Let's start with the big picture. Courts *love* men like Reginald—hot-headed, financially robust, fueled by a personal vendetta, and zero concern for what the kids actually need. Why? Because those guys keep the system well-fed with fees and drama. If I'd been granted primary custody early on, the legal juggernaut would've ground to a halt. I would've left the courtroom quietly, paid my last invoice, and lived my life. *How boring!* So, of course, they took one look at a raging, vindictive cardiothoracic surgeon with an ego the size of Texas and practically rolled out the red carpet. Jackpot. Lawyers like Karen—fueled by a bottomless appetite for conflict—were ready to wring every cent from Reginald's bitterness.

Judges like Falkenhausen, who appear to delight in condescending scoldings, got a perfect puppet show. Mental health evaluators who love "problem patients" found a gold mine in a man who is borderline clinically paranoid yet has an "M.D." behind his name: a trifecta of chaos that funds a hundred more country club memberships.

Not everyone was awful, though. I stumbled upon attorneys like Melissa, Marty, Joseph, and now Nancy, who actually seemed to have heartbeats and moral compasses. They're the unicorns you never expect in the legal system, the ones who make you say, "Oh, so it's not *all* about the money." But the rest? I can practically see them salivating when Reginald walks in—his fury, his jealousy, his inflated sense of self—and think, *Let's keep this train rolling*, because men like him will fight forever, even if it means wrecking their own kids.

This leads me to a reality that took me too long to accept: *You can't beat someone who's willing to burn their own children's well-being to the ground.* I'm simply unwilling to cause further damage to my kids by matching his scorched-earth tactics. So, I gave up on chasing primary custody.

Some might say I surrendered, but the way I see it, I refused to stoop to his level. He'd drag the kids through every psychological shredder imaginable. They've endured enough. Even Greg, my husband, concluded that continuing to fight Reginald was like wrestling a crocodile in a kiddie pool—pointless, with the real risk of someone losing a limb.

Meanwhile, Reginald's ploys get more bizarre: He keeps telling the children that Greg abused them (he did *not*), hoping they'll recant the truth. But they're older now. They remember the Bible verses he used to guilt them into lying ("Obey your parents!"), and they're done being manipulated. Only April mentions Greg spanking her *once*—and oh dear, we all know one spank does not an abuser make. But Reginald can't compute that. He's a pro at rewriting reality, especially if it makes him the saint and us the villains.

Hypocrisy and Hysteria in Reginald's Parenting

The twisted irony is that Reginald once proudly admitted he spanked my older daughter, Liza—multiple times, in fact. I'm not saying she was a perfect angel who didn't deserve a reprimand or two, but this man used *pressure points*, wrestling moves, and borderline chokeholds on a teenage girl. Then he has the nerve to call Greg a monster for a single, mild disciplinary moment.

It's like a bank robber accusing someone of petty theft and demanding the moral high ground. I look back and shudder at how I ever imagined Reginald would treat Liza decently. Even her biological father, who struggled with a diagnosed mental illness, showed more restraint.

Reginald's hair-trigger temper and manipulative tactics proved lethal to the peace of my home. The day I told him, "If I'd known you'd treat Liza like this, I would never have married you," was the same day I realized I was in far deeper trouble than a standard marital spat.

Now, Greg—contrary to Reginald's melodramatic spin—is the gentlest soul. Sure, he's a chatterbox. I sometimes joke that he has "verbal diarrhea," especially in text form. But never once has he laid an abusive hand on me or the kids.

Meanwhile, Reginald literally pinned my daughter against the wall and brags about how "holy" he is compared to us. The fact that Greg is a Black man in Reginald's eyes, apparently, screams "scary."

Let's just say the real *scary* figure is the one who thinks a teenage meltdown calls for an MMA lock.

Thankfully, Greg has shifted focus to our new baby girl, letting Reginald wallow in his delusions. We're no longer dancing to Reginald's beat. I've found it's best to let him think he's got the starring role while we quietly build a stable life that doesn't revolve around legal depositions and random accusations.

Full Circle Pity and the Downfall of an *Untouchable* Surgeon

Weirdly, I oscillate between anger and pity for Reginald. On the one hand, he tried to bankrupt me, yank my medical license, and force me to commute to San Diego every first, third, and fifth weekend so I'd lose my job. He wanted me on my knees, dependent and defeated, while he soared on a hospital's payroll. Plot twist: *He's* the one who lost his contract after being found negligent in a patient's death. The hospital severed ties with him, presumably paying out a hefty settlement.

Now, he's a self-employed cardiothoracic surgeon with more free time than ever. More money, too, ironically. But as we've all heard, money can't buy you peace or fill that gaping hole where empathy and decency should be.

He's even got a fiancée, or domestic partner, who's been by his side for three years. I hear she survived childhood cancer—which is nothing to scoff at, especially since I lost my baby brother to cancer—but unfortunately, the treatments have rendered her infertile, bittersweet mercy, perhaps ensuring Reginald couldn't father more kids he'd eventually mistreat.

Talk about cosmic justice. I glean that he has zero intention of actually marrying her, but it looks good for his image to have a stable *partner.* If I had the energy left to care, I might even feel sorry for her, too, stuck in the orbit of a man who cycles through vendettas like it's a daily vitamin.

Meanwhile, the kids no longer do their extended Chicago summers because Reginald's parents are in poor health. That means the children, ironically, are missing school here and there to help out in Illinois, which is pretty far from the "stable environment" he boasted about to the court. I chuckle darkly when I recall how his parents once suggested that he let the kids stay with me so he could chase more money.

Instead, he doubled down on snatching them purely for ego. So now they're bouncing around taking care of grandparents, and I'm left to reflect on how *full-circle* karma can be.

As for me, I got a slice of peace. No more new court cases are lurking (knock on wood). Greg dove into real estate, allowing us to buy an investment property where the kids can comfortably stay. I no longer have to plan visits around whichever Airbnb is cheap and available. The kids can come, toss their bags in their own rooms, and live like normal children for a few days.

Finding Slivers of Hope Through Hurricanes and Travel

Life's not perfect—far from it. I spent a year not hugging my children, immersing myself in my career to stave off heartbreak. I nabbed multiple promotions and even snagged "Physician of the Year" at my clinic's Christmas party—talk about a bittersweet victory. Then, finally, Veronica's birthday arrived, and I saw them for the first time in ages. The difference from her lonely party last year was night and day: This time, it was a joyous affair with so many gifts they could've opened a toy store. My kids fell asleep mid-laughter, the house echoing with a sense of normalcy I thought was forever lost.

From there, we resumed the standard first, third, and fifth weekend visits, plus some holiday get-togethers. Thanksgiving in Chicago let the kids reconnect with cousins, and we turned New Year's into a full-blown extravaganza—baking classes, magical light shows, children's museums, you name it. That momentum carried into a milestone I'd been longing for: Six consecutive weeks with them over the summer, the first time since 2018. I was ecstatic… until Hurricane Beryl decided to greet us, knocking out electricity in our Airbnb for a solid week.

We were trapped in sauna-like heat with no relief in sight. Veronica, normally the carefree one, practically shoved water bottles at me to keep me conscious. My mother managed to snag comfort with Greg and our toddler, but me and the older kids? We were stuck, panting like dogs. April's asthma flared, Veronica started feeling faint, and we took refuge in the car's A/C, which felt like déjà vu from the time Reginald left the stove gas on during Mother's Day 2018. By day four, we found a distant hotel with a vacancy, but not before I nearly lost my mind, scrambling for gas. I even picked up an extra shift at work just so the kids could hang out in an air-conditioned clinic. Adversity aside, we made it out intact—bonded, sweaty, but intact. Later, I secured passports for them, determined to show them more of the world than random flights to Chicago. They'd been to Taiwan once—Reginald, Veronica, Liza, both sets of grandparents—but claim they hardly remember it. Meanwhile, he never fulfilled his big Disneyland promise, so I decided I'd step up, taking them on new adventures. This time, they joined me in Aruba.

Although they couldn't attend the vow renewal with Greg, they got to spend time with Greg's mother, his brother, his friends, and my own circle of friends and family. I even had to move from hotel to hotel—splitting our stay between two different locations on opposite sides of the island—to keep everything together. And all the while, Reginald had a PI following me and the children under the guise of their protection. Because that's what normal exes do—stalk their child's mother (and her kids) on a tropical island notorious for its missing-person legends, right? The man's hubris is a case study in itself. Meanwhile, I was just trying to sip a piña colada on the beach without having a paranoid meltdown.

Nanny Kidnappings, Protective Orders, and Why I'm Still Standing

Some might read this and think I'm paranoid. Maybe so. But I've seen enough of Reginald's stunts and know too many tragic tales from my fellow physicians—some lost their lives in custody exchanges, some were cornered in public spaces, and a few took their own lives out of sheer hopelessness. I told Reginald through our *Talking Parents* app that I was never coming to San Diego, and I meant it. *Never.* If that means missing my kids' school recitals or field trips, well, I'd rather stay alive to see them grow up. Harsh but true.

And don't get me started on the nanny fiascos. Elda and her cohort managed to orchestrate a near-kidnapping (with Reginald's blessing!) by claiming I was too busy, newly married, and not *present.* They saw how uninvolved Reginald was, realized he was easy to manipulate, and the next thing I knew, they had the kids. I tried protecting them by switching daycares and removing certain nannies from pick-up lists, but Reginald re-added them behind my back. Everyone from the principal to the child services investigators wondered, "Why didn't he consult you first?" Good question. Because sabotaging me was more important than ensuring the kids' safety. It left me with enough PTSD about nannies that my youngest will likely never see one. *Thanks, Reginald.*

In a moment of desperation, I attempted to get a protective order, but Karen (Reginald's lawyer) apparently told the ADA's office that I was just playing custody games. Meanwhile, Reginald once told me, "You've suffered so much trauma in childhood; you can handle more pain." He threatened to kill me if I ever cheated. He left the gas on. He abused his childhood family dog by bludgeoning the poor dog with a baseball bat. He basically said my life has no value. Yet the system found no reason to protect me—no big surprise.

This same system forced me to pay child support to a man who fully acknowledges I'm a loving mom but sees me as disposable. He even mocks me for "showing no remorse," claiming he's the real victim because I left him.

Tacking on more emotional baggage, I decided to finalize a Catholic annulment. I wanted to sever every spiritual tie. It was painful: multiple meetings, prying questions, testimonies from family about the trauma. Reginald responded by admitting some wrongdoing but labeled me a narcissist. *Facepalm.* At least the church recognized that our union was built on a shaky foundation of intimidation, not love. I felt a bit more closure after that.

Lessons in Surviving (Not Conquering)

If I had a dollar for every time someone asked, "How do you co-parent with him?" I'd be living on my private island. The truth is, I *don't.* Co-parenting with Reginald is like playing chess with an opponent who sets the board on fire whenever you make a decent move. I regret being so flexible when I had custody, letting him see the kids anytime. I thought goodwill might yield goodwill in return. Instead, once he got custody, he slammed every door shut. I told the court: "I never even tried for his retirement or assets in the divorce. I just wanted peace."

They looked at me like I was speaking Martian. Because in a system built on conflict, *peace* might as well be a four-letter word. Yet, ironically, I'm finding a measure of that elusive peace. Greg and I have a stable home and a real estate venture, and the kids have actual rooms to stay in when they visit. We survived a year of no physical contact, overcame a meltdown of missed birthdays and lonely holidays, and then resurrected our connection with an epic six-week summer—punctuated by a hurricane that nearly turned us into sweaty puddles.

We came out stronger, inhalers and all. I even took them abroad, forging new memories to overshadow the gloom. Sure, they missed my vow renewal because Reginald blocked it, but they've tasted real freedom on other trips. And if that means we're forever looking over our shoulders for Reginald's hired private investigator snapping photos from behind a palm tree, so be it. Let him creep. I'm too busy living to care.

My cousin Abeena from L.A. once told me to remember we're African women; resilience is in our DNA. She compared my situation to those women who leave third-world countries, toiling away so they can eventually send for their kids and give them a better life. I see the truth in her analogy. This fiasco might be stateside, but it's the same spirit: I endure the nightmares so my kids can have a shot at normalcy eventually. She also cited Kelly Clarkson, Halle Berry, and Britney Spears, who ended up paying child support to men who made far less. Indeed, no one's untouchable in family court. If that's the standard, I guess I should be thankful I'm in interesting company.

In the end, I cling to the knowledge that I'm still here. I didn't lose my career, my sanity, or my life. I gave up certain battles for the sake of the kids' emotional health. I watched Reginald's grand plan to break me implode when his own contract fell through. He might make more money freelancing, but he lacks any real anchor.

The grandparents he once used as a dumping ground for the kids are now frail, forcing them to miss school to provide care. The father who bragged about Disneyland never took them anywhere but Chicago. Meanwhile, I keep forging new memories with them: teaching them to ride bikes, surviving power outages, and scouring the globe for family-friendly adventures. Their father might have custody on paper, but he'll never own the fullness of who they are.

Final Reflections: My Peace, Not His Permission

If there's one takeaway, it's that a broken system can only break you if you let it. I choose not to let Reginald define my existence. He's tried everything: humiliation, false accusations, forging alliances with incompetent nannies who ended up traumatizing the kids. I can't stop him from being who he is. I can only protect myself and the children as best I can, even if that means never stepping foot in San Diego. A protective order? Sure, it sounds good, but it's worthless if the man in question sees me as an expendable nuisance.

And from experience, the system often sides with the most determined liar. I hope no one reading this thinks, Oh, so that's how you gain custody—just make up false claims and manipulate the system. Because it's not a success story, it's a cautionary tale of how one man discovered a rickety county with questionable oversight and hammered it to his advantage: deniable plausibility, rigged jury, law school buddies on the bench—like a script from a cheap legal drama. Meanwhile, I had a buffoon for a lawyer who filed an interim band-aid order at the worst time. It was a perfect storm, and justice never stood a chance.

Still, if you ask me how I feel today, I'll tell you: surprisingly, at peace. I see my kids enough to shower them with the love and normalcy they deserve. Greg and I are building a life that's free from the chaos of my ex-husband's phone alerts. Sure, there's an ache; any mother who's forcibly separated from her kids feels it. But I'm done being the star in Reginald's horror show. The best revenge is living well, forging ahead, and letting him spin his wheels in anger.

I regret allowing him unsupervised visits when I had custody—turns out, a bit of graciousness can be exploited in the family court system. But I don't regret the mindset behind it; I was simply trying to do right by my children. Reginald, however, sees only an opportunity for more chaos. At the end of the day, I know I remain the better parent. The system might award him custody, but it can't change the truth about who truly holds these children's hearts. Every memory I create with them—baking cookies, braving hurricanes, traveling to new destinations—outshines the gloom Reginald attempts to cast. And that's the final chapter: I refuse to let him, or any broken system, define our story. The children will grow, they'll come to understand the truth, and, one day, they might even laugh with me about the sheer absurdity of these events. Until then, I'll keep forging peace, one day at a time, with or without a judge's permission. Because I am a working mother—an African woman in my bones, as my cousin says—built to endure and determined to flourish. And that, my dear reader, is how I must close this perpetually ongoing tale.

References

Beesley, J. (2022, December 24). *Yaa Asantewa.* Team Queens. https://teamqueens.org/yaa-asantewa/

Fadiman, A. (1998, September 30). *The spirit catches you and you fall down.* Google Books. https://books.google.com.uy/books?id=DUHAXXvSUeYC&printsec=frontcover&hl=es#v=onepage&q&f=false

Frakt, A. (2020, December 30). *What can be learned from differing rates of suicide among groups. The New York Times.* https://www.nytimes.com/2020/12/30/upshot/suicide-demographic-differences.html

New international version. (2011). Bible Gateway. https://www.biblegateway.com/passage/?search=Proverbs%203%3A5-6&version=NIV (Original work published 1973)

The history of Nana Yaa Asantewaa (resistance fighter) queen mother of the Asante kingdom. (n.d.). YAPGA. https://yaaasantewaa.co.uk/history/

The End

www.ingramcontent.com/pod-product-compliance
Lightning Source LLC
La Vergne TN
LVHW090311210926
848480LV00001B/203